Eyewitness to the Fetterman Fight

Eyewitness
to the
Fetterman Fight

Indian Views

Edited by John H. Monnett

UNIVERSITY OF OKLAHOMA PRESS : NORMAN

Publication of this book is made possible through
the generosity of Edith Kinney Gaylord.

Library of Congress Cataloging-in-Publication Data

Names: Monnett, John H., editor of compilation.
Title: Eyewitness to the Fetterman Fight : Indian views / edited by John H. Monnett.
Description: Norman, OK : University of Oklahoma Press, [2017] | Includes index.
Identifiers: LCCN 2016033853 | ISBN 978-0-8061-5582-1 (cloth) |
    ISBN 978-0-8061-6188-4 (paper)
Subjects: LCSH: Fetterman Fight, Wyo., 1866—Personal narratives. | Cheyenne
    Indians—History—19th century. | Lakota Indians—History—19th century. |
    Cheyenne Indians—Biography. | Lakota Indians—Biography.
Classification: LCC E83.866 .E94 2017 | DDC 978.004/97353—dc23
LC record available at https://lccn.loc.gov/2016033853

For all my students, maybe 10,000 or so

Since Indians could not write [in the 1860s,] the history of their wars has been set down by their enemies.

While their [the Indians'] culture differs from ours in some respects, fundamentally they are like ourselves.

—*George B. Grinnell, 1915, 1923*

Contents

Illustrations

Figures

Maps

Eyewitness to the Fetterman Fight

Introduction

Evening, December 21, 1866—

As temperatures plummeted well below freezing on the winter solstice of 1866, and the sun dipped behind Cloud Peak in the Bighorn Mountains above Fort Phil Kearny in Dakota Territory,[1] a train of blue army wagons lumbered south on the Bozeman Trail toward the fort's open gate. Inside the wagons the remains of forty-nine American soldiers killed that morning were piled in heaps. They had died in a fierce battle with Indians. Sergeant Frank Fessenden never forgot the sight: "There were arms and legs in all shapes, divulging the horrible manner in which our brave comrades had died. It was a horrible and sickening sight, and brought tears to every eye, to see how those men, many of whom had served four years in the War of the Rebellion, meeting with such an awful death on the western Plains." A few days' ride away by horseback in a Lakota village on Tongue River, a small Oglala Lakota lad, Black Elk, waited for the return of his warrior father. Years later Black Elk remembered, his first vivid childhood memory: "It must be the fear I remember most. All this time I was not allowed to play very far away from our tepee, and my mother would say, 'If you are not good the Wasicus [whites] will get you.'"

On that morning of December 21, 1866, a well-organized force of 1,500 to 2,000 Oglala and Miniconjou Lakotas, perhaps a few Brûlé and Hunkpapa, Northern Cheyenne, and Arapaho warriors annihilated a detachment of forty-nine federal soldiers from companies A, C, E, and H of the Second Battalion of the Eighteenth U.S. Infantry; twenty-seven troopers of Company C, Second U.S. Cavalry; and two civilian contractors, James S. Wheatley and Isaac Fisher, all under the command of Captain William Judd Fetterman. The Indians would also kill Fetterman and two other officers of the command that day, Captain Frederick H. Brown and Second Lieutenant George W. Grummond, all commissioned in the Eighteenth Infantry. The Fetterman Fight is the worst defeat suffered by the U.S. Army in the West during the 1860s, accounting for more military casualties along the Bozeman Trail in the Powder River Country than all other events of Red Cloud's War (1866–1868) combined and almost 8 percent of the army's killed-in-action losses with Indians in a half century of warfare in the trans-Mississippi West.[2]

Second only to the Battle of the Little Big Horn (or Bighorn), the Fetterman Fight is the most complete strategic and tactical equestrian Plains Indian victory over elements of the U.S. Army in Western history. Because the struggle resulted in the annihilation of Fetterman's entire command, federal authorities quickly raised immediate questions regarding responsibility for what it called the "disaster." Although the press immediately placed blame on Colonel Henry B. Carrington, Fort Phil Kearny's commander, two federal investigations exonerated him. Carrington's manipulative legal defense cast blame squarely on the dead Captain Fetterman for disobeying direct orders not to cross Lodge Trail Ridge north of the fort in pursuit of Lakota and Cheyenne warriors. Fetterman's alleged disobedience, Carrington would assert, resulted in an ambush of Fetterman's entire command by the numerically superior force of the Indians. Subsequent books by Carrington's two wives in 1868 and 1910 further condemned Fetterman as irrational.[3] Building on the Carrington accounts, early histories portray Fetterman as a brash, arrogant, "fire eating," irresponsible soldier whose disobedience of orders is mostly to blame for the destruction of his entire command. Historians have continued to portray Fetterman this way in both nonfiction and fiction through the years.[4]

Until recently Carrington's version of the famous fight has remained largely unchallenged. Voluminous government reports, combined with civilian testimonies attempting to ascribe blame for the event, are available in the literature.[5] Yet despite alternative explanations for Fetterman's actions, scholars, enthusiasts, and interested readers continue to focus on Fetterman's hubris and disobedience of orders as reasons for the demise of his command. Much reader interest in this lingering question comes at the expense of considering the testimonies of the only eyewitnesses to the battle. After all, a number of Lakotas and Cheyennes who were there lived into the twentieth century to tell their stories.[6] The purpose of this study is to present as fully as possible those Indian voices and to answer the question: Do the early Indian interviews corroborate with the non-Indian depictions of the event? This book is *not* another narrative history of all the events of the Fetterman Fight. Rather, it seeks to understand the validity of the relevant Indian views collected in interviews by non-Indian ethnologists through the early decades of the twentieth century.

≡≡

Readers should be mindful while reading these testimonies that defense of the resource-rich Powder River Country (today's Wyoming) was of utmost importance for both Lakotas and the Northern Cheyennes. After about 1846 the previous biomass that supported all equestrian societies on the plains began to change drastically. The late 1840s witnessed the beginning of a prolonged period of severe drought and a steady but subtle rise in temperature, although striking paradoxical extremes still occurred. This drop in annual precipitation marked the end of a three-centuries-long cool, moist period in the Earth's northern hemisphere that geologists call the Little Ice Age. Buffalo and people with their horses would now frequent reliably drought-resistant areas such as the Powder River Country, creating, in the words of historian Dan Flores, "a traffic jam of natural resource consumers, both four-legged and two-legged."[7] This drought at the end of the Little Ice Age would swiftly wither some buffalo ranges, pushing herds eastward on to the plains where mid-grass prairies beckoned. The climate shift would threaten ways of equestrian life for years to come. Plenty of game still roamed the verdant parts of the upper Powder River Country by 1860 because shallow coal deposits, or scoriae, provided more adequate aquifers. Bison, pronghorn, elk, and deer proliferated in the region. Although the entire Sioux Nation grew and expanded during the early to mid-nineteenth century, their natural resources were steadily shrinking, exclusive of slowly declining game numbers. With the decade-long drought during the 1850s the Powder River Country held even more significance

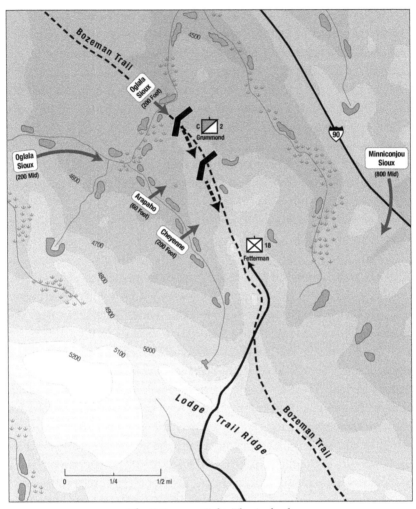

The Fetterman Fight: The Ambush.
Drawn by Erin Greb after a Combat Studies Institute map.

to tribes and bands, large and small, all of whom were constricted by the same exacting life-giving requirements of wood, grass, and water. Although environmental factors contributed to the concentration of wild game in the Powder River Country, so too did human interaction, especially the Crow War. With white migration threatening the ecological integrity of the Platte River Valley, Oglalas and other Lakotas ventured northward in 1857 to challenge

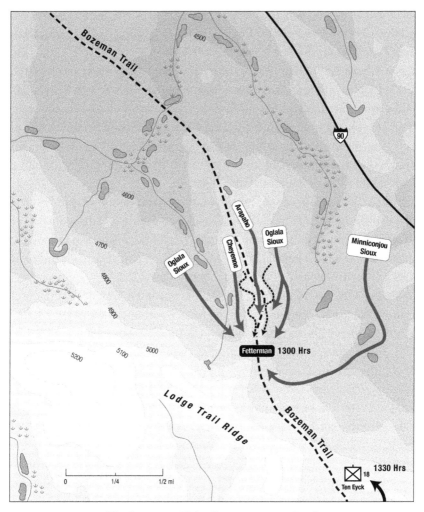

The Fetterman Fight: Fetterman's Last Stand.
Drawn by Erin Greb after a Combat Studies Institute map.

the Crows for the shrinking resources of the northern plains. Their intent
was to drive the Crows from lands the United States recognized as Crow
domain by the Horse Creek Treaty of 1851. The Crow War became a brutal
affair of conquest that drove the Crows west of the Bighorn Mountains. The
art of Amos Bad Heart Bull illustrates the battles of the Crow War as being
on a scale equal to or greater than the Sioux Wars with whites.[8]

In less than a decade, prospectors appeared on the scene to extract gold northwest of the Powder River Country in the new Montana Territory (1864). Travel north from the Platte Road bisected the newly won Oglala lands via the Bozeman Trail. From 1863 to 1865, using state volunteer army units, the United States attempted unsuccessfully to pacify Lakotas and Cheyennes in the area, but problems of primitive transportation and logistics thwarted their efforts. Then, in 1866 the federal government sought a new treaty at Fort Laramie to allow three new forts to be constructed along the Bozeman Trail, a proposal unacceptable to most of the chiefs and war leaders, including Red Cloud, a rising star among the Oglalas.

Thus, the convergence of Indian peoples, Montana-bound gold seekers, and supply contractors in the region combined with a decade and a half of drought and the decline of natural resources (noticeable to the Indians) to make conflict almost inevitable by 1866. As Civil War armies made their way back to hearth and home, the federal government's decision to protect travel to Montana by garrisoning new forts on the Bozeman Trail in the middle of prime Lakota and Cheyenne hunting grounds without a new treaty fostered armed conflict with the tribesmen. For the Indians, who had just witnessed Civil War volunteer units vacate the area, the arrival in 1866 of new regular army troops intent on establishing a permanent presence in the Powder River Country was simply too much. For the allied tribes, these lands so recently hard won from the Crows had to be defended. Red Cloud's War followed, sweeping the northern plains with fury. By rethinking the importance of the hotly contested Powder River ecosystem to the continued prosperity and endurance of the Lakotas and Cheyennes, the stories in the following eyewitness testimonies reveal a forceful, almost desperate, determination on the part of those tribes to keep and protect the ecological integrity of their hunting ranges and trade routes. They also reveal an intersection of increasingly visible ecological concerns, which they believed justified war. As such they take on meaningful new significance today and illuminate the importance of this era to understanding American Indian foresight for environmental preservation, an issue still relevant to our historical understanding of that matter today.[9]

Note on American Indian Testimony

In the twenty-first century most serious scholars of the nineteenth-century U.S. military in the West believe it is no longer appropriate to tell the story of this important era strictly from the viewpoint and written documents of the conquering society.[1] Problems arise, however, given the comparative scarcity of original Indian sources. Indian voices are too often silent in the early records. Where they do exist, they are usually transferred by a kind of filtering process through the cultural lenses of interested, scholarly-minded white interviewers, who, during the first three decades of the twentieth century, befriended surviving Native veterans of the Indian wars and recorded what they said about various events. The Lakota and Northern Cheyenne accounts of the Fetterman Fight are assembled here (no original transcribed eyewitness Arapaho accounts exist).

In this study one may learn almost as much about the interviewers as the Indian warriors and chiefs they interviewed. Here the reader will meet Walter S. Campbell, a.k.a. Stanley Vestal, a professor of English at the University of Oklahoma. Campbell is followed by John G. Neihardt, poet laureate of Nebraska; Eli S. Riker, a Nebraska attorney and judge; Addison E. Sheldon, director of the Nebraska State Historical Society; George E. Hyde, researcher and book dealer; mixed-heritage (Southern Cheyenne and white) George Bent, warrior, trader, news reporter; George Bird Grinnell, scientist, naturalist, ethnologist; Thomas Marquis, physician; John Stands In Timber, Northern

Cheyenne elder; and others. All these men shared an interest in chronicling the traditional culture of their Indian friends during a time when common belief held that Indians would soon be dead, and their stories had to be recorded for posterity and larger reading audiences. Certainly, they all questioned and wrote through the cultural lens of Euro-American interests they thought white audiences would favor. Chronicling large battles with whites was a common interest, especially those battles where no white eyewitnesses survived to tell the tale. Other true ethnologists, like George A. Dorsey and E. Adamson Hoebel, focused their endeavors with elderly tribesmen more on capturing the cultural forms of Plains Indians for anthropology, rather than on the battles that fascinated the larger mainstream society. Grinnell and Hyde admirably bridged both areas of interest.[2]

Often, in large battles like that at Little Big Horn, Indian accounts are highly individualistic, relating only the Indian veteran's memories of his personal exploits and with the range of that individual's personal experience on the battlefield. Although Plains warriors would indeed often fight for individual glory once engaged in close-quarter combat, their strategy and tactics were, as we find in the early literature, nonetheless often well planned, scrupulously organized, and closely monitored.

The stories told by Lakota and Northern Cheyenne participants in the Fetterman Fight are, with a couple of exceptions, highly corroborative with one another regarding the major sequences of the battle, given that the stories were told to different interviewers. They also parallel much of the original government documents deduced from forensics, although no white soldiers survived north of Lodge Trail Ridge to relate eyewitness experiences. There are no original Indian sources attesting to Fetterman's disobedience of orders in crossing over Lodge Trail Ridge. Stories of personal experiences are the means by which preliterate tribal members conveyed their history. Oral transmission of eyewitness history through storytelling, often disregarded by non-Indian scholars, is still favored among Indian people today. Oral stories, once transmitted past one or two generations, are important in tribal efforts to contextualize the indigenous voice within the American historical narrative, and to use that voice to shape legal arguments for restitution of land claims disputed with the government. Modern oral stories on such particulars as who were and who were not leaders conform to interviews conducted during the early twentieth century.

How much historians can rely on generationally transmitted oral histories that are more than a century removed from the events in question, however, remains arguable. Many historians think such sources can be relied upon to some extent. Historian Ned Blackhawk points out that family histories highlight "the power of narrative both to define a people's essence and to instill a deep sense of cultural pride."[3] But what about time gaps in the record? How far can we go in assigning individual actions played out in known events through assumptions based not on specific written or journalistically transcribed evidence, especially eyewitness testimony, but rather on known cultural customs, practices, traditions, and beliefs?

My research corroborating written documents with Indian art (such as that depicted in ledger drawings and winter counts of the Plains Indians for example), does indeed convince me that such cultural materials like ledger art and winter counts *do* qualify as original historical source documents. As this book was being written, a forgotten ledger book, recovered by the relief detail and burial party after the Battle of Little Big Horn and gathering dust on a shelf in Cambridge, Massachusetts, had been identified by the Houghton Museum/Library staff at Harvard by anthropologist Castle McLaughlin. Professor McLaughlin, with the help of art history experts, historians, and tribal scholars, has determined the drawings in the book as the work of several Lakota and possibly Cheyenne artists during Red Cloud's War of 1866–1868. If so, the diversity of artists in the book supports scholar Kingsley Bray's assertion: that by the late 1860s Lakota divisions and Northern Cheyennes had formed a coalition, which for all practical purposes comprised a new "Northern Nation" of tribesmen fighting to protect the Powder River Country.[4]

Non-Indians often consider latter-day oral testimonies two or three generations removed from the events in question, however, to be problematic. Stories fabricated by whites likewise creep into Indian oral tradition just as they do into secondary documentary history. Yellowstone National Park historian Lee H. Whittlesey finds that in over a century of storytelling by park interpreters, of one ilk or another, "there are a great number of so-called 'Indian stories' that can be dismissed as tales made up by whites, probably to explain what Indians should have thought. Indian stories originated by whites are often written too slickly and [have] too much perfectly balanced drama—to ring true as real Indian legend."[5] If modern oral sources are to be used in historical narrative, historians should seek oral stories directly from Indian people, and interpretations should be limited in number so as to not obfuscate original eyewitness testimonies upon which they are based.

One may argue that military documents, likewise, can be no less misleading and sometimes even more self-serving than Indian eyewitness testimonies. In documents usually written as "official reports" of one form or another, now housed in the National Archives, officers would often attempt to put themselves and their immediate commands in the best possible light. This was especially so in an age of a "peace-time army" when opportunities for combat were infrequent and promotions slow. One officer's report would sometimes conflict with that of another officer's report, or with Indian accounts, and with the reminiscences of enlisted men, which were given as testimony in federal investigations or recounted in memoirs written years later.[6] Sometimes, though less frequently, officers' reports could be condemnatory of fellow officers in order to cast blame for a failed action, or to redirect intention and blame away from themselves and onto other officers. With all the controversy surrounding the Fetterman Fight this unfortunate reality is rife with such *official* reports, court testimonies, and reminiscences.[7]

In my fifteen years researching the Fetterman Fight I have found that the Lakota and Cheyenne sources presented here are more valid and reliable—especially as they relate to the elements of the actual fight—than are the speculative, controversial, contentious, and conflicting military reports and court testimonies, especially those of officers who had personal agendas regarding blame for the "disaster," as well as individual loyalties and responsibilities, especially within the senior officer corps. Although the Indians' testimonials and personal stories, whether published or taken in my research from the original interview notes and statements, sometimes differ in some details, they show no indication of conflicting egos and no irregular or questionable attempts to exaggerate personal combat glory at the expense of others. No boastful conflict exists in these early stories that might be interpreted as intense tribal rivalry among Lakotas, Cheyennes, and Arapahos. Yet there was always the chance in interviews that an aging warrior remembering the romantic exploits of his youth might exaggerate a few individual details—a natural tendency that might be called "magnified memory" caused by the passage of time.

But we are fortunate indeed to have these stories, given that the white transcribers demonstrate in their notes a greater interest in finding from their friends the truth of the Little Big Horn fight and who killed George Armstrong Custer. The Fetterman material they would obtain from the veteran warriors was almost an afterthought. These interviewers of the early twentieth century seemed uninterested in which warrior personally dispatched Captain Fetterman, whom they regarded as inferior in profile compared to Custer. With one exception (American Horse) the interviewed warriors are totally silent on the subject. Again, most interviewers, writers, and historians of the era were also more interested in shoot-'em-ups between whites and Indians and whites versus whites than they were in learning about intertribal warfare, and thus had only a passing interest in Indian culture and tribal political organization. As such, they occasionally repeated oft-accepted conventional wisdom of the age. Of interest also is the lack of information on, or perceived unimportance of, obtaining stories regarding the specific role the great Oglala warrior Crazy Horse may have played in the Fetterman Fight. The interviewers seemed more interested at this time in finding out whether Red Cloud was present at the battle and what role he might have played in the fighting.

Still, the information they obtained is credible and useful today. As historian Jerome A. Greene points out, Indian accounts add another "on-site dimension to understanding what specific actions transpired on a battlefield."[8] He believes that "[r]eminiscent testimony, by its distance from an event, was more often bias-free for both giver and receiver than testimony delivered soon afterwards," when a warrior might be diffident or remain silent, out of fear of possible retribution to his family. Avoided in this study therefore are extremely brief statements by Indian participants that cannot be corroborated for validity by other eyewitnesses or by later, more "ethnologically" based testimonies at the military investigations shortly after the battle. The purposes of these inquires at the hearings were to seek culpability for the annihilation of Fetterman's command. This is true especially in the case of those few short statements by Indian participants at the "Special Commission to Investigate the Fetterman Massacre," conducted in 1867 prior to the recognized end of Red Cloud's War and the Treaty of 1868. Indian speeches at the treaty hearings itself are included in the appendix. Once such concerns were no longer threatening, accurate testimonies could be freely given. As Greene states, "Veracity was important in tribal society, and so was memory. Remembering such minute data was instilled as part of Indian storytelling ritual," Greene contends.[9] Passing down exact details of events and ritual from generation to generation is essential in Plains Indian societies and is instilled as part of the formal storytelling ritual today. As such, modern historians are recognizing the validity of eyewitness Indian testimony as well as the value of oral stories if they have been properly vetted and corroborated.

The accounts presented in Parts 1–4 are eyewitness reminiscences, not "hearsay," and thus offer a clearer rendition of the Fetterman Fight north of Lodge Trail Ridge. We must be aware, however, that interviewers and writers of Indian testimonies would often cherry-pick information they thought their non-Indian readers most desired. The information interviewers considered important to themselves and the general public at the dawn of the twentieth century reveals much about America's Indian wars at a specific point in time and thus adds some insight into the developing historiography of the topic through the years.

Given the obligatory need for accuracy among Indian peoples in passing down history, even latter-day oral storytelling is useful to demonstrate how Indians continue to maintain pride and reverence for their history and their heroes as a means of cultural celebration. My own conversations with Indian students in my university classes and on the Northern Cheyenne Indian Reservation reflect strong pride in their historical heroes. Among many Indian people today oral tradition holds greater weight than among non-Indians. According to Lydia Whirlwind Soldier, a Lakota, "The oral tradition is some-times considered [by non-Indians] as legend or myth without the credibility that these stories deserve. Most tribal members who have heard our relatives tell the stories, however, read the non-Indians' historical accounts with doubt and sometimes disbelief."[10] For Indian people, oral "family" history is essential to augment written sources of their history that differs from non-Indian sources. Historical thinking is thus viewed as circular (the Medicine Way) rather than linear, whereby events of the deep past are just as significant to cultural and historical understanding today as they were when those early events occurred.

Part 4 of this study expressly deals with "historical memory" regarding what Lakotas and Cheyennes consider important today about the Fetterman Fight. To test the validity of oral history more than two generations removed from the events in question, anthropologists contrast it against eyewitness accounts, written or otherwise.[11] Gordon M. Day argues, "The validity of the oral tradition is enhanced by its goodness of fit with the historical data." He refers to such methodology as "oral history as complement."[12] Indian storytell-ers sometimes disagree with Day's premise and believe their stories should stand as original rather than "complement." Storytelling has become more acceptable in the fields of ethnohistory and cultural anthropology, although many armchair historians, due to their interest in the small particulars of an event, still want to corroborate modern testimony with older or written eyewitness accounts.

If ethnohistorians are correct in emphasizing that Indians know their history better than non-Indians, ethnohistorical methodology is appropriate to understanding frontier military history.[13] The method the historian applies is a critical factor. Due to popularity of their subject matter among the general public, frontier military historians find they need to appeal to different (and often a wider variety of) audiences than ethnohistorians, and are thus often cautious in employing latter-day oral testimony. Such is often the case with some strictly military histories written prior to about the 1980s. For the authors of such histories, Gordon M. Day's strategy rings true: ethnohis-torical methodologies and latter-day family histories should be corroborated when possible with multiple sources of evidence. This approach in no way undermines my basic belief that Indian histories, oral or written, can stand alone if the comprehensive factual record of the pertinent events is utilized. The modern oral statements and stories I gathered for this work generally conform to the original eyewitness core testimonies. I encountered none that did not conform.

Somewhat questionable with the Fetterman Fight, however, is the validity of many secondary sources written about Indian participants beginning in the 1940s, composed by white authors after the deaths of the last surviving Lakota and Cheyenne veterans. Prior to and following each story presented here in its original form, I analyze the account as to its corroboration or conflict with other eyewitness accounts, and I examine the manner in which the account is used or not used in modern secondary sources, whether its transmission comes by way of personal interview or correspondence. I also consider how this information has been contextualized within secondary works. I then examine what we may learn from the account, not only about the fight itself, but also regarding tribal and individualized cultural martial practices of the 1860s. Reliability of original sources is established by comparison and corroboration. The testimonies here are not all equal in length. White Bull's account (Miniconjou), and that of Cheyenne White Elk, are substantial, while others such as that of Oglala Rocky Bear are short statements but no less important. Where no words exist from important historical actors like Red Cloud and Crazy Horse, I consider the testimonies of other eyewitnesses in logically evaluating their likely presence and roles in the Fetterman Fight. A few testimonies, like that of the Oglala warriors Rocky Bear and White Bear, have not previously been published. Where available, and where cursive words can be deciphered, I offer original unpublished interview notes that the reader may contrast with the corresponding published account. Part 4, "Memory and Legacy of the Fetterman Fight," considers how these eyewitness sources have been transmitted through the years and how they might reveal more modern concerns.

PART ONE

A Miniconjou Account

On a summer day in 1930 a forty-three-year-old English professor from the University of Oklahoma by the name of Walter S. Campbell sat on the ground outside a rustic log cabin on the Cheyenne River Indian Reservation in South Dakota. Campbell spoke through an interpreter to a man with whom he was rapidly developing an enduring friendship, Miniconjou Lakota Sioux chief Pte San Hunka (Joseph White Bull). Interested in writing a biography of Thathanke Iyotake (Sitting Bull), Campbell longed to meet Joseph White Bull, a nephew of the great Hunkpapa. White Bull, still a vigorous man at eighty-one, counted many coups in his youth and acquired a reputation as one of the great Miniconjou fighting men in the Sioux wars of resistance with whites. In 1926 White Bull, because of his reputation, led surviving Lakota warriors in a ceremonial ride across the Little Big Horn battlefield during the fiftieth anniversary of the battle. White Bull proved such a knowledgeable source on Northern Plains Indian warfare and its practices that Campbell decided to write the chief's biography. White Bull in turn adopted Campbell as a son, naming him Ocastonka, "Famous." Unlike many of his generation who spoke of the past only to his own people, White Bull was anxious to convey the story of his life to the outside world.

Campbell gathered the complete story of White Bull's life upon returning to the Cheyenne River Reservation during the summer of 1932. For nine hours a day interviews continued practically without interruption. Other aging warriors attended the talks and vouched for the veracity of White Bull's statements. White Bull's generation of Lakota fighting men judged their reputations by the exploits and demonstrations

White Bull and Walter S. Campbell.
Courtesy of the Western History Collections, University of Oklahoma Libraries.

of bravery they exhibited during their youthful years. No other deeds compared to this for their claims of respect. White Bull could write the Lakota language by the 1930s, although his writing style was still unpolished. Others translated his writings, resulting in some dubious representations. In 1968, James H. Howard mistranslated such a transcript White Bull had written for Usher L. Burdick in 1931, and mistakenly claimed White Bull was the actual slayer of Custer at Little Big Horn.[1] Campbell's notes are more faithful and he included a translation of White Bull's winter count calendar in the appendix of the chief's biography. Joseph White Bull passed away on July 21, 1947, at the age of ninety-eight. By that time his biography enjoyed classic status in Indian historiography, published as *Warpath: The True Story of the Fighting Sioux Told in a Biography of Chief White Bull*, by Houghton Mifflin in 1934.[2] Walter S. Campbell, now well lettered with the pen name of Stanley Vestal, survived White Bull by a decade, passing away at seventy in 1957. Today Campbell's work stands as important transcribed primary source information of the seminal years of the Lakota Sioux on the northern plains of the nineteenth century.

Joseph White Bull

Pte San Hunka, 1849–1947

The account of the Fetterman Fight that follows in its entirety is from *Warpath*, Chapter 6, "One-Hundred-White-Men-Killed." Campbell chose to write the biography in the third person so that he could interject military events he garnered from the *Records of the Special Commission to Investigate the Fetterman Massacre and the State of Indian Affairs, 1867*, in the National Archives, between statements made by White Bull. The account is the best known of the Indian testimonies of the Fetterman Fight to be found in this study. Readers will easily discern Campbell's inclusions around White Bull's words in his account of the action in the Fetterman Fight. The first four paragraphs of the account are Campbell's words, as well as the ending paragraphs and a few paragraphs in between. His narrative filler is obvious but contextually necessary in places throughout the account.

Campbell's unpublished rough interview notes in the Western History Collections of the University of Oklahoma Libraries reveal a few minor but significant facts, which are not found in *Warpath*, regarding the chronology and circumstances of the battle. White Bull reveals that Oglalas, Miniconjous, and Cheyennes, with the few Arapahos present, not only camped separately once reaching the Peno Valley but moved separately from their Tongue River camps as well. The notes reveal that White Bull believed the Indians deployed for the ambush in the ravines about 8:00 a.m. on December 21. Although in the published work Campbell names important chiefs present, White Bull stated, as revealed in the interview notes, that there was no central organizational leader over all the Indians, which attests to the ability of all chiefs and headmen to agree and organize as a democratic group. Many secondary works infer that the last remnants of Fetterman's command assembled on Monument Hill behind the boulders found there. White Bull reveals that a majority fought and died among the boulders while lying down in prone positions. As with other accounts White Bull states, in both his initial interviews and in *Warpath*, that Fetterman's command all fought and died bravely, fighting to the end rather than aborting tactical cohesion and trying to escape their fate in a flight of panic at the conclusion of the battle.[1]

White Bull was only seventeen in 1866 and this was his first major engagement. As such the recollections of the aging chief remembering his impetuous teenage years are passionate. White Bull paints himself as a somewhat reckless daredevil, and perhaps a little fortunate. White Bull's account is not without some problems. On occasion, as will be examined in the analysis below, White Bull's and Campbell's placement of Fetterman's troops north-south dispositions is confusing, transposing the infantry and cavalry positions at one point, something that is not evident in Campbell's original field notes. Still, White Bull's account is one of the most extensive and best-known eyewitness Indian testimonies of the Fetterman Fight, and the only Miniconjou reckoning from their southeastern position on the field. Thus it provides a benchmark from which other Indian accounts are compared.

Since the founding of the United States, American arms have suffered two great disasters, which no soldier survived. The first of these was the so-called Fetterman Fight, or Fort Phil Kearny "Massacre," when the Sioux and Cheyennes destroyed the entire force of Captain W. J. Fetterman, December 21, 1866. The second was the fight on the Little Big Horn River, in which General George Armstrong Custer and five troops of the Seventh Cavalry were wiped out by the same Indians, June 25, 1876. Only the celebrated affair at the Alamo can compare with these disasters. On the monument that commemorates the heroic combat of the Texans against the Mexicans under Santa Anna is this inscription: "Thermopylae had her messenger of defeat; the Alamo had none." This inscription might serve equally well on the monuments on Massacre Hill, Wyoming, and on the Custer Battlefield.

Few Indians now survive who can tell of even the more recent of these two battles, and naturally the white men's histories have little to relate concerning them. But there is one man living who has the distinction of having taken part in both the Fetterman and Custer fights. Not only that. He took a leading part in both. That man is Chief Joseph White Bull. Here we have his account of the first one, known to the Indians as One-Hundred-White-Men-Killed.

The Sioux fought for glory. To strike an enemy [count coup], to capture a weapon or a horse, or to be hit in battle were all rated as war honors, and in each of these battles White Bull won them all. The Miniconjou Sioux were governed by six hereditary chiefs or Scalp-Shirt Men. In 1866 these were Brave Bear, Makes-Room, White-Hollow-Horn, Black Shield, One Horn, and White Swan. Lame Deer and Fire Thunder were then vice-chiefs. Of these, White Swan in particular hated the whites, and thought he had good reason to. He had fought them often. It is said that some drunken soldiers once looted his home in his absence, and before they left, defiled it. This insult he could not forget nor forgive. When his time had come to die, White Swan had himself dressed up in his war-clothes, had his face painted ready for burial, and then summoned his head men and comrades-in-arms to the bedside. When they had assembled, he uttered his last request. "Friends," he said, "you must look out for yourselves and protect your people. Try to kill white men, for the white men have come here to kill you. I am about to die. I can kill no more. Therefore I look to you. Carry on." White Swan died, but the Miniconjou did not forget his last words.

The headmen decided to organize a great war party to carry out his wish. Accordingly they summoned the Oglala under Crazy Horse to join them. Early in December 1866, the Miniconjou, a large number of Oglala, and some Cheyennes were in camp on Tongue River near the White (Big Horn) Mountains. The Cheyennes were about to go against the Shoshoni Indians, as they considered themselves at peace with the white men. But when the Sioux asked them to join the expedition, they could not refuse. The Sioux and Cheyennes had always been allies. Moreover, recently the troops had fired at some Cheyenne young men passing a fort.

The chiefs decided to organize a great party and attack the troops at Fort Phil Kearny. War parties were organized in different ways. Sometimes an individual would call in his friends and ask them to join. Again a large party might be organized by some Warrior Society, which would hold a feast to elect officers on the understanding that next morning the officers-elect would lead the Society in battle. In this camp, however, the warriors were so numerous that two Societies held elections the same day. First the Mandan (Miwatani) Society elected officers, and afterward the Fox Soldiers.

White Bull had so distinguished himself on the warpath that the herald of the Fox Soldiers called out his name first of all and invited him to come and feast with the members of the Society. After him, the herald summoned Little Soldier, Thunder Hoop, Bear-Grabs, Thunder Hawk, Bear-Loves, Lazy Ghost, these seven. White Bull led the way into the lodge of the Society and was shown a seat at the right end of the place of honor opposite the door.

Each of the seven men was then given the insignia of his new office. Two were given whips; these acted as dance leaders. Two were given war bonnets covered with crow feathers; two were given lances, and White Bull, as the first one summoned, was given a big drum painted red, with four ornamented sticks on which to hang it when in use, and six drumsticks. The man who owned the drum was always head chief of this Society. Each of the new officers was given an eagle-bone whistle. They were expected to distinguish themselves and lead the way in the fight, but not, of course, to direct the movements of the war party. That was the duty of the regular chiefs.

Seeing their son so honored, Makes-Room and Good Feather came to the lodge leading two horses. At that time the Sioux were—for a wonder—at peace with the Crow Indians, and as several Crows stood there looking on, White Bull's parents gave the horses to these visitors. Before the meeting broke up, the former leader of the Fox Society made a speech. Said he: "I have been the leader of this Society. The members appointed me to this post. Now these young men here are to be the leaders and we must all stand together with them. We are all supposed to look after each other on the warpath and to consider the wishes of our people. It is not likely that these new leaders just appointed will be living long. Probably they will soon be killed. We all live but once. Friends, love each other. If you do this, I will love you. Help the poor and the old folks with donations. Of all things between heaven and earth, food is the most important. If you are eating, and someone comes into your lodge, share with him. If you wish to amuse yourselves, bring in some food, and two or three couples, and dance. If you see someone about to do something wrong, bring him into our Society lodge, get him to smoke the peace pipe, and quiet him down. That is my advice." Next day the whole camp moved up Tongue River toward the fort. The Miniconjou and the Cheyennes were more than a thousand men, and besides these there were numerous Oglala.

They moved along by stages. Black Shield was the principal chief leading the Miniconjou. They rode first, followed by the Oglala and Cheyennes.

It was cold weather and there was snow in places. White Bull had put on a pair of buffalo-fur moccasins with high tops, which his mother had made for him. He was wearing plain leggings of dark woolen cloth and a red flannel gee-string, but no shirt. Some of his comrades wore buckskin shirts with the hair outside. But White Bull preferred to wear his buffalo robe with the hair turned in, belted around him. He wore no mittens and no cloth on his head; he left such protections to old men.

Like the others, he was riding his laden packhorse and leading his war-horse by the lariat. His saddle he had made himself; it had only one cinch. On his saddle he carried some pemmican and a wooden cup, and a war-bag containing his dress clothes. He had a four-point Nor'west blanket, red as blood, strapped to the cantle. In his belt on the left side he carried his knife in a sheath, but had no whetstone. His weapons consisted of a quiver containing his bow and forty arrows, and a lance. His father had made the iron points of those arrows from a frying pan.

As he moved along with his comrades, he sometimes joined a group, which turned aside to kill buffalo or deer, and would take as much meat as he could carry on the saddle. Early each day eight scouts were sent out with instructions to return if they saw nothing, but if they saw enemies to signal back with hand-mirrors from the highest hilltop. They all started about sunup every day and halted for an hour about noon to rest their horses. They always chose a trail through the coulees and gulches, avoiding the hilltops. At sundown they would make camp. Each of the three tribes camped separately in a circle in the creek bottom, the three circles in the brush extending more than a quarter of a mile.

When making camp, White Bull and his comrades planted poles or willow shoots in the ground in a circle, covering them part way up with saddle blankets all around and building a fire in the center of this windbreak. Ten men slept with White Bull in his shelter. He used his buffalo robe and his red blanket for bedding. At night, guards were used. These guards did not walk a post, but generally sat in a group and kept their ears open. It was the custom for anyone who waked during the night to get up and walk around the camp to see that everything was all right. Indian warriors could determine in advance their hour of rising by regulating the amount of water drunk before going to bed. Of course every warrior had his weapons ready, and in enemy country the men never undressed. White Bull kept his face painted red as a protection against the weather.

This large party was full of patriotic spirit. White Bull's relatives were very proud because of the honor done him by the Fox Soldiers. Uncle Flying-Hawk accordingly called these relatives to council—Long Ghost, Crazy Thunder, Fast Horse, Runs-Against, and Powerful. He told them they ought to make a donation and confer another title upon their brave nephew. They agreed, and each man present contributed two arrows, making twelve in all. They decided upon the name of a distinguished ancestor for the young man. Then Flying Hawk called over two singers, men with good voices, Two Herd and Wrinkled Leg. Flying Hawk explained what he wished announced and gave each of them six arrows. They walked out into the camp and called aloud: "Hear ye, hear ye, Bull-Standing-With-Cow is going to leave that name here. From this day you will call him Big-In-The-Center."

This announcement was a complete surprise to White Bull, who was still commonly known as Bull-Standing-With-Cow. Even his father had said nothing of any change. No sooner had his name been changed than he heard someone calling from another camp. It was Long Forelock, who belonged to the Don't-Eat-Dog Band. He was calling: "Big in the Center, my friend, you have a good name. So I am inviting you to come and feast with me." White Bull was pleased to go, for Long Forelock was one of the best fighters in the whole tribe.

When that great war party reached a point some ten miles northwest of the fort, the Indians halted and made camp. There the chiefs held council. They knew that Indians armed only with bows and lances could not hope to capture the fort by assault. They therefore decided to lure the troops out of the fort and along the Trail into the rough country to the north. In the forks of Peno Creek, five miles from the fort, was a long narrow ridge [Massacre Ridge], high and steep. The Trail passed along the top of this ridge. The plan was to lie in wait on each side of this ridge and send a few young men on fast horses to tempt the troops out of the fort and lead them into the trap. By means of this ambush the chiefs hoped to kill all the soldiers and afterward burn the fort. Six young Sioux [two Arapahos] and several Cheyennes were chosen to act as decoys.[2]

At daybreak next morning these young men rode off to the fort to make an attack, and at sunrise all the warriors saddled up, mounted, and followed

Peno Creek up to the forks. There they halted to conceal themselves. As the Cheyennes were guests of the Sioux, they were given their choice of positions. They and the Oglala chose the west side of the ridge. Some who were on foot stopped near the lower (north) end of the ridge, close to the stream. Those on horseback went on higher and took position almost a mile distant from the Trail. The Miniconjou hid themselves behind a ridge to the east of the road within half a mile. White Bull was with them.

Young White Bull stood with the others behind the ridge, armed with a lance, a bow, and forty arrows, holding his gray war-horse and eagerly waiting for a chance to show his valor. He had his four-point Nor'west blanket, red as blood, and because of the cold he folded this blanket and fastened it around him like a short coat. He had two eagle feathers in his hair. Beside him stood Fine Weather, Long Forelock, Little Bear, Thunder-with-Horns, and Runs-Against.

When White Bull peeped out of his covert he could see no one; all the Indians were hidden. Straight ahead of him to the west were the grassy flats and the shallow stream from which the road climbed up the ridge to his left and disappeared in the direction of the fort five miles away. The Indians stood quiet, waiting to spring their trap.

At Fort Phil Kearny that morning there were less than four hundred soldiers. The commanding officer, Colonel Henry B. Carrington, well knew the dangers which surrounded the little post, and felt a heavy responsibility for the women and children there. He knew how brave the Sioux and Cheyenne warriors were. Some of his officers, however, knew nothing of Indian warfare and were eager, overconfident, and impatient of Colonel Carrington's cautious methods. Captain F. H. Brown was so anxious for a fight that he slept in his uniform with his spurs fastened in the buttonholes of his coat and side arms handy, ready day and night. He had orders to go to Fort Laramie and said he "must have one scalp" before leaving the post. Captain (Brevet Lieutenant-Colonel) W. J. Fetterman, who had never fought Indians, talked of "taking Red Cloud's scalp," [this was Captain Brown, not Fetterman] and boasted that "with eighty men I can ride through the whole Sioux Nation." He led just that number of men into the ambush, and none of them ever came out of it.[3]

At about eleven o'clock the morning of December 21, the lookout on Pilot Hill signaled "many Indians," and orders were given to send a detachment to the relief of the wood-train then corralled some distance west of the fort. At his own request Captain Fetterman took command of the detachment, which Captain Brown joined without orders. The little force consisted of three commissioned officers, seventy-six enlisted men, and two civilians. As they moved out, Colonel Carrington gave orders "to relieve the wood-train, but under no circumstances to go beyond Lodge Trail Ridge." It was with great anxiety [but not evident by his next inactions] that Carrington saw Fetterman's command moving straight for Lodge Trail Ridge instead of going toward the wood-train as ordered.

All this time White Bull and his comrades had been waiting in their concealment. Suddenly far away to the southeast White Bull heard on the frosty air a faint sound of firing. It lasted only a few minutes. After a silence he heard it again. It seemed nearer, but did not last long. After a time came a third burst of shooting, not far off this time. Within a few minutes he saw the decoys at the top of the ridge riding back and forth across the Trail in their retreat, and shooting as if trying to stand off the soldiers and save someone behind them. Immediately after, the blue-coated soldiers came into sight and the Sioux began to get ready, grasping their weapons and pinching the nostrils of their ponies to keep them from whinnying to the troop horses. They were all waiting for the signal to charge.

Down the Trail along the ridge came the soldiers, almost a hundred of them, in two bodies, half of them afoot, half mounted, the cavalry in the lead. They were in no hurry, they kept on coming slowly down the ridge, firing at the decoys until the cavalry reached the flat near the forks of Peno Creek and the infantry behind them were already well within the trap. Then the decoys forded the little stream at the end of the ridge and divided into two parties. These two parties separated and rode in opposite directions, then turned and crossed each other. When White Bull saw this signal, he cried out, "Come on! We must start!" The Indians on both sides jumped on their horses and rushed yelling out of the ambush. The Miniconjou, being nearer the Trail than most of the Oglala and Cheyennes, reached the soldiers first. Thunder Hawk was in the lead. He was first to strike a soldier.

When the soldiers saw them coming, they halted, but when the Indians came close and arrows began to fly and one or two of the soldiers were shot down, the infantry quickly fell back up the hill to some large rocks which lay on the slope [separated from the element of infantry remaining in the advance position a few hundred yards downslope]. They flung themselves down behind these rocks and began to shoot. The cavalry did not join the infantry, but moved back and took a position on the hillside about a hundred yards [north] above the infantry [advanced position].

This left the infantry between the Indians and the cavalry [as the warriors swept around and cut off any possibility of retreat to the fort], and the Indians therefore spent their first fury upon the infantry among the rocks. The Oglala and Cheyennes swept around the infantry to the north and east, the Miniconjou circled to the south and west, and for a short time there was hot fighting in which the cavalry took little part. The infantrymen defended themselves bravely, firing their muzzle-loading rifles at the circling Sioux. The Indians greatly outnumbered the whites, but their advantage in numbers was balanced by their lack of firearms. It took courage for a man armed only with a bow or lance to charge in the face of forty rifles, especially as the two civilians with the troops had up-to-date Henry rifles. Nevertheless one brave Miniconjou, Eats-Meat, rode his horse right through the infantry. They shot him down after he had passed. He was the first Indian killed.

The Indians kept riding around, hanging on the sides of their horses, loosing arrows at the infantry, and there were so many of them that the fight with the infantry did not last long. But it lasted long enough to kill and wound a number of Indians and their horses.

The Sioux always carried off their wounded and dead, if possible. But when Bull Eagle was shot, the fire of the soldiers was so hot that no one dared go to his rescue. After most of the infantry had been killed, three of the survivors jumped up and ran up the slope to join the cavalry. When the Sioux saw these three men running past, they all rushed them. Bull Eagle, on foot, was in the lead. He ran forward with raised bow, ready to strike his victim. He ran right up within two paces of the foremost soldier. One of them fired and dropped him. He lay on the prairie, shot through the right thigh, unable to move. When his comrades saw him lying there, they ran to cover. No one went to his rescue.

Then young White Bull remembered his duty as Drum Keeper of the Fox Soldiers. When he saw his friend lying there helpless, he jumped off his horse, ran out to him under fire. Bull Eagle was bleeding freely and groaning—but like a wounded bear, to show that he still had a strong heart. A white man would have cursed for the same reason. White Bull seized Bull Eagle by the wrists and dragged him away over the edge of the ridge to safety. There the wounded man's uncle took charge of him. Then White Bull ran back to his horse, mounted, and joined in the charge. The Sioux were killing the infantry one by one with their arrows; the rifle fire was steadily lessening; the white smoke drifted away. Suddenly, as White Bull dashed along, circling the rocks, he was shot from his horse. He fell with a thud on his shoulder, but managed to keep hold on the lariat tied about the horse's neck. A bullet had passed through the red blanket behind his left shoulder and had knocked him off his horse without touching him. There were two holes through the blanket.

White Bull ran to his horse and remounted. Being knocked off his horse that way made him angry instead of afraid. Soon after, the Indians killed the last of the infantry. When they had wiped out the doughboys, they turned their attention to the cavalry farther up the ridge.

Up to this time the cavalry had held their ground about a hundred yards south [?] of the [advanced element of] infantry, but now, as the Indians rushed them from all sides, the troopers began to fall back toward the fort, slowly fighting their way up the ridge. They moved in a compact body, shooting all the time. They were half-hidden in the powder smoke. Some of them were on foot leading their horses. Others, whose horses had been shot, would stop, and kneel, and fire, then go on. In the rear White Bull saw one trooper on foot, facing the Indians, running backward, and yelling at the top of his voice. He carried a carbine, threatening the Indians, pointing it first one way and then another.

Young White Bull thought he saw a chance to distinguish himself. He made up his mind to charge that man. Quirting his pony on both flanks, he raced forward ahead of all the Sioux, holding an arrow on his bowstring, expecting the soldier to shoot. When within ten feet of the trooper, he drew his arrow to the head. The trooper seemed too much excited to resist. He did not try to shoot until White Bull was almost on top of him. White Bull let his arrow go, shot the man in front, through the heart. As he fell on his back, White Bull cracked him across the head with his lance, knocking the man's cap off. Thus he was first to strike that soldier. He counted a first coup.

White Bull's charge put heart into his comrades, and after this soldier was killed the Indians swarmed up the icy slopes more and more, while the cavalry made more and more haste up the ridge. Almost every minute White Bull shot an arrow at the troops. In that way he killed a troop horse. All the

Indians were shooting, arrows were flying in every direction. Indeed, even some of the Indians were hit by arrows, among them Thunder Hump and King. The ground was so covered with arrows that a warrior did not have to use his own, he could pick one up almost anywhere.

Under this hail of arrows many of the troop-horses were hit, became frightened, and broke away. Finally the soldiers reached the upper end of the long ridge and all at once let all their horses go. The Indians were all eager to capture a cavalry horse. They stopped shooting then, and raced after these animals. This gave the soldiers time to breathe. They ran up and flung themselves down behind some boulders, which lay close together at the top (south end) of the ridge. White Bull took after the horses also, though the ground was very steep and icy, and his own horse was slow. He caught none; the other Indians out rode him. When all the horses had been captured, the Indians came back to the fight.

The ridge on which the troopers had flung themselves down was high and narrow, only about forty feet wide, just where the monument stands now. On every side but the south the ridge fell away very steeply into the bottoms far below. That was no place for horsemanship, more especially as the slopes were covered with snow and ice, and the weather had now become so cold that blood froze as it flowed from a wound. The chiefs called out, ordering the Indians to leave their horses in the ravines and to fight on foot.

Up to this time White Bull had been fighting to the north and west of the troops, but now he crossed the ridge and joined the warriors who were creeping up the eastern slope. The fight with the infantry had occupied only a few minutes, but the destruction of the cavalrymen among the rocks on the steep ridge was a longer business. The cavalrymen were armed with single-shot breech-loading carbines, using percussion caps: they could fire more rapidly than the infantry had done. For all that, the Indians kept advancing, swarming up the slopes and shooting back and forth across the ridge. The air was full of arrows. All this time the Indians kept encouraging each other, and advancing foot by foot toward the doomed troopers. White Bull moved forward side by side with his friend Charging-Crow, a Miniconjou Sioux. He says that the Miniconjou braves did most of the fighting at this end of the field.

When the Indians were already crowded close up to the top of the ridge on both sides, Long Fox, leader of the Miniconjou on the west side, stood up and yelled, "Hopo! Let's go!"

Then all the Indians jumped up and rushed forward. White Bull and Charging-Crow reached the top of the ridge at the same moment. An instant later Charging-Crow tumbled at the boy's feet, shot dead. This man's death frightened the boy for a moment; he dropped to the ground. Immediately after, his uncle Flying Hawk fell dead there, shot through the right breast. The other Indians rushed on—right in among the rocks. They fought hand-to-hand with the troopers, stabbing and scuffling there in the smoke and dust. It was a dreadful mix-up, the kind of fight that the Sioux call "stirring gravy." That charge ended the battle and killed the last white man. Because of his delay when Charging-Crow fell, young White Bull got there just as the last soldier was killed. But he was in time to capture a carbine.

After that the Indians stripped the soldiers, and White Bull took two pairs of trousers. He cut off the legs so that his father could use them for leggings, and threw the seat of the pants away. In the pockets of the troopers, he and other Indians found paper money and silver coins. They knew the value of the silver, but paper money was unknown to them. They saved only the new bills; they thought the children at home might like to play with them. White Bull also got one overcoat from the troops and some cartridges. He says that less than half the ammunition carried by the soldiers had been used in the fight. He himself had shot away twenty of his forty arrows. The length of the fight, estimated by those in the fort by the duration of the firing, was hardly more than forty minutes. If each of the other two thousand Indians present shot as many arrows as White Bull, one can imagine how the ground was littered with those feathered shafts. White Bull picked up many of these arrows and filled his quiver with them, for arrows were valuable and hard to make. Others did the same. They left only the broken or blunted arrows.

All the troopers were killed in the battle, fighting, with weapons in their hands and ammunition in their possession. It was therefore no "massacre," as it has been called. It was all over about noon. When Colonel Carrington at the fort heard all that heavy firing, he knew that a desperate fight was going on beyond Lodge Trail Ridge. Within twelve minutes Captain T. Ten Eyck was dispatched from the fort with infantry and cavalry, two wagons, ambulances, and two surgeons. He went on the run, but just as he reached the hillside overlooking the battlefield, all firing ceased. He saw the Peno Valley full of circling Indians. At first they beckoned him to come down, but he stood his ground until they left the battlefield, soon after.

Then he advanced and found Captain Fetterman, Captain Brown, and more than half the command lying in a space about forty feet in diameter. A few cavalry horses lay dead not far off, all with their heads toward the fort. Following the road down the ridge he found the naked bodies of the [advanced element of] infantrymen, [and farther along] the two civilians, and Lieutenant G. W. Grummond [found a short distance north of the others], surrounded by ten dead Indian ponies and sixty-five pools of dark and clotted blood [these near Wheatley-Fisher Rocks on the north end of the field]. Only six of the command showed gunshot wounds. Captain Fetterman and Captain Brown were found shot through the temple, with powder burns around the wounds. These officers had declared that they would not be taken alive by Indians; they feared torture. It was supposed that they had committed suicide. The dead soldiers had been stripped, cut to pieces by the Indians, scalped, and shot full of arrows. One man had more than a hundred arrows in his body. All the bodies lay along, or near, the road on the ridge.

White Bull was only a boy of seventeen at this time, but he thinks the Indians cut these enemies to pieces because they had put up such a good fight and had killed so many Indians. Of the Sioux the soldiers killed or mortally wounded Bear Ears, Little Crow, Yellow White Man, Lone Bear, Clown Horse, Male Eagle, He Dog, Eats Meat, Fine Weather, Charging-Crow, Eagle-Stays-In-The-Air, Broken Hand, Eats-Pemmican, and Flying Hawk. Flying Hawk was White Bull's uncle, the brother of his father, Makes-Room. The dead man's two brothers, Long Ghost and Crazy Thunder, took his weapons and horse home with them. The Indians laid away their dead a few miles from the battlefield, wrapped up well in blankets and covered with rocks to keep the wolves away.

When Captain Ten Eyck returned to Fort Phil Kearny with forty-nine dead bodies and the dreadful news of the disaster, those in the fort were terrified. Guards were doubled, and every man slept in his clothes with loaded weapons at hand. The officers did not sleep at all, expecting an immediate attack. The women and children were placed in the powder magazine, which had been stocked with water, crackers, and other supplies. There an officer was on duty pledged not to allow the women to be taken alive, if the Indians should get over the stockade. Colonel Carrington then set out to bring in the remaining bodies left on the field.

All these precautions were unnecessary. The Indians were satisfied with their victory. They knew they could not take the fort. Had they wished more fighting, they might have attacked Captain Ten Eyck. Instead, they rode home to the camp on Tongue River. There, four days later, they danced the Victory Dance.

This Victory Dance was the first occasion on which White Bull began to pay attention to the girls. He was only a boy, seventeen years old. The girls must have been friendly toward him, however, when he came home with a captured carbine, a "wound," and a coup to his credit.

The monument on the battlefield gives Chief Red Cloud of the Oglala Sioux credit for leading the Indians in this battle, but all the Indian testimony, both Sioux and Cheyenne, is unanimous in stating that Red Cloud was not present, and took no part in the fight, or in planning it. Crazy Horse was the leader of the Oglala, Black Shield of the Miniconjou. Many of the chiefs besides Red Cloud led their warriors against the white men in that year of '66. Every wagon train, which passed over the Bozeman Trail, was attacked. More than a thousand head of horses and mules were captured and about two hundred whites were killed and wounded. It was the most sustained warfare the whites had ever encountered from the Sioux. But the biggest battle of all was only the fulfillment of the wish of a dying man, Chief White Swan.

Of all the warriors who took part in this fight, few showed more courage or won more honor than young White Bull, now also called Big-in-the-Center.

White Bull was surprised to learn recently that Captain Fetterman committed suicide. He says he never knew an Indian to do such a thing, in a fight. As to torture of captives, he is unable to recall any instance among the Prairie Sioux, though he does remember an instance or two of assault upon Indians of enemy tribes when visiting the Sioux camp. The Plains Sioux, he says, killed their enemies in the fight, or else adopted them, or turned them loose. That was the custom.

I knew, of course, that stories of Indian atrocities had been hugely exaggerated on the frontier—often for very base motives. Still, I thought he might remember some atrocity, if pressed, and so continued to question him on this point. And to make it easy for him, I told how white men sometimes burned Negroes at the stake. The chief turned upon me in horror, and cried: "Would you burn a Negro?" I hastily explained that I personally would not, but that many whites had been guilty of such cruelty. The chief was so upset by this news that he could not go on with the talk for some little time. Had I confessed to such a crime, I am certain that he would have broken off our friendship then and there.

No man knows the Plains Indians better than George Bird Grinnell, and he writes: "There was practically no torture of captives by the Western Indians." Atrocities do occur, of course, in all wars; but the Plains Sioux had no deliberate policy of frightfulness. The fact is that the White men brought with them from the East a ready-made notion of Indians, which did not fit the Plains tribes at all.

≡ ≡

What may we learn from Chief Joseph White Bull? Readers should be mindful that Campbell crafted his interview questions during a period in American history that, in the midst of the Great Depression, would suddenly shift concerns from nostalgia for the old West and its vanishing cultures to concerns of poverty, unemployment, and New Dealism in the face of immediate financial crisis. Concern for the survival of peoples who had known poverty since military conquest ended in the late nineteenth century would temporarily replace reverence for the old heroes of this bygone era. Ironically, these new economic calamities belied a general belief that Indians constituted "vanishing Americans." Although the federal government largely ignored much of their financial need during the Great Depression, John Collier's Indian Reorganization Act (IRA), or the "Indian New Deal," in 1934 started the quest for tribal self-determinism by returning some elements of indigenous local governance back to the tribes.[4]

With American citizenship barely a decade old and the IRA not yet fully implemented when *Warpath* first appeared in print, many Indian people looked ahead for better times that largely would not come for several more decades. Many non-Natives however, were also changing their attitudes toward American Indians. They were ending an era of thirst for capturing evocative stories of America's now-bygone frontier cultures confirmed by the Pan American Exposition of 1915 in San Francisco, a gala that celebrated the defeat of savagery by the most civilized society in the world and the fulfillment of their Manifest Destiny. Visitors to the exposition marveled at a two-story iconic sculpture symbolizing that powerful fulfillment, James Earl Fraser's interpretation of a weary and defeated Plains Indian, *The End of the Trail*. The once proud warrior sleeps bent over the mane of his exhausted horse while riding slowly toward an unknown future. Seemingly a chapter had come to an end. But Indians did not vanish, and many Americans' attitudes toward Indian people from the 1940s on became not as romantic as they had once been.

But writers during the generation between the Great War and the Depression, in which Campbell brought up the rear, sought out the tales of old soldiers, pioneer settlers, and Indian warrior veterans during this era of nostalgia. Writers' motivations to present stories of interest about Indians to white audiences predominate during this era. Many of these aging Indian people were often amazed their stories of travail, toil, and survival were now actually remolding them as mythic historical actors in the American pageant of success yet also shadowed past and present exploitation of encountered peoples. As such, the stories of figures like White Bull were romanticized and enshrined in a kind of politics-free time capsule, which portrayed a mythic individuality that was thought to characterize frontier partisans—Indian and white alike, heroic figures who would soon vanish and become irrelevant in the future. Men like Walter Campbell, and perhaps White Bull himself, strived to insert this image of romantic heroism and self-sacrifice into America's romantic historical memory, if not yet into the contextual reality of the master narrative.

Campbell literally enshrined White Bull as a heroic figure of a defeated people. "To me, at least," he writes, "it is no small thing to have known and talked to a man straight out of Homer." Predictably then, White Bull's account focuses on the chivalry of individualized warfare, "stirring gravy," in White Bull's words, as being unique and as vanished and anachronistic as the frontier itself. This iconic, chivalric, and perhaps subtly self-righteous image contrasted sharply and thus more sanitarily with the most recent realities of the mass industrialized and mechanized carnage of the First World War, of which Campbell was a veteran, having served barely a decade previously. White Bull, anxious to foster outside interest in his experiences, gratefully obliged Campbell. The time for determined rhetoric about seeking decolonization had not yet arrived. The reader will detect that White Bull's testimony of the Fetterman Fight as related through Campbell is rather an amazing accounting of planning, organization, and cooperation in achieving counter-offensive success against U.S. troops that, until 1876, was without equal in Lakota-Cheyenne military history on the Plains. In this regard, Campbell's interest in the Indians' "style of warfare" takes total precedence over why war came to the Powder River Country in 1866 to begin with and what were its consequences. Ironically it also belies the myth that Indian warfare was always individualized and stresses the fact of strict organization in planning and deployment until engagement, with individual exploits taking over once shooting started.

White Bull clearly reflects the Miniconjou feeling that the ambush at Fort Phil Kearny was simply the fulfillment of a wish by the dying headman White Swan, who had suffered past wrongs by the whites. In 1866 the Lakotas and Cheyennes still held the balance of power and superior population numbers in the Powder River Country. The knowledge that the recently constructed forts on the Bozeman Trail were far removed from supply sources at Fort Laramie and food supplies from Virginia City, Montana, gave them a strategic and tactical advantage of which they were well aware. They used this advantage on an almost daily basis in keeping Fort Phil Kearny, the mid-point on the supply and communication chain, in a virtual state of siege. With a couple of exceptions the northern tribes were yet to be defeated and had gained confidence with their command over the environment and their grass-fed horses. This was as opposed to the logistical nightmare of supplying grain for army horses on long military offensive campaigns, exemplified by the trials of Patrick Conner's expedition of the previous year.[5]

As will be seen in the following accounts, the Oglalas, due to their bloody war with the Crows in 1857, grasped the full extent of the potential for disaster to their way of life with white occupation of the Powder River Country. As for the government's concern in keeping the Bozeman Trail open to Montana prior to rail connections reaching Salt Lake City, Campbell leaves us not a word. White Bull's lack of awareness or concern in retrospect for the political consequences of the war in 1866, or as those possibilities later became realities, reveal not only Campbell's immediate interests in capturing descriptions of cultural martial practices but also the eagerness of a "retired" accomplished warrior to remember the impetuous exploits of youth.[6]

White Bull's daring and dangerous actions are not at all unusual for Lakota warriors, and remembering those years in maturity as heroic is understandable. Lakota youth were expected to be daring in risking their individual lives to insure success of the group as a whole. Lakota confidence in military success and personal risk is based in long-standing cultural belief of superiority to all other enemies and ethnicities. Institutionalized thinking in this regard became characterized as expected roles for the individual being beneficial to the group—what one scholar has called "systematic auto-suggestion."[7] With Lakota balance of power yet unbroken by whites in the Powder River Country, White Bull's confidence in his daring actions was admirable in the eyes of his fellows despite his young age of seventeen.

White Bull recalls especially his close calls with death—a bullet through his blanket, being knocked from his horse, then seeing a friend and his uncle killed next to him. His account establishes the use of bows and clubs as principal Indian weapons in the fight, a fact corroborated by other accounts. Perhaps most importantly in reconstructing positions and movements, White Bull places the Miniconjou in the

White Bull, wearing his red Nor'west blanket, counts his first coup on a soldier in this
drawing of himself. The bullet holes in White Bull's blanket can clearly be seen. The
dress of the soldier suggests he may be a cavalryman with a shell jacket and a kepi
White Bull drew over the visible crown of the man's head. Although the lack of cavalry
boots is problematic, White Bull speaks of fighting the cavalry. The absence of the
boots may be explained by the shortages of extraneous supplies to Fort Phil Kearny.
A copy of this drawing is in the author's personal collection.

southeastern ravines, hidden below the ridge and the Bozeman Trail, and reveals
how his peoples swept around to the south, moving east to west, thus cutting
the troops' avenue of retreat and escape back to Fort Phil Kearny and completing
the envelopment of Fetterman's doomed command. He confirms that surviving
cavalrymen retreating south up the ridge turned loose their horses and scrambled
for the rocks on Monument Hill. White Bull corroborates other Native sources in
describing how the warriors amazingly kept their horses from whinnying in the ravines
in order to maintain silence until Fetterman's entire command was well within the
trap set for them. Neither White Bull nor Campbell leave readers with a sense of time,
motion, and distance between the infantry positions and the farthest cavalry position
(a mile total south to north) in either Campbell's field notes or the final manuscript
of *Warpath*.[8] Neither are they clear on the cavalry's split from the infantry from the

summit of Lodge Trail Ridge. Lieutenant Grummond charged ahead at that point, possibly of his own usual impulsive volition, to a distance north of almost a mile, down a ravine west of the infantry to the Peno Creek forks. Upon being engaged by overwhelming numbers of warriors, he and most of his men attempted to retreat back up the ridge and took a position on what is now known as Cavalry Hill, about midway up the ridge. Survivors of the limited engagement there, of which Grummond may or may not have been one at that point, scrambled up to the rocks on Monument Hill, releasing their horses somewhere along the way of their retreat.

Simple errors in the transcription of White Bull's memories are rendered by Campbell, not White Bull, in recounting the army reports and especially in Campbell's lack of understanding of armaments prevalent at the Fetterman Fight. Spencer rifles and carbines were seven-shot lever action repeating cartridge weapons, not single-shot breech-loading guns requiring "percussion caps." Captains Fetterman and Brown did not commit suicide jointly. And, according to most battle reconstructions and archaeology not all of the Infantry was destroyed before the cavalry. Neither was the advance infantry position likely "north" of the farthest penetration point of the cavalry until surviving cavalrymen who had not remained at Wheatley-Fisher Rocks raced past the farthest infantry position in an attempt to reach the protection of the rocks on Monument Hill, on the south end of the line where Fetterman and some remaining infantrymen had also retreated and fought during much of the battle. Recent and previous "known" archaeology suggests any "stand" taking place on Cavalry Hill was of short duration given the scarcity of artifact evidence.[9] Campbell correctly ascertains that the fight was not a "massacre" as the soldiers were armed and in pursuit of Indian combatants with the intent of engaging them in battle.[10]

Despite its geographical and sequential ambiguity, in the estimation of anthropologist Raymond J. DeMallie, White Bull's account of his life as a warrior gives the reader, more than any other reminiscence in the vast literature of the Sioux, "an appreciation for the values of plains Indian warfare in practice." White Bull is the antithesis of the dreamer/philosopher Black Elk.

"White Bull's story," states DeMallie, is "graphic and direct."[11] Today White Bull's stories of the Fetterman Fight serve to complement his many other memories by inserting the Indian voice into the decades of the 1860s and 1870s, thus helping to give Miniconjou Lakotas ownership of their history.

PART TWO

Oglala Accounts

Oglala Lakotas likely constituted the largest contingent of warriors in the Fetterman Fight. They also had the most reason to protect the Powder River Country from white intrusion. During the 1840s the Oglalas were the most numerous of the seven council fires, or *ospaye*, of the Lakota people. The seven *ospaye*, in turn, make up the sacred hoop (*cangleska waken*)—a metaphor for Lakota society. Inhabiting the rich Platte Valley with the Brûlé, and often, Miniconjou Lakotas, the Oglalas enjoyed excellent trade relations with Fort Laramie and other permanent trading sites. During the 1850s, wagon migration took its toll on the fragile grasses along the Platte River Road, as well as affecting buffalo migration patterns. With an extended period of drought after circa 1846 at the end of the so-called Little Ice Age, the sustainability of the Platte Valley ecology and its effects on Plains Indian economy would become challenged. Following the punitive military expedition in 1855 under General William S. Harney against the Lakotas for the killing of Lieutenant John Grattan the previous year, the band of Oglalas known as the Smoke People decided to move north to the ecologically viable Powder River Country. There they joined with northern Lakotas and Northern Cheyenne allies, who moved north simultaneously from the Republican and Solomon Valleys in Kansas and Nebraska. They all wrested this coveted hunting ground from their enemies the Crows, whom the United States had recognized as suzerains in the region by the Horse Creek Treaty of 1851.

The Crow War of 1856–59 became a brutal affair, with two large battles, Captive Hill, and Rain (or Rainy) Hill, claiming more lives than any subsequent fights with

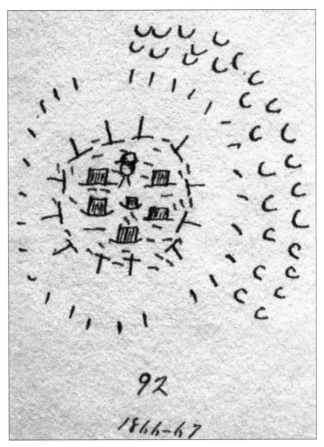

The Fetterman Fight, American Horse Winter Count Mnemonic
for 1866–1867. The mnemonic illustrates the envelopment of the
remains of Fetterman's command on Monument Hill. The "u"
symbols represent horseshoes, while the vertical dashes represent
warriors closing in on foot. The "T" markings are hand-to-hand
combat with the soldiers among the rocks (small hash mark)
within the encirclement. The empty "Hardee" campaign hats
ostensibly represent slain infantrymen, while there appears to be
a soldier standing with a kepi, likely either a cavalryman or officer.
Courtesy of the American Bureau of Ethnology, Smithsonian Institution.

Americans. The drawings of Oglala Amos Bad Heart Bull illustrates the Captive Hill fight as being greater in scope and numbers than Little Big Horn in 1876. Outnumbered and defeated, the Crows by 1859 retreated north and west of the Bighorn Mountains. The Lakotas, until 1877, with their Northern Cheyenne allies, tenaciously defended their "right of conquest" in the Powder River Country from Indian enemies, American soldiers, and government treaty makers. Stated Northern Cheyenne Chief Black Horse to Colonel Henry Carrington during the colonel's botched peace talks at Fort Laramie in 1866: "The Sioux helped us. We stole the hunting grounds of the Crows because they were best. The white man is along the great waters [Missouri and Platte Rivers], and we wanted more room. We fight the Crows because they will not take half and give us peace with the other half." In 1866, the Lakota and Northern Cheyenne northern alliance was not about to allow whites to build permanent forts in this rich country, won with blood only seven years previous.[1]

The Smoke People, named for the followers of Oglala Chief Old Smoke, who came north to the Powder River Country in the 1850s, were part of a highly sophisticated and well-organized tribal political structure whose decisions were made mostly through a representative democratic council system similar to all Plains tribes. The Oglalas as a whole, as previously stated, were one of seven *ospayes*. The Smoke People, in American minds, constituted a "band" which in Lakota translates to *tiyospaye*. A *tiyospaye* generally incorporated ten or more extended families, although charismatic leaders might attract more families, in which case a *tiyospaye* would be sub-divided into several camps (*wicoti*), each of which still bore the name of the original *tiyospaye*. The *tiyospaye* was the basic functional unit of Oglala daily life and social practice. *Itancans* led the *tiyospaye* by regulating camp life, occasionally trying to influence domestic disputes. Most often the head *itancan* inherited his position. Lesser *itancans* within the larger *tiyospayes* also held responsibilities within the bands. *Itancans* were supposed to be diplomatic, generous, kind, and brave. Americans occasionally misinterpreted *itancans* as being "head band chiefs," but in Oglala society their status is not that of a tribal decision-maker. They often had little such authority, although they might speak in a council if they had important things to say.

Lakotas in 1866 recognized no centralized executive authority. The *owoglake* (council), understood by Americans as the Chiefs' Council, conferred over matters of tribal importance beyond band matters, such as war and peace, treaty negotiation, and so forth. Individuals could call councils at times of crisis or when significant matters needed to be discussed and decisions made. *Itancans* with important issues might speak at a council, as could the *blotahunkas* (war party leaders), and *akicitas*, a form of police that enforced decisions and standard practices on the hunt, in the village, and during war. Holy men might attend council as could anyone else important to the matters being discussed. "Shirtwearers" might speak at a council. The White Horse Rider soldier society selected prominent warriors from across the bands as shirtwearers. These men were considered impeccable Lakotas who epitomized the virtues of bravery, generosity, and wisdom. Shirtwearers took oaths to protect their people in war and peace and provide for their needs and protection.[2]

Councils made decisions by consensus rather than majority rule, which often frustrated whites (Wasicus) in treaty talks and peace negotiations. Eventually, Lakotas selected a small delegation to negotiate with the Americans and then seek consensus with the important leaders of the tribe during council. By one estimate, in 1861–67 over 11,000 warriors (probably exaggerated) were at war with Americans on the northern plains. Their numbers included all seven *ospayes* or council fires of the Lakotas, some Yanktonais and Santees, as well as Northern Cheyennes and Northern Arapahos. No wonder confusion reigned among the Americans throughout the 1860s with their attempts to negotiate with Plains Indians, all of whom practiced similar political systems with some specialized differences. Separating peaceful bands or smaller groups from those at war became an even bigger headache in the Powder River Country of 1866. Colonel Carrington would often issue letters of safe passage to warriors who then proved to be problematic by deciding later to go to war.[3]

But the principal Oglala *tiyospaye* that had moved north to challenge the Crows in the late fifties, and then the Americans in the 1860s, was the Smoke People, the *Hunkpatila*, commonly nicknamed, the "Bad Faces" (*Ite Sica*). Their principal *itancan* was Old Smoke (d. 1864), succeeded by his son, Man Afraid of His Horses (d. 1889), and then succeeded in the reservation years by his son, Young Man Afraid of His Horses. Red Cloud in 1866 became an influential *blotahunka* of the Bad Faces. Following Carrington's peace conference in June 1866, a principal Southern Oglala *tiyospaye*, the Kiyuska, under head *itancan* Little Wound, struck their lodges and moved to the South Platte and Republican valleys. They renewed their friendship with the Southern Cheyennes and attempt to remain at peace following the short-lived and unratified Treaty of the Little Arkansas in 1865. By December, a number of these warriors went north to the Powder River Country, including the famous Kiyuska warrior Pawnee Killer where they would participate in the Fetterman Fight. Others, about 850, mostly elderly men and women, moved to the Republican Valley to hunt with Spotted Tail's Brûlés. Followers of Northern Cheyenne council chief Dull Knife may have been with them for a while and may have then gone north for a short time, but later that winter they camped near Fort Sedgwick in Colorado Territory. Dull Knife's presence at the Fetterman Fight is unclear.[4]

The Oglalas who later would relate their experiences of the Fetterman Fight are important men. But unlike the Cheyenne accounts in Part 3, their accounts are brief, reflecting again the interests, interactive abilities, and any charm possessed by the particular interviewer. Black Elk is the first account in this section. As we shall see, fear determined certain proscribed actions in tribal warfare. John G. Neihardt is meticulous in presenting not only Black Elk's story but also the voice of aged Fire Thunder in the first person, one of the finest of the Oglala Accounts. Eli S. Ricker was less meticulous in his interview with American Horse. Yet the brief tale told by American Horse of the death of Captain William J. Fetterman is revealing. Doane Robinson and Addison E. Sheldon give us even briefer, unpublished accounts of White Face, Eagle Hawk, Red Fly, and Rocky Bear, and the statements of others. Sheldon's interview with American Horse, however, is more substantial than Ricker's. Sheldon, Robinson, and Ricker appear not to have established long-term relationships with their Indian friends.

Finally, the voice of Red Cloud is mostly silent regarding the battle itself. His presence and role in the battle is still a topic of disagreement among aficionados of the Fetterman Fight. By examining and analyzing little-known encounters with Red Cloud's white contemporaries, this section attempts to resolve that issue. A later essay in this section considers historical memory in the cultural celebration of Crazy Horse with the earlier written record.

⇒ 2 ⇐

Black Elk

Heȟáka Sápa, 1863–August 9, 1950

Black Elk Speaks, transcribed by John G. Neihardt, is widely known the world over as one of the great religious masterpieces of the twentieth century and the best book ever of the translated words of an American Indian. John G. Neihardt captured the spiritual essence of the Lakotas at their critical time of transition from hegemonic warriors of the northern plains to a defeated people attempting to adapt to the monumental upheaval and changes of reservation life. Like Joseph White Bull and Walter S. Campbell, Black Elk and Neihardt became lifelong friends. Black Elk named Neihardt "Flaming Rainbow." Important eyewitness history is recorded in Black Elk's narrative.

Born in 1863, Black Elk was only three years old at the time of the Fetterman Fight and living with his parents in the 1866 Oglala camp circle on the Tongue River, more than a day's horseback travel from Fort Phil Kearny. Black Elk's father's name was also Black Elk. The young child could not have had lucid memories of the Fetterman Fight. Yet a lifetime later, imprinted in his subconscious, the aftermath of the great battle in which his father suffered with a broken foot or leg is perhaps the earliest impression the young boy acquired. Black Elk's emotion is exacerbated by the commotion after the warriors returned from the battle. He told Neihardt of sensing, even as a small child, communal *fear* of what might happen next. In the following years, of course, family and tribal elders told Black Elk the specific circumstances of the fight. The elderly Black Elk deferred these stories to Fire Thunder to relate them to Neihardt. Fire Thunder was in the thick of the fight.

Black Elk teaching Broken Nose's children with Two Roads catechism, 1920s.
Courtesy St. Francis Mission and Marquette University, Saint Francis Mission Records, ID ITS 00042.

Although widely read, Black Elk's reflections on the Fetterman Fight are excerpted here from *Black Elk Speaks* to add continuity to this study by allowing readers to examine the constant fear of retribution that must have spread through the Tongue River camps, especially for children, following the battle.[1] Also, as opposed to some noted battles of the American Indian wars, there are no known references or accounts regarding women at or near the Fetterman Fight, although some accounts presented here attest to some Cheyenne women, who had accompanied family members, being present along Peno Creek. Some women could reasonably have followed husbands, brothers, or fathers; we simply do not know their specific identities. Black Elk discusses a furtive memory of his mother putting him in a pony drag next to another travois holding his father with his broken foot while moving out of the Tongue River village. Both women and children were ever on the alert for danger from enemies in their vicinity. Women were well practiced in breaking camp, taking down lodges, making travois from poles, and packing belongings and supplies in a very short period of time. No evidence exists that the Indians were in a huge hurry to move camps after this battle. They took time for a victory dance and to care for their dead and wounded. When they finally exited the Tongue Valley toward the west, as Black Elk believed, they faced one of the bitterest snowy winters on the northern plains many could remember before they returned to assaulting the forts on the Bozeman Trail in 1867.[2]

———

I can remember that winter of the Hundred Slain as a man may remember some bad dream he dreamed when I was little, but I can not tell you just how much I heard when I was bigger and how much I understood when I was little. It was like some fearful thing in a fog, for it was a time when everything seemed troubled and afraid.

I had never seen a Wasicu then, and did not know what one looked like; but every one was saying that the Wasicus were coming and that they were going to take our country and rub us all out and that we should all have to die fighting. It was the Wasicus who got rubbed out in that battle, and all the people were talking about it for a long while; but a hundred Wasicus was not much if there were others and others without number where those came from.

I remember once that I asked my grandfather about this. I said: "When the souls come back from seeing the prairie full of bison somewhere, the people say the Wasicus are coming; and when strange men are coming to kill us all, they say the Wasicus are coming. What does it mean?" And he said, "That they are many."

When I was older, I learned what the fighting was about that winter and the next summer. Up on the Madison Fork the Wasicus had found much of the yellow metal that they worship and that makes them crazy, and they wanted to have a road up through our country to the place where the yellow metal was; but my people did not want the road. It would scare the bison and make them go away, and also it would let the other Wasicus come in like a river. They told us that they wanted only to use a little land, as much as a wagon would take between the wheels; but our people knew better. And when you look about you now, you can see what it was they wanted.

Once we were happy in our own country and we were seldom hungry, for then the two-leggeds and the four-leggeds lived together like relatives, and there was plenty for them and for us.

But the Wasicus came, and they have made little islands for us and other little islands for the four-leggeds, and always these islands are becoming smaller, for around them surges the gnawing flood of the Wasicus, and it is dirty with lies and greed. A long time ago my father told me what his father told him, that there was once a Lakota holy man, called Drinks Water, who dreamed what was to be; and this was long before the coming of the Wasicus. He dreamed that the four-leggeds were going back into the earth and that a strange race had woven a spider's web all around the Lakotas. And he said: "When this happens, you shall live in square gray houses, in a barren land, and beside those square gray houses you shall starve." They say he went back to Mother Earth soon after he saw this vision, and it was sorrow that killed him. You can look about you now and see that he meant these dirt-roofed houses we are living in, and that all the rest was true. Sometimes dreams are wiser than waking. And so when the soldiers came and built themselves a town of logs there on the Piney Fork of the Powder, my people knew they meant to have their road and take our country and maybe kill us all when they were strong enough. Crazy Horse was only about 19 years old then [twenty-six], and Red Cloud was still our great chief [only a *blotahunka*].[3] In the Moon of the Changing Season (October) he called together all the scattered bands of the Lakota for a big council on the Powder River and when we went on the warpath against the soldiers, a [man on] horseback could ride through our villages from sunrise until the day was above his head, so far did our camp stretch along the valley of the river; for many of our friends, the Shyela [Cheyennes] and the Blue Clouds [Arapahos] had come to help us fight.

I am quite sure that I remember the time when my father came home with a broken leg that he got from killing so many Wasicus, and it seems that I can remember all about the battle too, but I think I could not. It must be the fear that I remember most. All this time I was not allowed to play very far away from our tepee, and my mother would say, "If you are not good the Wasicus will get you."

We must have broken camp at the mouth of the Peno soon after the battle, for I can remember my father lying on a pony drag with bison robes all around him, like a baby, and my mother riding the pony. The snow was deep and it was very cold, and I remember [being] in another pony drag beside my father and mother, all wrapped up in fur. We were going away from where the soldiers were, and I do not know where we went, but it was west.

It was a hungry winter, for the deep snow made it hard to find the elk; and also many of the people went snow blind. We wandered a long time, and some of the bands got lost from each other. Then at last we were camping in the woods beside a creek somewhere, and the hunters came back with meat.

I think it was this same winter when a medicine man, by the name of Creeping, went around among the people curing snowblinds. He would put snow upon their eyes, and after he had sung a certain sacred song that he had heard in a dream, he would blow on the backs of their heads and they would see again, so I have heard. It was about the dragonfly that he sang, for that was where he got his power, they say.[4]

⇒ 3 ⇐

Fire Thunder

Wakinyan Peta

"I was born at the mouth of Beaver Creek in Wyoming during the year when the Indians died of cramps [1849]," Fire Thunder told John G. Neihardt on May 10, 1931.[1] One of the last surviving veterans of the Fetterman Fight, Wakinyan Peta (Fire Thunder) gathered with four other Oglala "elders," Heȟáka Sápa (Black Elk, age sixty-seven), Mato Najin (Standing Bear, age seventy-two), and Sinte Sapa Wakan (Holy Black Tail Deer, age seventy-four). The men had assembled at the home of Black Elk to tell their stories of the past to Neihardt, a professor at the University of Missouri who was soon to become poet laureate of Nebraska. Neihardt's purpose was to interview and record the life, history, and spiritual beliefs of Black Elk, which in 1932 became his masterpiece, *Black Elk Speaks*. Fire Thunder and the other elders became instrumental in verifying Black Elk's tribal stories, and telling of Black Elk's early history prior to the time Black Elk could remember.

Neihardt's daughter Enid, whom Black Elk named She Walks with a Sacred Stick, recorded the interviews in shorthand and then quickly transcribed them in narrative form using a typewriter. *Black Elk Speaks* differs slightly from the original transcription. Offered here first is this original transcription of Fire Thunder's story of the Fetterman Fight. It is followed, for readers concerned with the specific minor differentials in the two accounts, by the version of Fire Thunder's story in *Black Elk Speaks*. Fire Thunder's narrative corroborates the other Indian accounts regarding the disposition of the Oglalas in the fighting and the locations of the tribes within the geography of the staged ambush site.[2] Fire Thunder was positioned at the bottom of the ridge and slightly to the west on the north side of Peno Creek. He describes chasing the cavalry all the way to the top of the ridge. Fire Thunder also faithfully corroborates the fighting on Monument Hill at the end of the battle. Readers will detect, as with White Bull's account, the excitement of a teenage warrior out to win honors in one of his first fights with the Americans. Fire Thunder's story is one of the best Oglala accounts of the Fetterman Fight.[3]

Enid Neihardt's Transcription of Fire Thunder's Account

I was sixteen years old at the Fetterman fight. We camped on Tongue River. A man by the name of Big Road was the chief of our band at this time. Red Cloud was, of course, over all of us [as a *blotahunka*]. We decided to go on a warpath, several different bands all taking part on horseback. We were out to fight anything, but particularly we were after the soldiers. We started out, camping twice from Tongue River the same day. We were going toward the Piney Creek Fort [Fort Phil Kearny]. We had come out to attack the fort. Sent ten men ahead to coax them out of the fort and then we were going to hide there nearby. There is a hill there and this band of ours divided into two parts and stood on either side of this hill. We waited there for an hour or so and heard a shot soon and knew that meant the soldiers were coming. This happened right on the north side of Piney Creek. I was on the west side of the hill. The riders were coaxing the soldiers back. Some got off their horses, leading them, pretending they were worn out. The Indians came first downhill and the soldiers followed, firing on the running Indians all the time. My weapons were six-shooters and bow and arrows, which I had traded for. As the Indians got down the hill, [and] got to a little flat, the soldiers in between them began to holler. I was riding a sorrel horse and just as I was about to get on my horse, the soldiers stopped and began to fight the Indians back up the hill. I hung on to my sorrel. As they charged I pulled out my six-shooter and began killing them. There were lots of bullets and lots of arrows—like locusts. The soldiers did not kill all the Indians that were killed, as the Indians killed each other [by over-shooting] as well as the soldiers. I saw them shot through the arms and legs. They charged up the hill [little by little], losing men as they went. There were only a few left. There was no place to hide so they got on the hill and we surrounded them. As they charged up the hill some of the soldiers let go of their horses and the Indians tried to capture some of the horses. I tried to catch a horse, but I thought it was a good day to die so I just went ahead fighting. I wasn't after horses—I was after white men. Just as I was going up the hill I saw there were seven horses left, so I just caught one of them, as it came right by me. We were told to crawl inch by inch onto the soldiers, so I got off my horse. When we got closer someone hollered: "Let's go; this is a good day to die. If we don't, someone is going to die today, and at home our women are hungry!" Then they all hollered "Hoka He!" Then we all jumped up and went for them. I was pretty quick on my feet and was first to get there and I scalped a soldier lying there. I killed five or six of these soldiers myself—three with my six-shooter and three with arrows. Some of the soldiers that we were among now were dead and [a few] of them were alive. They all got up and fought hard. There were none of them left at the end of the fight. The only living thing was a dog. We didn't kill the dog because he looked too sweet. After the fight was over, we picked up our wounded and started back to the Tongue and just left the dead lying there. It was pretty cold weather to bury anything—the ground was frozen solid. We did bury a few by just turning them over in the hollow ground. There was a terribly big blizzard that night and we lost most of our wounded going home, and most of the [remaining] wounded died when they did get home. This was the same time when Black Elk's father was wounded.

Fire Thunder in *Black Elk Speaks*

I was 16 years old when this happened, and after the big council on the Powder we had moved over to the Tongue River where we were camping at the mouth of Peno Creek. There were many of us there. Red Cloud was over all of us, but the chief of our band was Big Road.[4] We started out on horseback just about sunrise, riding up the creek toward the soldiers' town on the Piney, for we were going to attack it. The sun was about halfway up when we stopped at the place where the Wasicu's road came down a steep, narrow ridge and crossed the creek. It was a good place to fight, so we sent some men ahead to coax the soldiers out. While they were gone, we divided into two parts and hid in the gullies on both sides of the ridge and waited. After a long while we heard a shot up over the hill, and we knew the soldiers were coming. So we held the noses of our ponies that they might not whinny at the soldiers' horses. Soon we saw our men coming back, and some of them were walking and leading their horses, so that the soldiers would think they were worn out. Then the men we had sent ahead came running down the road between us, and the soldiers on horseback followed, shooting. When they came to the flat at the bottom of the hill, the fighting began all at once. I had a sorrel horse, and just as I was going to get on him, the soldiers turned around and began to fight their way back up the hill. I had a six-shooter that I had traded for, and also a bow and arrow. When the soldiers started back, I held my sorrel with one hand and began killing them with the six-shooter, for they came close to me. There were many bullets, but there were more arrows—so many that it was like a cloud of grasshoppers all above and around the soldiers; and our people, shooting across, hit each other. The soldiers were falling all the while they were fighting back up the hill and their horses got loose. Many of our people chased the horses, but I was not after horses; I was after Wasicus. When the soldiers got on top, there were not many of them left and they had no place to hide. They were fighting hard. We were told to crawl up on them, and we did. When we were close, someone yelled: "Let us go! This is a good day to die. Think of the helpless ones at home!" Then we all cried, "Hoka hey!" and rushed at them. I was young then and quick on my feet, and I was one of the first to get in among the soldiers. They got up and fought very hard until not one of them was alive. They had a dog with them, and he started back up the road for the soldiers' town, howling as he ran. He was the only one left. I did not shoot at him because he looked too sweet; but many did shoot, and he died full of arrows. So there was nobody left of the soldiers. Dead men and horses and wounded Indians were scattered all the way up the hill, and their blood was frozen, for a storm had come up and it was very cold and getting colder all the time. We left all the dead lying there, for the ground was solid, and we picked up our wounded and started back; but we lost most of them before we reached our camp at the mouth of the Peno. There was a big blizzard that night; and some of the wounded that did not die on the way, died after we got home. This was the time when Black Elk's father had his leg broken.

American Horse

Wašíču Thašúnke

American Horse, a Khiyaksa Oglala, is best remembered as a progressive leader during the reservation years at Pine Ridge. Prior to his death in 1908, he held close ties with his father-in-law Red Cloud as an advocate and statesman for the Oglalas, He visited Washington with other important counselors. In 1877, he feared the influence of Crazy Horse and some speculate he urged the arrest and imprisonment of Crazy Horse.[1] Hunkpapa historian Josephine Waggoner places his date of birth as 1842, while Oglala winter counts assert 1840. American Horse told Judge Eli S. Ricker he was born in 1839.[2] We find American Horse as a man in his mid-twenties at the time of the Fetterman Fight and already recognized as a superior warrior who would soon become a shirtwearer. He was not yet an *itancan* but became one during the reservation years.[3]

The earliest account of the Fetterman Fight that American Horse leaves to history is the mnemonic for 1866–1867 on his family winter count (pictured at the heading of Part 2). His graphic clearly shows the remaining Fetterman troops from the early stages of the fight now congregated on Monument Hill while being enveloped by Lakotas and Cheyennes fighting on foot during the last stages of the battle.[4]

The Ricker Interview with American Horse

Nebraska judge Eli S. Ricker interviewed American Horse, then in his sixties, at the Agate Springs Stock Farm in Sioux County, Nebraska, on June 16, 1905, where American Horse and his close friend Red Cloud often sought respite and enjoyed

American Horse.
Courtesy of Nebraska State Historical Society, Lincoln.

the hospitality of proprietor James S. Cook. Rafael Romero (nicknamed "Romeo"), a longtime government employee, interpreted. Ricker, like his contemporaries, became fascinated with the tales of frontiersmen and aging warriors during this era of nostalgia in the early twentieth century. Ricker took reams of handwritten notes, often in a kind of shorthand that has defied translators over the years. Like other contemporaries, he recorded his information grammatically in the third-person. He intended to use his notes for a book but never undertook the task. Ricker scribbled his notes on writing tablets, which are located in the archives of the Nebraska State Historical Society today, and are a rich source of information for historians and other researchers. The portion of the American Horse interview below is found in tablet no. 16 and now published in Richard E. Jensen's *Voices of the American West*, Volume 1, *The Indian Interviews of Eli S. Ricker, 1903–1919*, (Lincoln: University of Nebraska Press, 2005), 277–85.

Although the complete interview is longer than what is presented here, I have reproduced only that portion relative to American Horse's participation in the wiping out of Fetterman's troops on December 21, 1866. One significant aspect of American Horse's account is that he "may have" been one of the few "decoys" on Lodge Trail Ridge, which led Fetterman over the rise and into the trap set for him. From his account American Horse fought his way to Monument Hill with other Oglalas and was in on the last of the fighting. As in the other accounts in this study, American Horse's perception of time regarding the duration of the battle is different from others. The accounts vary from thirty minutes to ninety minutes. As with most testimonies, American Horse's casualty list attests to the dead and wounded warriors he personally witnessed in the battle or heard about and thus differs from other eyewitness accounts. But the major significance of this account is American Horse's assertion that he personally killed Captain Fetterman by slashing his throat with his knife after dismounting and hitting Fetterman with his war club. The Ricker–American Horse account is important in understanding the concluding stages of the battle.

List of Indian Casualties at Phil Kearny as given by Am. Horse to me [Ricker];
Killed:

1	Lone Bear	Oglala Sioux	
2	Yellow White Man	"	"
3	Horse Looking	"	"
4	Little Bear	"	"
5	Bird head	Arapahoe	
6	Good Shield	["]	
7	Bear Robe	Cheyenne	

and Eight is [*sic*] wounded

American Horse says he killed the chief officer in command (who was Colonel Fetterman) & he tells how he did it as follows: When Colonel Fetterman and party were on [the] wagon trail to wood camp American Horse and 8 other Oglala warriors met and attacked them. The mounted soldiers were riding in advance in column of fours, the dismounted men following closely. After firing at the troops Am. Horse & his party slowly retreated into rough ground over

[the] ridge where 2 long lines of warriors were lying in ambush, troops rushed into the trap set for them and were completely surrounded. In one hour and a half every soldier was killed, also 2 civilians who were with the party. One of those civilians was a swarthy looking man that looked like a mixed blood. Those 2 men got into a pile of rocks and did a lot of shooting before they were killed. The soldiers when they discovered that they were trapped by hundreds, if not thousands of Indians, were badly demoralized and did poor shooting. The Indians had only 7 killed and 8 wounded.[5] American Horse himself ran his horse at full speed directly on to Colonel Fetterman knocking him down. Then he jumped down upon him and killed him with his knife. One of the Inds. killed, having a brave heart succeeded in riding into the midst of the soldiers shooting right and left. After the battle the Inds. scattered, the various bands going in different directions to secure game for food.

Over the years, secondary sources of the Fetterman Fight continue to cite Colonel Carrington's initial report of the fight in which he claimed that both captains Fetterman and Brown committed suicide together with gunshot wounds to the head.[6] But the assistant surgeon at Fort Phil Kearny, Dr. Samuel M. Horton, who tended the bodies afterward, testified at the hearings of the special commission to investigate the battle that although Captain Frederick Brown likely took his own life, Fetterman did not: "[Brevet] Colonel Fetterman's body showed his thorax to have been cut crosswise with a knife, deep into the viscera; his throat and entire neck were cut to the cervical spine all around. . . . Brown's body showed gashes inside of both thighs, to the bone, from his body to his knees, both ears had been cut off and his body otherwise horribly mutilated and a hole made in his left temple by a small pistol ball; the latter most probably caused his death."[7] Horton's report is consistent with American Horse's account, and Horton never met American Horse at any time.

The fact that American Horse's account corroborated with Assistant Surgeon Horton's 1867 testimony should put to rest the myth of Fetterman and Brown's joint suicides.[8]

The Sheldon Interview with American Horse

In 1903, Addison E. Sheldon of the Nebraska State Historical Society visited the Pine Ridge and Rosebud Reservations to interview aging Oglala chiefs and warriors. Primarily interested in obtaining information on Red Cloud possibly for a biography

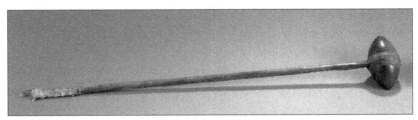

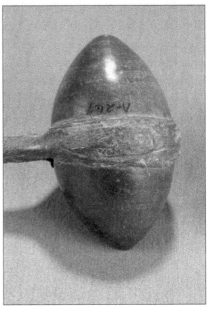

American Horse's war club, allegedly
used against Wm. J. Fetterman.
*Courtesy National Park Service, Museum
Management Program and Agate Fossil Beds
National Monument, Nebraska, AGFO-55.*

he never completed, Sheldon recorded some interesting firsthand testimony of the Fetterman Fight. One of the lengthier interviews was with American Horse on July 30. American Horse did not speak to Sheldon about personally killing Fetterman but rather, at Sheldon's obvious prompting, opened up with information concerning Red Cloud's role in the fight, a subject that will be probed more in depth later in chapter 6. Although there exist some disparities of time (American Horse was sixty-four years old remembering events thirty-seven years previous), his account in the portion of this previously unpublished interview relating to the Fetterman Fight is nonetheless revealing. By the time of this interview in the early 1900s, American Horse was an *itancan* and a chief in the American sense of recognition. He went to Washington on several occasions and was known among his people and Americans as an eloquent statesman. He died at Pine Ridge, South Dakota, in 1908. At the conclusion of his interview Sheldon described him as, "American Horse—the leading Indian at Pine Ridge—a man of energy, intelligence, and courage."[9]

[AH] Red Cloud and his band were in the Black Hills and Montana at this time. Red Cloud planned the fight in which the soldiers were killed. All the Oglalas were there, or nearly all—some Brûlés, some Miniconjous.

Sheldon: How many Warriors? More than 1,000?

[AH] Yes. Red Cloud was there. I saw him. I saw him before the fight. I saw him after the fight. No, I did not see him during the fight. It was all dust and smoke.

The fight was planned. Just a few Indians rode out toward the fort. They shot at the wood train. [Then] there were six or eight. They rode near the fort. Then Red Cloud and part of the Sioux rode on their horses up a deep canyon with trees and the right land [high above the ridge]. I was with them. Other chiefs rode up in the same way on the left. Some other Indians—I think mostly Miniconjous—stayed across the road, back a mile or two.

The soldiers came out of the fort to fight. They were on foot. The six or eight Indians began to retreat, slowly; they made believe their horses were lame. The soldiers ran to head them off. The Indians led them over one hill and then over another. Then the Indians hiding behind the ridges came up fast on both sides. The Miniconjous on ahead then turned back. They came up on all sides and shot the soldiers down very fast. The Indians became excited—so much so that they shot across into each other. The soldiers were all killed and scalped.

Sheldon: How many Sioux were killed?

[AH] They were all laid together in one place after the fight. There were thirty of them but some died after the battle.

They were buried where the white men could not find them. Then the Sioux scattered. Red Cloud and the Bad Faces went over on Rosebud Creek and stayed [in] that country. Red Cloud was the big leader. All the bands were broken up and stayed in different places.

Red Cloud planned the fight. Sitting Bull [the Oglala] and Crazy Horse were both there. Crazy Horse was one of the bravest.

The year before this fight Spotted Tail with some Brûlés and Oglalas killed seven soldiers up Powder River.

Sheldon, coaxing American Horse back on topic: Did the soldiers fight bravely?

[AH] Yes, but the Sioux were too many.

Sheldon: Did the cartridges [Spencer and Starr carbine and rifle cartridges] stick in their guns so they could not shoot?

[AH] Well, those near me could shoot all right. I didn't see any whose guns didn't go off.[10]

In Sheldon's interview American Horse did not claim to be one of the decoys on Lodge Trail Ridge but rather one of several chiefs who demonstrated in front of the fort to draw the soldiers out, drawing a Howitzer shell from the fort as a result, and then riding with Red Cloud onto one of the hills to the west of the ridge, then (probably) finally joining other Oglalas in the final assault on Monument Hill. This calls into question Ricker's interview transcript in respect to the decoy operations on Lodge Trail Ridge. American Horse also claims thirty Lakotas were killed, as opposed to the seven he identified to Ricker.[11]

George Sword

Ricker on April 29, 1907, interviewed George Sword, a shirtwearer and important statesman-chief during the reservation years. Sword said he was in the Fetterman Fight along with his brother, Sword Owner, who was one of the decoys. Ricker also interviewed George W. Colhoff, an Indian trader who clerked at western forts during the 1860s and knew the Sword family. Ricker wrote that Colhoff told him that Sword Owner "was the principal young man who headed the decoy party with American Horse at Fort Phil Kearny. He says that he has always understood that there were six or seven men in this decoy party. This old Sword [Sword Owner] died and was buried over about Ash Creek." Regardless of American Horse's role as a decoy, George Sword told Ricker: "These were young men thirsting for the fray. . . . In those days they were not looking up to chiefs."[12]

The Addison E. Sheldon
Short Interviews, 1903

"A busy man" best describes Addison E. Sheldon in his research visits to Pine Ridge, June–August 1903. In addition to American Horse (chapter 4), and Red Cloud (chapter 6), Sheldon conducted interviews with other Oglala chiefs and aging warriors in a quest for information about Red Cloud's life.[1] Many of these are short interviews, either due to the lack of willingness or energy of the participant, or because Sheldon did not think the interviews were of value to his research. The brief interviews here are unpublished sources from Sheldon's original notes of Indian eyewitness accounts of the Fetterman Fight. Interviews with White Face and Big White Horse (interviewed together), Red Fly, and Rocky Bear were conducted on July 30 along with American Horse. Sheldon had conducted the interview with Eagle Hawk two days earlier on July 28. As with the American Horse testimony, these interviews are important in themselves, but they also offer valuable information regarding Red Cloud, which shall be considered further in chapter 6.

White Face

White Face and Big White Horse, Sheldon noted, were eager to talk about the Fetterman Fight, but could not agree on some of the minor details of the battle.

Sheldon: Age 60 years—both. One of them (WF) small, compact, keen-eyed, athletic. The other larger, slightly compact, slower in action. They became

White Face, circa 1886 (no known photo exists of Big White Horse).

much interested in giving their story of the battle at Ft. Phil Kearny, Dec. 13 [*sic*], 1866, drawing a rough diagram of the locality of the ground and sometimes eagerly disputing over details of the day.

[WF and BWH] We were at Ft. Phil Kearny fight the battle where 90 soldiers were killed [*sic*]. We were young men then. It was in the wintertime. The white men built a fort on Lodge Pole Creek—up near the mountains. It was not white man's country. The big road [Bozeman Trail] ran past the fort to the Yellowstone. The white men were all this time traveling the big road. All the Indians were angry. As for Red Cloud, he was there, we saw him.

Eagle Hawk

Eagle Hawk reveals little regarding the Fetterman Fight. The 1841 killing of Bull Bear, a rival to Red Cloud's clan, interested him more. Eagle Hawk stated that he "was out on the head of Cheyenne River when they made [the] Treaty of 1868 at Ft. Laramie. Did not go in. Think we [were] in a war party out looking for Crows." Eagle Hawk was probably not present at the Fetterman Fight since he offers no eyewitness testimony of the battle. The only significant information he offered to Sheldon was quite possibly secondhand when he stated: "'The Stinger' [?] and Crazy Horse were in the fight at Ft. Phil Kearny."

Red Fly

The warrior Red Fly most definitely participated in the destruction of Fetterman's command. Sheldon described him as a "very old Indian sitting on a cracker box in a Pine Ridge grocery store. Red Fly was a man of some importance in the past as he accompanied Red Cloud as a statesman to Washington in 1871."

I was with Red Cloud at the fight near the Big Horn Mountains where we killed the hundred soldiers. I was with him also when we fought the soldiers in the wagon boxes. That was after the other fight. Red Cloud was the *chief soldier* [emphasis mine], the one who managed the war for the Sioux in all the wars with the whites until he came in and made peace. Red Cloud came in and made peace with the whites at Ft. Laramie the summer after the big fight we just talked about. I think it was 1869 or 1870 [actually 1868]. Yes, Red Cloud washed his hands in front of the big general at Laramie when he came in. I was there. I saw him.

While Red Fly offers little original in terms of events from the other Sheldon short interviews, his language is significant in an important way. Red Fly, as did White Bull, other Oglalas quoted elsewhere in the literature of the Indian Wars, Cheyennes, and others, sometimes referred to their fighting men as "soldiers." They thought of themselves as soldiers when fighting the Americans, and occasionally emulated them in battle.[2] The term "soldier" thus can be potentially misleading while reading original cursive notes of the whites who transcribed the words of these aging fighting men through interpreters as we shall see in the case of the interview with Rocky Bear.

Rocky Bear

Sheldon's interest in Rocky Bear's story centered more around the rivalry of Man Afraid of His Horses and Red Cloud's Bad Face *tiyospaye* with that of Bull Bear's clan in the 1850s. Rocky Bear's reminiscences of the Fetterman Fight consist of one paragraph in Sheldon's cursive. It is an important paragraph; indeed, it is one that may be interpreted by scholars in different ways unless put in larger contexts alongside corroborative, or noncorroborative, materials.

Sheldon: Ft. Phil Kearny:

[RB] I was there & Red Cloud was there. Another Indian wounded Red Dog. Sword & Crazy Horse toled [*sic*, to lead?] the soldiers on. Sent 8 soldiers on—main party of Indians in a circle. Infantry chased them. Several played [like] their horses [had] played out—Red Dog, Red Cloud. All the Oglalas—the Miniconjous, over 1,000.

Rocky Bear's brief statement, made ambiguous through Sheldon's writing, possibly due to a time factor, is the only eyewitness account of the Fetterman Fight that suggests Crazy Horse was one of the ten decoys to lure Fetterman over Lodge Trail Ridge. The interview with Eagle Hawk that appears prior to 1942 *might* lead scholars (given the writer's preconceptions) to conclude the same. "Sword" was also "toled" the soldiers. But, which Sword—George or Sword Owner, who was deceased by 1903? George Sword does not claim to be a decoy. But Rocky Bear, like Red Fly, uses the term "soldier" ("sent 8 soldiers on") to refer to fellow Oglala warriors. Did Rocky Bear mean that Crazy Horse and Sword were "to lead" the eight Oglala "soldiers" in a decoy maneuver "to lead" Fetterman's troops over Lodge Trail Ridge, or did Rocky Bear mean that Sword and Crazy Horse were, as historian Doane Robinson and George Hyde have suggested (chapter 7), to lead the Oglalas on in the general combat?[3] What is certain from the short interviews, however, is that Red Cloud has a far greater presence in the battle than many writers thought. Further consideration of the roles played by Red Cloud and Crazy Horse, and Crazy Horse's connection to Rocky Bear's reminiscences, are considered more fully in chapters 6 and 7.

The Question of Red Cloud

Maĥpíyalúta, 1822–December 10, 1909

What role did Red Cloud play in the Fetterman Fight? Should he be regarded as the central leader of the coalition that destroyed Fetterman's command? Is he the principal strategist of the ambush? These questions continue to be asked today. They continue to be answered in various and opposing ways by both Indian and non-Indian people, to the extent that Red Cloud is regarded as a mythic hero of Lakota resistance to the government and both a great warrior of the Bad Face Oglalas and later a statesman for all Lakota rights. He is honored today by the United States Postal Service with a ten-cent postage stamp of the Great Americans commemorative series. He is also a posthumous member of the Nebraska Hall of Fame.

Red Cloud was born in 1822 near the forks of the Platte River. His mother, Walks As She Thinks, was Oglala while his father was Brûlé. Both died young around 1825 so Red Cloud's uncle Old Smoke raised him traditionally in his mother's clan, which was Old Smoke's *tiyospaye*. Being both uncle and *itancan*, Old Smoke played a major role in the boy's upbringing. As such, Red Cloud as a nineteen-year-old budding warrior is implicated by some historians in the killing of Old Smoke's rival Bull Bear in 1841, on the Chugwater River in today's Wyoming. Little is known, however, of Red Cloud's childhood years.

During the late 1990s, historian R. Eli Paul rediscovered a forgotten manuscript purporting to be an autobiography of Red Cloud told during the closing years of his life to Sam Deon, a former trapper, who relayed the story to Charles Allen to edit and archive with the Nebraska State Historical Society. As Paul asserted, the

Red Cloud.
Courtesy of Nebraska State Historical Society, Lincoln.

manuscript's history is a mystery unto itself. Allen died before he did anything with the manuscript, which then passed on to E. Addison Sheldon by 1917. Sheldon, who, like Allen, entertained ideas of writing Red Cloud's life story, fumbled with it, while making sure it stayed away from his rivals Walter S. Campbell and George Hyde.

Finally, Mari Sandoz, who worked at the society, "conveniently lost" the manuscript for the next several decades. Sandoz in turn wrote her historical novel, *Crazy Horse: Strange Man of the Oglalas*, launching Crazy Horse into eternal prominence among the Bad Face Oglalas while trying her best to send Red Cloud into oblivion. Those who actually read the Red Cloud manuscript complained of it being written in the third person, thus questioning its accuracy. As we have seen here, most of these aging warriors' accounts were published in the third person from the transcriber's notes. In 1997, Paul published the manuscript, with his masterful introduction and validity analysis, so that today we have much filled-in information regarding Red Cloud's early years of his exploits in intertribal warfare.[1]

Undoubtedly Red Cloud attained an apex of his reputation among the Oglalas, in the Crow War of 1857–58. He likely fought whites for the first time as a member of the Waciska warrior society against the Eleventh Ohio Volunteer Cavalry at the Battle of Platte Bridge on July 25, 1865. About that time he became widely recognized by the Bad Face Oglalas as a shirtwearer and *blotahunka* of great courage and ability, a recognition he would carry throughout his years fighting against the U.S. Army, 1865–68.[2] Certainly Red Cloud's importance is reflected in his role as counselor, statesman, and delegate to Washington and New York in audience with presidents, Congress, and citizen groups. Sam Deon, in transcribing the autobiography, claimed that Red Cloud "has never been considered a great orator by his own people; there has always been a number of Indians that excelled him in this respect, and he always availed himself of the services of such as these, in the capacity of head men, sub-chiefs [?], etc., and largely through these orators have his thoughts and plans been conveyed to the multitude."[3] Perhaps Deon was not aware of Red Cloud's eloquent speech in New York at Cooper Union in 1870. Although Red Cloud's biographer, Robert Larson, questions how much of that speech was Red Cloud's words or those of Reverend Howard Crosby, an interpreter and a powerful orator in his own right, Red Cloud's charisma impressed the audience and would continue to do so through the remainder of his life.[4]

During the reservation years until his death in 1909, Americans considered Red Cloud a "chief" in the American sense because of his leadership in working for his peoples' rights, both on the reservation and in Washington. His words, today found in government records from the 1870s, are prolific and profound.

But Red Cloud is mostly silent about his years fighting the Americans. Margaret Irvin Carrington, Colonel Henry Carrington's first wife, gives us the first sizeable written account of Red Cloud's struggle for the Powder River Country in 1866 in her book, *Absaraka, Home of the Crows* (1868). In late May, Lakota headmen from all the divisions met at Fort Laramie for talks with Commissioner of Indian Affairs Nathaniel G. Taylor, for the purpose of seeking the consent of the Lakotas, Arapahos, and Cheyennes to construct three new forts to protect the Bozeman Trail. The Carringtons were present. Red Cloud's words and actions, despite being noticed by everyone, were not recorded verbatim. No official transcripts of the Taylor Peace Commission talks exist today. Red Cloud's words are thus secondhand hearsay, but still convey his feelings and actions at the council. In 1868 Margaret Carrington wrote: "The Man Afraid of His Horse[s] and Red Cloud made no secret of their opposition, and later with all his fighting men withdrew from all association with the treaty-makers, and in a very few days quite decidedly developed his hate and his schemes of mischief."[5]

Private William Murphy was present and apparently left his impressions, although Henry Carrington's second wife, Frances Grummond Carrington, did not record them until 1910. Frances was the widow of Lieutenant George Grummond, who was killed at the Fetterman Fight, and she later married Colonel Carrington following Margaret's death. She was not present at the treaty council. Murphy noted, and Frances likely paraphrased in 1910: "The powwow continued for some time until the hostile Sioux under Red Cloud withdrew, refusing to have any further counsel or to accept any presents."[6] Frances continues with words of her own and supposedly not Murphy's. They are probably elaborate embellishments of Margaret Carrington's *Absaraka*, and what her husband, Henry Carrington, told her over the years. Thus her account is hearsay:

> Red Cloud himself, it is "officially reported" [by whom?], when he saw Colonel Carrington at his visit to the council, upon his arrival threw his blanket around himself, refused an introduction, and left with his announcement of his views, pointing to the officer who had just arrived. "The Great Father sends us presents and wants us to sell him the road before the Indians say yes or no."[7]

In 1903, Henry Carrington paid an extended visit to writer Cyrus Townsend Brady at his home in Philadelphia. Brady had spent years as a missionary on the Great Plains in the late nineteenth century, and devoted his time to writing his bestseller, *Indian Fights and Fighters* (1904), which still finds its way into some bibliographies today. Carrington wanted to give his version of the Fetterman Fight and the events leading up to it in order to further his lifelong attempts after 1867 to re-establish his reputation for alleged culpability in the Fetterman Fight, commonly referred to at this time as "the disaster." Brady's version of the battle is basically that of Margaret and Henry Carrington's writings with some added drama. Brady is undoubtedly the author of the famous eighty-man boast supposedly uttered by Fetterman, "Give me eighty men and I will ride through the Sioux Nation," assuredly a paraphrase of Margaret Carrington's claim of what Fetterman actually said, and seconded by Fetterman's fellow junior authors, that "a company of regulars could whip a thousand and a regiment could whip the whole array of hostile tribes." Due to Brady's version of the boast a powerful irony was created from which Fetterman is long remembered in popular literature until today. The number eighty is the exact number of men under Fetterman's command that died with him on Lodge Trail Ridge.[8] Brady also captures the mood if not the exact words of Red Cloud at the Taylor Commission council:

> Red Cloud, noticing his [Carrington's] shoulder straps, hotly denounced him as "White Eagle," who had come to steal the road before the Indians said yes or no. In full view of the mass of Indians who occupied the parade ground he sprang from the platform under the shelter of pine boughs, struck his tepees, and went on the warpath.[9]

An early secondary source without documentation is from Doane Robinson of the South Dakota Historical Society in 1928. Robinson asserted that "Red Cloud leaped from the platform, caught up his rifle, saying, 'In this and the Great Spirit I trust for the right.'"[10]

Over the years, these sources that have no interview support have been cited as references to Red Cloud's specific words at the Taylor treaty talks at Fort Laramie. They are likely either paraphrases or fabrications that capture the essence of Red Cloud's defiance in 1866 over the idea of forts on the Bozeman Trail, through one of the last vibrant northern buffalo ranges that had been hard won with blood from the Crows eight years previous. Yet authors of popular nonfiction literature to the present day continue to put words into Red Cloud's mouth and thoughts into his head to exaggerate a degree of centralized authority he did not actually possess outside his immediate Oglala ospaye.[11]

Among Americans present in the Powder River Country in 1866, Red Cloud was and continues to be a powerful force as a war leader of the Oglalas, to the extent that many whites view him as the central leader, planner, strategist, and tactician of the Fetterman Fight. Actually, as we shall see in Part 3, "Northern Cheyenne Accounts," the Cheyennes do not recognize his presence at the battle. Neither do the Miniconjous. White Bull (Part 1), in his talks with Walter S. Campbell in the 1930s, implies instead there were no central leaders in the battle.[12] George Sword (chapter 4) stated to Sheldon that, "warriors were not looking up to chiefs in those days."[13] But did Sword mean warriors were not looking up to itancans or blotahunkas? Probably he meant the former, as blotahunkas possessed more immediate influence on the actual field of combat.

George E. Hyde asserts that the Miniconjou High-Backbone (Hump) was the man actually issuing the orders and that Red Cloud was not present, but was in the Tongue River camps at the time. The fight, writes Hyde, "was primarily a Miniconjou affair [and] is admitted by all the Sioux, but the Indians did not agree as to who the leaders were. It seems this misunderstanding," Hyde continued, "arises from the failure of the Indians themselves to make any distinction between general and active leadership."[14] Likely, High-Backbone (Hump) was directing Miniconjous in the fighting. From the Cheyenne stories in Part 3 we will see that the planning and strategy for the Fetterman Fight was made by consensus of leaders of all principal tribes and *ospayes* present: Miniconjous, Oglalas, Northern Cheyennes, and Northern Arapahos.

Each tribe began the fighting as individual groups at various points along Lodge Trail Ridge and Peno Creek under their own warrior headmen. They mixed together mostly toward the end of the fight on the upper (south) incline of the ridge, possibly Cavalry Hill, and Monument Hill. As we have seen from the work of Catherine Price, no single Oglala *blotahunka* would have wielded total centralized authority and overall control, as writers often attribute to Red Cloud. Not even during the reservation years, when Red Cloud's true significance in American history emerged, and is well documented, did he have any supreme power in decision-making for the Oglalas, although Americans continued to view him, in their conceptual universe, as "the Big Chief." Price wrote of the later years: "Moreover, neither civilian agent nor army officer . . . had weakened, let alone destroyed, the political customs or influence of the Oglala multiband council."[15] Any proven young warrior could organize and lead a small horse-stealing raid or even a modest war party, but a large general battle, with a significant contingent of the enemy, required consensus, especially among a coalition that did not always agree, or instead made decisions in their own best interests.[16]

But there is little doubt that fellow Oglalas honored Red Cloud's skills and his leadership as a masterful *blotahunka*, if not a true chief or central commander. By 1867 more than one hundred lodges had gathered around him after the Fetterman Fight. Red Cloud's voluntary following rivaled that of the Bad Face true *itancan*, Man Afraid of His Horses, and his son, Young Man Afraid of His Horses. Certainly the Americans accorded him this status. Red Cloud likely first attained that fierce reputation with the army and the press from his histrionics at Fort Laramie during the Taylor peace talks in May. As the previous Oglala accounts attest, his presence near Lodge Trail Ridge is confirmed. But did Red Cloud leave to history any words specifically about the Fetterman Fight?

During the reservation years, both Red Cloud and American Horse would seek respite with their families away from tribal politics, on the ranch of their white friend James H. Cook, a rancher at Agate Springs, Nebraska, where they would set up their lodges for extended periods of time. Cook had spent most of his adult life on the frontier as a trader, rancher, and with other enterprises. Cook was perhaps the only white friend Red Cloud could fully confide in with his personal stories of the past. In his *Fifty Years on the Old Frontier*, Cook wrote: "A number of white men in the past had tried to get him [Red Cloud] to do this [tell of his role in the Fetterman Fight], but that he did not want to say anything for white men to write down in order to make money for themselves by selling his words." But, Cook continued, "we planned that some time the story should be told and recorded. But the years slipped by, and the old Chief's memory was so clouded the greater part of the time during his last visits to my house that it was impossible for him to tell the story that would have added so much to our knowledge of the Indian life west of the Missouri River before the building of wagon roads and iron rails through the land of the Sioux." Cook planned to hire a "first rate interpreter" and stenographer for Red Cloud's tales but never got around to it.

In 1923, fourteen years after Red Cloud's death, Cook recorded what he could remember of what the old man, then deceased, had told him of the Fetterman Fight:

My dear friend Major Tenedore [*sic*] Ten Eyck, now passed away, but in 1866 a captain at Fort Phil Kearny, was the man sent out with a relief party to bring in the bodies of his comrades whom Red Cloud's warriors had slain. Later, he often sent word to his old enemy, through me, that when he looked back to the conditions that existed at the time of the fight at Fort Phil Kearny, he could think with less enmity of those who had killed his companions-in-arms with such seeming ruthlessness. Major Ten Eyck wanted me to learn, if possible, the number of Indians killed and wounded by Fetterman's command before they gave up their lives. When I asked Red Cloud for this information, his reply was that but few Indians, eleven in all he thought, were killed outright during the fight, but that a number were wounded, many of them so badly that they died later on in the camps which were quickly scattered all over the country. Red Cloud also told me that in this fight, his sub-chief, American Horse, killed Colonel Fetterman. American Horse has told me the same. These old Chiefs often talked with me about the details of this fight. Both told me that a number of the soldiers were so terrified, when they realized what a trap they had fallen into, that they seemed paralyzed and offered no resistance to the Indian warriors. The officers, however, did everything in their power, fighting gamely to the last. In the 1876 campaign Red Cloud took little if any part.

Many warriors from the Red Cloud Agency, however, were with the hostiles, and several old Indians who took part in the fight with Custer's command, and who have visited me in company with Red Cloud, have told me of the day when they wiped out the courageous General and so many soldiers. Their victory, as they well knew, was due only to their overwhelming numbers and to the fact that the cavalrymen were forced to fight on foot.[17]

About the same time as Cook's recollections (1922), Wyoming historian Grace Raymond Hebard, in her acclaimed tome of that day, *The Bozeman Trail*, acknowledged Red Cloud's leadership in the Fetterman Fight, but in a statement that could be viewed as racist today, she chided Red Cloud for not following up his victory. She wrote:

> Had the Fetterman battle been won by any other fighting force than the Indians, the victory would have been followed up by an attack on the hated fort of Phil Kearney [*sic*], which, with it its depleted fighting force, might have been completely overcome, destroying that symbol of invasion, and wiping out all evidence of the white man's possession of the Powder River Country. The American Indian with his semi-trained mind did not possess the genius in military warfare of following up a victory after an advantage ground had been won—an art of war, which seems to be the special property of the white man.

Hebard must have forgotten Meade at Gettysburg, who did not follow up the Union victory there. The tribal coalition never considered facing the howitzers of the walled fortification in an all-out assault. Carrington still had 312 effectives and 119 civilian contractors, and the chiefs and headmen knew it, since nighttime reconnaissance continued almost daily.[18]

Red Cloud's words in the first person then are few. Not surprisingly, only fellow Bad Face Crazy Horse exceeds Red Cloud in an almost total lack of loquaciousness. Red Cloud found formal white interviewers who visited him at Pine Ridge an anathema when they asked him for his stories and exploits in military engagements with the Americans. As such, without Indian voice, the question of his presence at the fight continues to be asked by historians today despite the eyewitness testimony of others. So, to fully answer that question, we must revisit those eyewitness testimonies of Oglalas who actually fought in the battle.

The previous unpublished A. E. Sheldon Short Interviews (chapter 5) attest to

Red Cloud's presence and leadership among the Oglalas at the Fetterman Fight.

White Face: As for Red Cloud, he was there, we saw him.[19]

Rocky Bear: Fort Phil Kearny: I was there & Red Cloud was there.[20]

Red Fly: I was with Red Cloud at the fight near the Big Horn Mountains where they killed the hundred soldiers. . . . Red Cloud was the chief soldier, the one who managed the wars for the Sioux in all the wars with the whites [in the 1860s] until he came in and made peace.[21]

American Horse: Yes. Red Cloud was there. I saw him before the fight. I saw him after the fight. No, I did not see him during the fight. It was all dust and smoke.[22]

Clearly, these aging Oglala headmen attest in their own words to Red Cloud's role as a primary *blotahunka* for the Oglalas' deployment, at least prior to the fight. As American Horse suggests, he was probably behind the lines during the battle, on a hill, possibly directing some actions by Oglala warriors, and certainly, at age forty-four, allowing the young men to count coup, take scalps, and attain war honors.

Ohiyesa (Charles Eastman), a mixed-blood Santee Dakota, met and befriended Red Cloud at Pine Ridge when he served as an agency physician. The two frequently met to talk. Nine years following Red Cloud's death Eastman published one of his best-known books, *Indian Heroes and Great Chieftains* (1918), still in print today. The life of his friend Red Cloud is featured as chapter 1. In Eastman's assessment of the Powder River war, he quotes Red Cloud verbatim speaking to fellow Oglalas just prior to the Fetterman Fight. Did Eastman remember this famous, often-cited quote by heart or is it a paraphrase of Red Cloud, by then deceased, as to what he was thinking at the time?

Hear ye, Dakotas [Lakotas]! When the Great Father at Washington sent us his chief Soldier (General Harney) to ask for a path through our hunting ground, a way through our hunting grounds, a way for an iron road to the mountains and western sea, we were told that they wished merely to pass through our country, not to tarry among us, but to seek for gold in the far west. Our old chiefs thought to show their friendship and good will, when they allowed this dangerous snake in our midst. They promised to protect the wayfarers.

Yet before the ashes of the council fire are cold, the Great Father is building

The 1905 Fetterman monument. The point marked with the arrow in the distance
is the approximate location where Red Cloud and other leaders observed the
development of the ambush and the battle. He likely used binoculars,
a common and sought-after trade item, enabling him to view the
entire scope of the Bozeman Trail along "Massacre Ridge."
Author's photo.

his forts among us. You have heard the sound of the white soldier's ax upon
the Little Piney. His presence here is an insult and a threat. It is an insult to
the spirits of our ancestors. Are we then to give up their sacred graves to be
plowed for corn? [L]akotas, I am for war!

Eastman collapses different events in his remembrance of Red Cloud's statement.
General William S. Harney counseled with Lakotas and other tribes following the
Battle of Blue Water Creek in 1855, seven years prior to the passage of the Pacific
Railroad Act of 1862 and more than a decade before Union Pacific rails reached below
the Powder River Country. Colonel Henry Carrington, not Harney, is the officer who
attempted to get Lakota agreement for building forts on the Bozeman Road in 1866.
Although Red Cloud would use the term "White Father" ubiquitously in his speeches
to American diplomats during the 1870s, during the war years he would most likely

have used the Lakota term "Wasicu" in reference to the coming of the Americans and the forces of their government.[23]

Are there any direct words of Red Cloud's recorded on the spot by interviewers that speak to his role in the 1866–68 war that today bears his name? In 1903, A. E. Sheldon succeeded, where many others had failed, to prompt Red Cloud to speak a few brief words about his days in the Powder River War of 1866–68. Red Cloud still hedged his memories.

Red Cloud: I never went to war with the White Men. The first time I ever made peace with the White men was at Fort Laramie—the Treaty of 1868, with General Sanborn. In the old time the Sioux broke up into small bands and went hunting the buffalo. They sometimes struck White Men and fought them—the same as other Indians. The first time I went to war with the Crows I stole two horses. That was a long time ago.

Sheldon: Where were you at the time the soldiers were killed at Ft. Phil Kearny?

Red Cloud: I never was in that trouble with the whites.[24]

Denial was Red Cloud's tool for talking to whites, especially Sheldon, whom he suspected of profiting from his story as an enemy of the United States.

Ricker Interview with Red Cloud

November 24, 1906, Pine Ridge, Clarence Three Stars, Interpreter

Three years prior to his death in 1909, Red Cloud finally opened up to Judge Eli S. Ricker. Understandably, Red Cloud mostly wanted to talk about his grievances about the Fort Laramie Treaty of 1868. But toward the end of the interview he answered a couple of Ricker's questions. The following interview is presented here in two parts. Below are Red Cloud's ambiguous statements about the Fetterman Fight. In Appendix D is found the earlier, more specific, and loquacious words of the chief about the Treaty of 1868, as told to Ricker.

"There were some battles fought after the Treaty of 1851. I remember the one where 100 soldiers were killed and where 30 [Grattan Affair, 1854] were killed. I have no hesitation to tell you all I can recall about the fighting that was done. The Indians were right; they were defending themselves and their country, as they had the right to do so."

To answer my question why the Indians speak of the Fetterman Massacre as the fight where a Hundred were Killed when there were but 81 killed he replied that, when they saw the soldiers coming, "they counted them alive and made out one hundred. They did not count them after they had fallen."

Asked as to the number of Indians slain he did not know of more than about ten; "there might have been others who died of wounds," it was hard to know their own loss, because when the battle was ended the Indians broke into their several bands and dispersed.[25]

The formal title for the events of 1866–68, "Red Cloud's War," is elusive in its origins. Surely it was used informally from earlier times but it is hard to track as any kind of familiar *label* until recent years. Margaret Carrington and Frances Carrington do not use the three-word term. It is missing from the works of Cyrus Townsend Brady (1903 and 1904), and not present as late as Dee Brown's *Fort Phil Kearny* (1962). Writer Dorothy M. Johnson titles a chapter in her *The Bloody Bozeman* (1971), "Red Cloud Wins His War," while not listing Red Cloud in her index, and thus supporting Hyde in questioning his presence in the Fetterman Fight. But the term is not frequent in the literature until the last twenty years or so.[26]

The eyewitness testimony and contemporary secondary-source literature support the fact that Red Cloud was present at the Fetterman Fight and, according to the Lakotas, received all the war honors.[27] His leadership as a *blotahunka* (war party leader) was likely pronounced among the Oglalas. He likely managed what he could with some of those warriors as a director behind the battle lines, and perhaps in the company of other headmen and chiefs of the other tribes. He did not single-handedly "plan" the strategy for the deception and ambush. He would have been subject to "council" with other Oglala headmen present as well as those of the Miniconjous, Cheyennes, and Arapahos. He was not a supreme leader of the entire multi-tribal coalition. He likely gained such reputation among the Americans who witnessed his dramatic exodus from Fort Laramie during the talks with the Taylor Commission in May 1866 and his defiance in the Powder River Country afterwards. Red Cloud does confirm that American Horse killed Fetterman. Certainly, after the American media "crowned" him formally a "chief" because he ostensibly won *his* war, at least in combat if not in treaty, his people recognized him during the reservation years as an *itancan*, if not a hereditary one because of his Brûlé father. Among Americans he remains an icon, and rightly so, because of his diplomatic abilities to express the feelings of his peoples' councils during the important years of agency politics, religious and economic reform, assimilation efforts, and severalty policies of the government.[28]

Although important to Lakota heritage, Red Cloud should be remembered not simply as an enemy of the United States, or even as a great war leader in general, or as an ardent opponent to westward expansion, but as an even greater diplomat and iconic inspiration for the rights of the Oglalas and all Lakotas. Even now, in an age of instant social media, a powerful mythology adds to his iconic stature with the words: "They made us many promises, more than I can remember, but they never kept but one; they promised to take our land and they took it." The eloquent statement appropriately summarizes Red Cloud's estimation and memory of events despite his Homeric efforts to advocate for the rights of his people during a vital eighty-two years of Lakota and American history. Sadly too, perhaps, despite the passion these words evoke as a summation of Red Cloud's life, they also add to the mystery surrounding the man. He never made this statement.[29]

⇒ 7 ⇐

The Enigma of Crazy Horse

Thašúnke Witcó

The most glamorous figure of the Fetterman Fight leaves no words at all about his role in the battle. Indeed, Crazy Horse (Oglala/Miniconjou) presents historians with a conundrum. He is even difficult to specifically locate on Lodge Trail Ridge. From the tales of descendants we know his concern for the environmental integrity and protection of the Powder River Country and the Black Hills was heroic. Undoubtedly, evidence supports that he was instrumental in wiping out Fetterman's forces.[1] According to popular accounts he is supposed to have played a major role as a member of the small decoy party (perhaps even the leader of the decoys) that lured Fetterman's command over Lodge Trail Ridge to their deaths. By some recent accounts Crazy Horse bravely played the "wounded quail," dismounting on several occasions to examine the hoof of his seemingly injured pony so that the soldiers could not resist the temptation to pursue him.[2]

The stories told in the many secondary sources are what many readers believe about Crazy Horse. Thus they need to be considered for their accuracy or inaccuracy. A problem, however, is that the original sources are ambiguous. Crazy Horse could have taken part in any of three different decoy movements. Of course, no original military sources place Crazy Horse on Lodge Trail Ridge because none of the whites at Fort Phil Kearny, with the possible exception of scout Jim Bridger, who was not present in the fight, had yet heard of him in 1866.[3] Crazy Horse was only in his mid-twenties at the time (Black Elk states mistakenly that he was about nineteen) and had not yet gained the reputation among the whites that would shadow him

Crazy Horse memorial.
Photo courtesy of http://www.goodfreephotos.com.

to his death following the campaigns of the 1870s. No known photograph of him exists and no white in the fight that otherwise might have remembered any such figure from the battle lived to tell about it. But what stories do the Indian participants in the fight have to tell? Until the mid-twentieth century the voices of oral tradition were fairly silent on the matter outside Indian country. The voices of the few Lakota and Cheyenne eyewitnesses to the battle, who told their stories to white journalists and ethnographers, are, perhaps surprisingly, vague. But Lakotas, at least, attest to his presence and bravery.[4]

The death of Crazy Horse is well chronicled by white sources. But the exploits of his early life are more obscure than his exploits at the Battle of the Little Big Horn a decade after Fetterman's demise. Although the scant eyewitness sources attest to his presence, there is only one eyewitness (Rocky Bear), who infers that he was one of the handpicked decoys who demonstrated on Lodge Trail Ridge and lured Fetterman's command to their demise, so pervasive in the popular secondary literature. The testimony of the Miniconjou warrior White Bull (Part 1) is flimsy as it pertains to Crazy Horse. White Bull declares that Red Cloud was not present at the Fetterman Fight and that (or is this interviewer Walter S. Campbell's assumption in

1932?) "Crazy Horse led the Oglalas." White Bull goes on to state in the next sentence that "many of the chiefs besides Red Cloud led their warriors against the white men in that year of '66." But on Crazy Horse being a member of the small, now almost legendary decoy party, White Bull makes no mention. White Bull did tell Campbell that Crazy Horse rode up the Tongue River toward Fort Phil Kearny with He Dog and other Oglalas a few days prior to the fight, but there is nothing else in Campbell's notes other than White Bull's short ambiguous statement that would pinpoint Crazy Horse among the Lodge Trail Ridge decoys.[5]

Another original reference to Crazy Horse at the time of the Fetterman Fight is a statement made in 1904 by a warrior named Whitewash (White Bear) to Doane Robinson, the secretary of the South Dakota Department of History: "Crazy Horse, though inferior in standing to Man Afraid [of His Horses], was Red Cloud's principal lieutenant among the Oglalas and Roman Nose from among the Cheyennes." This statement too is ambiguous. In his book *A History of the Dakota or Sioux Indians* (1904), Robinson relates this testimony early in a chapter on the Fetterman Fight in context with events occurring before the fight itself. In his narrative of the actual fight Robinson makes no mention of Crazy Horse's presence. Whitewash's claim, while probably true, still does not identify Crazy Horse as being one of the famous decoys. His statement regarding Roman Nose as a "chief lieutenant" of Red Cloud's for the Cheyennes is inaccurate. Roman Nose, a prominent Cheyenne Crooked Lance warrior, but not a chief, had come south to Kansas earlier in the year to fight with the Dog Soldiers and was not present in the Powder River Country during the fall of 1866 and, as a Cheyenne, would not have been under Red Cloud's direction.[6]

Wooden Leg, a Northern Cheyenne warrior of Little Wolf's clan, interviewed extensively by physician Thomas B. Marquis in 1922, asserts that in the fall of 1866 Crazy Horse was a principal war leader of the Oglalas, and a shirtwearer—likely attained sometime during the war; but already a *blotahunka*? We do not know this for certain.[7] But he does not place him specifically in the battle or as a member of the decoy party. Wooden Leg, as we shall see in Part 3, was only nine years old at the time of the Fetterman Fight and thus did not participate in the action, although his elder brother, Strong Wind Blowing, was killed in the fight.[8]

A most compelling case for Crazy Horse being in the general action at the Fetterman Fight is made by frontiersman and scout Frank Grouard. Captured by Hunkpapas about 1870, Grouard later found his way to Crazy Horse's camp in 1873 and befriended him. In Grouard's later years Joe De Barthe recorded his adventures. Grouard was not in the Powder River Country in 1866. But De Barthe relates a secondhand tale of Grouard's, if it can be believed (Grouard tended to be melodramatic at times), of Crazy Horse coming to the aid of his friend the mortally wounded Lone Bear following the Fetterman Fight. Lone Bear is a confirmed Oglala casualty of the battle, corroborated by American Horse and White Bull. Of Lone Bear, De Barthe writes as told to him by Grouard: "His limbs and body were frozen terribly. He died in the arms of Crazy Horse while Hump [High Backbone] stood by, weeping." Grouard however, mentions nothing of Crazy Horse being a decoy.[9]

George B. Grinnell was a bit more meticulous. He talked with a number of Cheyennes who were in the battle, most notably White Elk, who took him over the battlefield, pointing out the route of the soldiers, where the Indians were hiding, and showing him spots where groups of soldiers fell. White Elk's story, as we shall see in Part 3, is detailed. He relates that Miniconjou chiefs Black Shield and Black Leg were the principal leaders of the Lakotas in the fight. He does not mention the presence of Crazy Horse's close friend High Backbone (Hump) of the Miniconjous, although he certainly was in the fight. There is no mention of Crazy Horse whatsoever as having been involved in the Fetterman Fight, although Grinnell discusses his presence numerous times regarding events of the 1870s.[10]

The other principal Cheyenne account, that of Two Moons, who claimed to have been in the fight but later denied it, comes to us through the letters of George Bent, who was one of George Hyde's primary informants. Hyde asserts in *Red Cloud's Folk* (1936) that Two Moons claimed in 1912 through Bent that Crazy Horse led the decoys but offers no elaborate details regarding his specific exploits. There is no mention by Bent in any of his letters to Hyde (written early in the twentieth century) or in *The Life of George Bent Written from His Letters* (completed by 1918 but not published until 1968) of any participation by Crazy Horse in wiping out Fetterman's command. Hyde's reference to Two Moons' assertion of 1912 does not exist in Bent's correspondence. No mention is made by Two Moons of Crazy Horse in an interview with William Camp in 1913 or earlier with Grinnell in 1908. All interviews of Two Moons are presented in Part 3. Thus Hyde's statement about Crazy Horse leading the decoys is suspect, although it is the earliest source claiming Crazy Horse was a decoy at the fight. In any event Hyde (Two Moons?) does not attribute any elaborate deeds to Crazy Horse in the fight as so many modern writers have done, although many decoys did play the wounded quail.[11]

In *Red Cloud's Folk*, published eighteen years after the Bent material was shelved in the Denver Public Library, and all but forgotten until rescued by Savoie Lottinville in the 1960s, Hyde also accepts White Bull's 1932 statement that Crazy Horse "led the Oglalas." But in the earlier 1918 Bent manuscript, Hyde had already written Two Moons' version of the Fetterman Fight with no mention of Crazy Horse whatsoever. Two Moons' account that appeared in Hyde's *Life of George Bent* (1918) was based on a letter from Bent, who interviewed Two Moons in 1904. Two Moons does not mention Crazy Horse in any of his letters to Hyde. In addition, in 1908 Two Moons denied to George B. Grinnell that he (Two Moons) was in the Fetterman Fight. Hyde asserts in 1918 in the Bent manuscript that Crazy Horse gained his reputation as a warrior in the 1870s. Hyde thus bases his premise of Crazy Horse's presence in *Red Cloud's Folk* (1936) on White Bull's and Campbell's 1932 statement with no elaboration and he offers no verified substantiation of Two Moons' alleged 1912 claim that is found in the text of that book. Hyde may have been referring to the 1913 unpublished interview with Two Moons by William Camp mentioned above. In a nutshell, the brief interview of Two Moons by Camp in Part 3 is what Two Moons states happened in the Fetterman Fight without mention of Crazy Horse.[12]

Even with the extensive interviews of Lakotas who knew Crazy Horse intimately, in the wake of his dramatic death at Fort Robinson, Nebraska, the great Oglala warrior cannot without question be located as a decoy in any one specific critical spot on Lodge Trail Ridge by his close friends. In 1907 Eli S. Ricker interviewed Crazy Horse's close companion from the time of their boyhood, Chips (Horn Chips). Ricker states: "Chips was in the Fetterman Massacre. . . . He says fourteen Indians were killed there. American Horse was there. American Horse did not lead the decoy party. Chips says he wants to tell the truth." If Chips did tell the truth, as he knew it, he certainly did not place his close boyhood friend Crazy Horse in the fight, let alone the decoy party. In fact, Chips does not even mention Crazy Horse in relation to activities in the Powder River Country in 1866 at all.[13] Neither did George Sword. George Sword, we know, was in the Fetterman Fight, while his brother, also named Sword (Sword Owner), was, by George W. Colhoff's account at least (albeit a secondhand account) a decoy in the Fetterman Fight, and possibly its leader.[14] American Horse also told Ricker that he (American Horse) was a decoy. But that interview, as we have seen, conflicts with Sheldon's interview with American Horse, where American Horse makes no mention that he might have been a decoy [chapter 4]. George Sword and American Horse likewise make no mention in their testimonies to Ricker and Sheldon of their fellow Oglala warrior Crazy Horse being one of the decoys or even that Crazy Horse was in the fight. Then again, by the time of Crazy Horse's death in 1877, political currents on the reservation had estranged Crazy Horse and American Horse, and some even believe American Horse was instrumental in Crazy Horse's arrest.[15]

The cornerstones of original source material on Crazy Horse are the so-called Hinman interviews, conducted by Eleanor H. Hinman and her assistant at the Nebraska State Historical Society, Mari Sandoz, in 1930. The two women interviewed several of the old "Long Hairs," as Neihardt referred to the aged warriors from the days of resistance, still living three decades into the twentieth century at Rosebud and Pine Ridge. The two women were specifically interested in the life of Crazy Horse, particularly the circumstances of his death. None of the old warriors they interviewed, including Crazy Horse's close friend He Dog, mentions Crazy Horse in respect to the Fetterman Fight. Then again He Dog had a reputation for keeping mum when it came to sensitive topics.[16]

Yet based on three short ambiguous phrases that may be acknowledged as original narrative testimony, an ever-expanding fanciful role for Crazy Horse as being a principal decoy on Lodge Trail Ridge has found its way, time and again and with much embellishment, into well-read secondary literature since the middle of the twentieth century.[17] These testimonies are: by Whitewash (White Bear) in Robinson (1904): "Crazy Horse . . . was Red Cloud's principal lieutenant among the Oglalas;" White Bull in Campbell (1932–34): "Crazy Horse was the leader of the Oglala;" and an unsupported assertion by Hyde in 1936 that Two Moons had claimed back in 1912 that "Crazy Horse led the decoy party." Reputable historians, not-so-reputable historians, popular writers, and filmmakers (one of the more recent depictions being Steven Spielberg's television miniseries on the Turner Network, *Into the West*) have dramatized Crazy Horse dismounting, rubbing his pony's hoof as if it were injured, and in the case of Spielberg, standing on the ridge within pistol range as Captain Fetterman himself personally took potshots at him.[18]

Much of this supposition as image-making comes to us from the marvelously entertaining tour de force (but historically flawed) semi-fictional biography, *Crazy Horse: Strange Man of the Oglalas*, written by Mari Sandoz in 1942.[19] As Eleanor Hinman's transcriber for the Crazy Horse interviews twelve years previous, Sandoz did not garner any information from He Dog or the others that would place Crazy Horse in such elaborate detail, and in such a daring role, on the slopes of Lodge Trail Ridge on December 21, 1866. Sandoz, who visited Lodge Trail Ridge in winter with her typed manuscript in hand for inspiration, wrote: "Several times Crazy Horse had to get off [his horse], once pretending to tie his war rope closer. . . . Once when they [the other decoys] had all stopped to turn back he sat down behind a bush as though hurt or worn out and built a little fire, the others going on, leaving him behind. Shots began to splatter around him." Eleanor Hinman, who relinquished to Sandoz her claim to write a biography of the great Oglala, had acquired no knowledge of these kinds of events as none of her interviews came close to supporting such melodrama. There is nothing in the extensive notes of Mari Sandoz that point to any original testimonies attributing such daring exploits to Crazy Horse as a decoy.[20]

Hinman asked Walter S. Campbell in 1932 what he had learned from White Bull and others through his reservation interviews. Campbell replied to Hinman, in a letter dated October 13, 1932 with a list of actions that White Bull and others claimed Crazy Horse participated in, with no mention of the Fetterman Fight. In an unaddressed typescript in his personal papers following his reply to Hinman, however, Campbell wrote: "When the Sioux decided to attack Fort Phil Kearney in Wyoming, which was guarding the Bozeman Trail to Montana, Crazy Horse was chosen to lead the Oglala detachment." Campbell made no mention of Crazy Horse being one of the ten decoys on Lodge Trail Ridge.[21]

Yet the "wounded quail" scenario has played out ever since Sandoz published *Crazy Horse* in 1942. Dee Brown echoed Sandoz in *Fort Phil Kearny: An American Saga* (1962), later re-titled *The Fetterman Massacre* over Brown's objections. "Crazy Horse won a great name for himself that day with his acts of defiance," Brown wrote, "sometimes dismounting within rifle range and pretending to ignore the presence of the soldiers and the screams of their bullets."[22] Stephen Ambrose in his lengthy trade-edition biography *Crazy Horse and Custer: The Parallel Lives of Two American Warriors* (1975), goes further than Brown in embellishing Sandoz, having Crazy Horse waving his blanket and whooping, feigning a general retreat of the decoys before Fetterman's onslaught: "The ambush was working," Ambrose wrote. "Crazy Horse took one look at the advancing soldiers, checked his own pony, and turned back toward Lodge Trail Ridge, using the old trick of pretending to beat the horse with one hand while actually holding it back with the other." Ambrose goes on to assert in his endnotes that his material for Crazy Horse's role at Fort Phil Kearny is taken from statements by Whitewash (White Bear) given to Doane Robinson in *A History of the Dakota* (1904), p. 361. Of course Ambrose is mistaken. Whitewash (White Bear) claims only that Crazy Horse was a "chief lieutenant of Red Cloud's," and offers no such elaborate details in Robinson's book. Ambrose's extrapolated drama, designed for the large trade market like that of Mari Sandoz, is creative but imaginary. So too are Drury and Clavin in *The Heart of Everything That Is*, who claim, based solely on a modern oral testimony, that the final straw that baited Fetterman over Lodge Trail Ridge was the sight of Crazy Horse "mooning" the captain on the south side of the slope.[23]

Others have been more cautious from the surveys of the literature in ascribing specific actions to Crazy Horse, including Cheyenne historian Father Peter John Powell, who still places Crazy Horse in a sentence or two as a decoy but without an endnote to support it.[24] Less assertive too is Larry McMurtry in his short form biography of Crazy Horse. While paraphrasing Dee Brown as to Crazy Horse's presence at the fight, McMurtry simply states that "his reputation was enhanced."[25] Although not the most illuminating modern biography of Crazy Horse, Mike Sajna's *Crazy Horse: The Life behind the Legend* (2000) is perhaps the most honest. Sajna wrote: "Many writers have Crazy Horse leading the decoy party, but that is difficult to support from primary sources. As the leader of the Oglala warriors [as White Bull claims] it seems more likely that he would have stayed back with the main force."[26] Unfortunately these misperceptions have been perpetuated to the present day. Joseph Marshall's inspirationally written *The Journey of Crazy Horse: A Lakota History* (2004) identifies his sources as being storytellers from the Rosebud and Pine Ridge Reservations. Unfortunately the book has no endnotes to correlate these oral sources with the statements in Marshall's narrative. His descriptions of Crazy Horse's exploits as a decoy at the Fetterman Fight strongly echo Sandoz, as does other modern oral tradition.[27] In what is overall the best biography of Crazy Horse to date, Kingsley Bray's *Crazy Horse: A Lakota Life* (2006) the same flaws persist, naming Crazy Horse as a decoy and ascribing personal individual actions to him on the slope of Lodge Trail Ridge.[28]

By revisiting the A. E. Sheldon 1903 Short Interviews (chapter 4) we may convincingly place Crazy Horse at the Fetterman Fight but not specifically on the southern slope of Lodge Trail Ridge as one of the famous decoys.

> Eagle Hawk, July 28, 1903: 'The Stinger' [?] and Crazy Horse were in the fight at Ft. Phil Kearny.
>
> American Horse, July 30, 1903: Sitting Bull [the Oglala] and Crazy Horse were both there. Crazy Horse was one of the bravest.
>
> Rocky Bear, 1903: Red Dog was wounded by another Indian. Sword & Crazy Horse toled [to lead?] the soldiers on. Sent 8 soldiers. Main party of Indians was in a circle. Infantry chased them. Several played [like] their horses, [had] played out—Red Dog, Red Cloud.

Rocky Bear's statement is intriguing and the only eyewitness account that could be interpreted as support for Crazy Horse being a decoy. But it is uncorroborated by any other person's eyewitness account. Sheldon's cursive of the word, "toled" in the 2003 interview is forever uncertain and confusing. Did Sheldon mean Crazy Horse was to lead "Fetterman's soldiers" on over the ridge or to lead the "Oglala soldiers" on in battle and thus "sent" eight Indian "soldiers" in the decoy party? We know from the testimony of Red Fly that the Oglalas applied the term "soldier" to their own warriors: "Red Cloud was the *chief soldier*" (emphasis mine) Red Fly stated. We may never know for certain, but either way it keeps Crazy Horse in the mix.[29]

The closest account of Crazy Horse being a decoy, however, *is* Rocky Bear. Besides his statement to Sheldon a reporter from the *Rapid City Journal* in 1907 wrote that: "Rocky Bear, an old Indian in Pine Ridge Reservation, says that Red Cloud, Young-man-afraid-of-his horses, Red Dog, and Crazy Horse were the principal leaders in this massacre. Red Cloud sent Crazy Horse with eight Indians to the fort to try and draw the soldiers out; they circled around the Fort at the same time firing upon it. This ruse was successful, and as soon as the little command under Capt. Fetterman was seen leaving the Fort, the Indians retreated, at the same time pretending that their horses were lame and tired."[30] The statement does not account for the amount of time lapsed between the encirclement of the fort and the egress of the wood train. Neither does it account for the amount of time lapsed between the wood train's egress from the fort, its attack, and Fetterman's exit from the fort. The Indians in the fight indeed executed what may be viewed as at least three decoy movements. The first one circling around the fort, the second, sometime later, a feint on the wood train to draw troops out of the fort, and a third one, luring Fetterman's force out of the fort and over Lodge Trail Ridge. Crazy Horse may have participated in one or more of these, which is likely but nonspecific in the Indian accounts.

Depending upon one's confirmation bias, Rocky Bear's statements may be interpreted in different ways and thus remains an objective mystery that has come into play only after the publication of Mari Sandoz's *Crazy Horse: The Strange Man of the Oglalas* in 1942. Possible meanings cannot be corroborated definitively to acceptable Ranke-prescribed scholarly standards with other eyewitness testimony. Then again, Crazy Horse is the "Strange Man of the Oglalas." He may well have been in more than one decoy action, or perhaps was one of many warriors making taunting feints that day, as some historians believe.[31]

Santee historian Ohiyesa (Charles Eastman) offers a semantic possibility about the feint on the wood train (second decoy action). Eastman never personally knew Crazy Horse but wrote his biography anyway in *Indian Heroes and Great Chieftains* (1918). Eastman wrote: "Crazy Horse was chosen to lead the attack on the 'woodchoppers' [emphasis mine], designed to draw the soldiers out of the fort, while an army of six hundred [1,500+] lay in wait for them. The success of this stratagem was further enhanced by his masterful handling of his men."[32]

Interestingly, the Indians designed the attack on the wood train (by white accounts, forty warriors) on the morning of December 21, 1866, to be a feint to draw troops out of the fort to protect the woodcutters. Once the troops left the fort the feint ended and the forty warriors retreated back to the east, behind the ridges separating them from the wood road and the fort, in a successful effort to lure the troops over the ridge to head them off, the soldiers not knowing what awaited them on the north side. Certainly this feint, designed as part of the ambush plan, can be viewed as a "decoy maneuver" every bit as much as the ten warriors demonstrating on the southern slope of Lodge Trail Ridge in order to bring the soldiers over the ridge, hopefully figuring they would think the ten men on the ridge were protecting the retreat of the forty on the other side. Demonstrations by warriors circling the fort, which Carrington dispersed with howitzer fire, can also be viewed as "decoy maneuvers." Could this too be a first intended decoy action by yet a different group of warriors, or were these men circling the fort the same small party of the famous ten decoys of Sandoz fame who, after a demonstration around the stockade, then fell back on Lodge Trail Ridge? Fetterman and his officers all had been tempted by small decoy parties previously, Grummond coming close to losing his life chasing one group on December 6. The garrison at Fort Phil Kearny had never yet met more than one hundred or so warriors outside the fort. At the least the troops certainly did not figure 1,500 Indians awaited them over Lodge Trail Ridge. Could the feint on the woodcutters be the first widely published genesis of the Crazy Horse decoy story? One can certainly visualize Crazy Horse leading any of these three maneuvers.[33]

So what we may conclude of Crazy Horse's presence on or over Lodge Trail Ridge on December 21, 1866, is that, based on specific eyewitness testimony, Crazy Horse was present at the Fetterman Fight and, as we shall see in Part 4, his inspirational and spiritual presence is heavily felt in the secondary literature and modern oral tradition. There is enough circumstantial evidence to conclude that Crazy Horse was an up-and-coming warrior in 1866 and perhaps indeed a primary "lieutenant" of Red Cloud by that date. Likely Crazy Horse and He Dog rode up the Tongue River to the Oglala camps a few days prior to the fight. Certainly, given his devotion to defend the ecological integrity of the lands of the Oglalas—the Powder River Country and the Black Hills—it would have by no means been out of character for him to be in the thick of the action. Neither is it illogical to assume that he would have enthusiastically led a decoy party and engaged in daring acts while doing so.

The weight of eyewitness evidence demonstrates that Crazy Horse was *somewhere* in the fight and performed bravely, but the exact details remain, at the least, uncorroborated, and virtually none of the specific daring and dramatic actions and deeds directly attributed to Crazy Horse as a leader or a member of the decoy party can be substantiated by *any* identifiable original sources, save Rocky Bear's ambiguous and undefined statement, and later, Hyde's short, paraphrased comment of Two Moons' (1936), which is highly suspect given his earlier 1918 account. All decoys used "wounded quail" tactics. These dramatic exploits first appear in print in Sandoz's *Crazy Horse* (1942) and have been repeated, embellished, and written into the secondary histories ever since.[34] Since the maneuver of ten decoys on Lodge Trail Ridge was an intertribal representative effort, surely one of those men interviewed would have recognized the deeds of Crazy Horse years later when he had become an icon. That Crazy Horse "distinguished himself that day" somewhere in the fight is certain, given American Horse's statement that he *was one of the bravest.* Many warriors, who have gone unnamed in the eyewitness accounts, possibly even Crazy Horse, distinguished themselves that day and they should be remembered in their family histories. Again, according to scholars at Fort Phil Kearny Historic Site, many individual warriors characteristically feinted and moved back on many parts of the field, with different groups of soldiers, to urge them into the arms of concealed warriors during the flow of the battle. Their individual stories simply were never told when they were alive or corroborated by eyewitness testimony to the outside world. Perhaps this is a more meaningful explanation for testimonies of warriors like American Horse and George Sword for also being decoys. Were Crazy Horse and the "famous ten" not unique?

The absolute truth undoubtedly died with Crazy Horse at Fort Robinson in September 1877, and possibly with White Bull who died seventy years after the battle, a converted Christian in 1947 at the age of ninety-eight, and one of the last surviving Lakota veterans to have fought against the United States. But the failure to prove the specific actions of Crazy Horse on December 21, 1866, in no way diminishes his iconic stature for all and his revered reputation as a leader of resistance and a source of spiritual enlightenment for his people in the past and in the present. Rocky Bear's almost forgotten account of Crazy Horse's alleged decoy actions keeps multiple possibilities alive, if not to the extent of the dramatic prose of Mari Sandoz then at least attesting to the bravery of many Lakotas and Cheyennes at the Fetterman Fight.

History is a discipline with multiple viewpoints, written, oral, and artistic, that are recognized and respected as part of a peoples' cultural celebration, as will be seen in

Part 4, "Memory and Legacy." Change over time of historical memory and celebration is likewise common to all societies and communities. The story told in this essay is one example of the legacy of Crazy Horse. The legendary acts attributed to Crazy Horse and the Indians' great victory in the Powder River Country in 1866 continue to commingle with the disputes as to who was to blame for the dramatic defeat of the Americans at Fort Phil Kearny. This combination of legend and uncertainty adds vigor to the mystique of and the debate over the Fetterman Fight, as do the dynamics of Crazy Horse's heroic but better-chronicled exploits at the Wagon Box Fight and Little Big Horn, as well as those of all Lakotas.[35]

Account of a Mixed-Heritage Scout, Mitch Bouyer

Kar-pash, 1837–June 25, 1876

Mitch Bouyer, a courier and interpreter at Fort Phil Kearny, who was traveling to Fort C. F. Smith at the time of the Fetterman fight, leaves history with the only account of a mixed-blood. Bouyer made his single sworn testimony at the official investigations of the Fetterman Fight, conducted in 1867. Bouyer is the son of Jean-Baptiste Bouyer, a French Canadian fur trapper for the American Fur Company. Jean-Baptiste died in an Indian attack while trapping in 1863. Bouyer's mother was a Santee Dakota. Bouyer died at the Battle of Little Big Horn on June 25, 1876, on what is today called the south skirmish line, while serving as a 7th Cavalry scout. Earlier that day Bouyer had warned Custer that the Lakota village on the Greasy Grass was the largest he had seen in thirty years. He gave away his possessions in anticipation of his own death. Bouyer's testimony before the investigating committee of the Fetterman Fight is a secondhand account given to him by an unnamed Lakota who was in the battle. This account corroborates well with the other Indian eyewitness accounts presented in this study.

On my way to Fort C. F. Smith last Spring, a Sioux Indian came into my camp on the Little Horn River, and remained with me that day and night and the next day and told me all about the massacre [Fetterman Fight]. He stated that there were eight Indians killed on the battle ground, and about fifty wounded and twenty-two of the wounded afterwards died. He also said that the soldiers fought bravely but huddling together it gave the Indians a better opportunity to kill them, than if they had scattered about. He said that the soldiers' ammunition did not give out, but they fired to the last. He said the Indians took all the ammunition the soldiers had left but some soldiers had no ammunition left. The great majority of Indians were Sioux. There were about 150 warriors of Cheyennes. There were about 60 Arrapahoes. I asked him why the Indians killed these soldiers. He said that the principal reason was that the whites were building forts in this country and traveling this road driving all their game, and if they allowed it to go on, in two years they would not have anything for their children to eat. Another reason was the principal Chief of the Missouri Sioux [Miniconjou] had died just before the massacre, and the bands had gotten together and determined to avenge his death. The chief's name was White Swan who died a natural death on the Powder River. He stated that there were 1800 [warriors] on the ground but only half of them engaged in the fight. That the fight did not last very long, about one hour. That some of the soldiers were a mile in advance of others, and when the Indians rose up from the ravines the advance and soldiers were killed in retreating to the main body and that the main body huddling together were killed as before stated.[36]

⇒⇐

The Lakota eyewitness accounts presented here represent a storied history and rich cultural tradition of a great people. The Fetterman Fight was truly one of the Lakota people's greatest victories alongside their Cheyenne and Arapaho allies, whose stories are presented in Parts 3 and 4.

PART THREE

Northern Cheyenne Accounts

The Omisis (Northern Cheyennes) give us some of the most vivid and important eyewitness accounts of fighting the Vehoé ("Spiders"/Whites) at the Fetterman battle thanks to the excellent interviews of George B. Grinnell, George Bent and George Hyde, and Thomas Marquis. Four individual Omisis leave these various original testimonies to history.

Once, before the whites contested the Great Plains, the Cheyennes had been a unified people living on the northern plains after crossing the Missouri River in the late eighteenth century. They had migrated from the north and east in the land of the Great Lakes, pushed west by Chippewa enemies, disease, and diminishing resources.[1] They call themselves *Tis-tis-Tas*, meaning, "people alike," or "called out people," or simply "the people." On the plains the much larger Lakota nation that followed them a bit later gave this Algonquian linguistic group the name Shaiena, or "people speaking a strange tongue." Not long after, whites corrupted the name in English to "Cheyenne."[2]

The pre-reservation political structure of the historic Cheyenne nation is less complex than that of the historic Lakotas. The principal decision-making group is the Council of Forty-Forty, council chiefs historically elected every seven to ten years and sometimes known as "old man chiefs," which has connotation for wisdom rather than chronological age. Presiding over the council was an elected "Sweet Medicine Chief," who is the embodiment of the values and virtues of Cheyenne culture hero Sweet Medicine, who taught the people the ways of the Great Plains as well as much of their moral and social structure. By most accounts, the Northern old man chief Little Wolf is credited with also being Sweet Medicine chief of all Cheyennes (the last Sweet Medicine chief) at the time of Red Cloud's War or shortly thereafter. The council chiefs usually presided over affairs of the village, settling domestic disputes, village movements, trade with outsiders, and, by the 1860s, negotiations with white officials. As such, the immediate followers of a particular council chief constituted a "band" within the tribe. The council chiefs led by example and exercised no formal absolute authority over decisions for war or peace that bound individual warriors or their military societies. Council chiefs were also designated as peace chiefs. As ethnologist E. Adamson Hoebel wrote: "The supreme authority of the tribe lies not in the hands of aggressive war leaders [military society headmen] but under the control of even-tempered peace chiefs. All peace chiefs are proven warriors, but when a [little] chief [headman] of a military association is raised to the rank of peace chief, he must resign his post in the military society. He retains his membership, but not his position as war leader."[3] The Cheyenne tribe consisted of seven military societies, although they did not all exist at all times during their history. They were:

Wŏhksēh'ētănui, Kit Fox Men or Fox Soldiers
Hĭm'ōwēyŭhk'ĭ̄s, Elks or Elk-Horn Scrapers or Crooked Lances
Hōtă'mit ă'niu, Dog Men, often erroneously called Dog Soldiers
Mǎhōhē'wǎs, Red Shields
Hotă'mi mǎssāu, Crazy Dogs
Him'ǎ'tǎno'his, Bowstrings
Wīh'iu nǔt'kīū, Chief Soldiers[4]

Decisions for war almost always resided with military society headmen (little chiefs), although individual factions within a military society or among the societies could choose to go raiding against enemies or to steal horses or both but there never existed a designated "war chief" of the entire tribe. By the 1860s bands often factionalized between war and peace. These splits became a problem for Southern Cheyennes following the Colorado Gold Rush, but not as much for the Omisis in the Powder River Country, then still unsettled by whites, though northern fighting men often came south to war with their southern relatives and friends.[5]

In pre-contact days, however, as a successive group of invaders on the Great Plains, the Cheyennes fought many wars with rival tribes for prime ecological biomes, especially buffalo ranges, before settling in the lands east of the Rockies on the northern plains. The center of their universe was Noahvose, the Sacred Mountain, known today as Bear Butte near the modern town of Sturgis, South Dakota. It was here that Maheo, the all-being, bestowed upon the Cheyennes, through the leadership of Sweet Medicine, Maahotse, the Sacred Arrows by which Maheo poured his divine life into the people. In the early years the Cheyennes cultivated corn and other crops. Bison is the resource that drastically transformed the Cheyenne way of life. Within a generation or so they became almost exclusively buffalo hunters. After acquiring the horse from peoples to the south, the Cheyennes formed powerful alliances with more populous nations, principally the Lakota. Now they followed the herds over the plains, expanding their territory into transition or neutral zones shared and contested with other tribes and eventually the Vehoé (whites). Sometime during this era the Cheyennes assimilated a small tribe on the northern plains known as the Suhati or So'aeo'o. The Suhati culture hero, Erect Horns, gave the Cheyenne people Esevone or Issiwun, the Sacred Buffalo Hat through which Maheo pours life into Cheyenne women and makes them fruitful.[6]

Around 1780 the Cheyennes numbered close to thirty-five hundred. By the dawn of the nineteenth century they had attained great affluence on the Great Plains as burgeoning middlemen in a system of trade that drew guns from the east and north and horses from the southwest. As trade facilitators they became even more reliant on horses. During the 1830s and 1840s the American fur trade would both benefit and corrupt the Cheyennes. They began dividing into two distinct geographical regions. One group, even before the Peace of 1840 with Comanches and Kiowas, became drawn to trade around Bent's Fort on the Arkansas River, in what today is Colorado, and spread east into Kansas. Others preferred to remain in the north, near the Tongue and Powder River valleys, the Black Hills, and the sacred mountain. Traditional bands and even the military societies were, to various degrees, fractured by this economic realignment.[7] Among the bands that remained in the north the most numerous were the Omisis, or Northern Eaters, the name selected in this study to distinguish the Northern Cheyennes.[8]

By this time all Cheyennes began to overuse their resources. Their vast pony herds overgrazed the prairies, especially after a cycle of drought on the plains during the 1850s and afterwards, with a warming period of the Earth at the end of the so-called Little Ice Age. Intertribal warfare, along with disease, took a calamitous toll. By trading with whites, even as centrally located facilitators, the Cheyennes would by the 1850s change their destiny by locking themselves into an economic dependency from which they could not escape. Essentially, as historian Elliott West writes, "the Cheyennes were caught up in an old theme of gain and cost. As they broadened their command over valuable resources, they became absolutely reliant on the essentials they were helping to destroy."[9]

The split between northern and southern people became further accentuated about 1830 or 1833 when Pawnees captured the Sacred Arrows in a disastrous battle, and again in 1837 when Pawnees practically annihilated the Bowstring military society. In the years to follow the Cheyennes suffered as never before, especially the peace factions of the splintered southern bands at the Sand Creek Massacre in Colorado Territory in 1864. The Pike's Peak gold rush in Colorado, the Treaty of Fort Wise in 1861, Sand Creek, and the expansion of the agricultural frontier in Kansas less than a decade later are perhaps the most catastrophic events in Southern Cheyenne history that resulted from the loss of the original Sacred Arrows.[10] White settlement thus drove a geographical wedge between the northern and southern groups. Warfare in the 1860s raged between the lands of the northern and southern people along a central corridor within the ancestral neutral grounds between the Platte and Arkansas Rivers, even before Sand Creek. But the Cheyennes had always considered themselves one people. Journeys to see friends and relatives between Northern Cheyennes and Southern Cheyennes continued frequently well into the 1870s and ultimately until today.[11]

Until 1865 most Northern Cheyennes fared better in their still-unsettled-by-whites Powder River Country. Some, who made their homes along the South Platte River joined their southern brethren, especially Bull Bear's and Tall Bull's Dog Men military society, now a full-fledged, separate but patrilineal band, which included families and fighting men from other traditional matrilineal bands, in raids of revenge for Sand Creek. Attacks on the express station of Julesburg, Colorado, and on volunteer regiments at Fort Sedgwick, Colorado, and at Platte Bridge and Mud Springs in Nebraska, in turn provoked a forlorn offensive military expedition under General Patrick Conner that only emboldened the northerners. In 1866, the renowned Northern Cheyenne warrior Roman Nose ventured south to help friends among the Dog Men try and clean out freight traffic on the overland trails, rather than fight the American troops on the Bozeman Trail with the Oglala and Miniconjou coalition. By most accounts Roman Nose would miss the Fetterman Fight and two years later lose his life at the Battle of Beecher Island on September 17, 1868, in Colorado.[12]

As such, the Northern Cheyennes, never a party to the 1865 Treaty of the Little Arkansas with the southern people, were technically still at war with whites when Carrington proposed his ill-fated agreement with the Bad Face Oglalas at Fort Laramie in 1866, resulting in Man Afraid of His Horses' and Red Cloud's defection from the council. Most Cheyenne accounts presented here assert that the Bad Face Oglalas invited the Omisis, who were camped along Rosebud Creek just below the confluence of Lame Deer Creek and the Rosebud in December 1866, to participate in the ambush of the soldiers at Fort Phil Kearny. At the staging of the ambush the Miniconjou chiefs allowed the participating Omisis warriors to choose on which side of the ridges along the Bozeman Trail they wished to hide for the intended ambush. These warriors were generally followers of headman Crazy Head, who believed in the medicine of the warrior Crazy Mule, who claimed not only immunity to bullets but also that his mere stare could cause soldiers to fall down and die. The Cheyennes (along with Arapahos) selected the middle or southern reaches in the ridges west of the Bozeman Trail. They wished to be in on the fight at the beginning. Cheyenne fighting men in the Fetterman Fight believed Crazy Mule's lethal stare at the enemy and his invulnerability would give them a quick victory.

"Did you ever hear about Crazy Mule?" an aged Cheyenne warrior (probably Sun Road) asked Thomas Marquis in the early 1920s. He continued:

The spirits worked for him more than any other Indian I ever knew. Bullets might hit him, but they would not go through his body. I saw a test made upon him, at a time when our tribal camp was far up the Tongue River. I was then 29 years old. He dressed his body with only a muslin shirt, this painted with his special medicine colors, and on his feet he wore a pair of moccasins beaded in a certain way, according to his medicine plan. Thus prepared, he placed himself in front of a big tree. Twenty-seven Cheyennes who had rifles were chosen to take a position a short distance in front of him. They rested their rifles in upright forked sticks and fired at the painted muslin shirt. As soon as the shots had been fired, Crazy Mule reached down and pulled off his moccasins. From them he emptied out the 27 bullets.

I saw Crazy Mule kill three Captains of white men soldiers, each one a long distance away, too far for bullets to carry. He just stood on a hill and looked steadily at them. They became dizzy, staggered in their walk, then were paralyzed and fell dead. He could do such acts at any time he might want to do them. But he was a good-hearted man, so he never harmed any Cheyenne.[13]

Cheyennes leave us with some of the best accounts of the prelude to and the beginning of the Fetterman Fight, thanks to the efforts of armchair ethnographers Thomas Marquis, George Hyde, George Bent, and ethnologist and naturalist George B. Grinnell. Marquis gives us the reminiscence of Wooden Leg, who like the Oglala

Black Elk was a child in 1866. Hyde relays the stories of Two Moons (often spelled Two Moon), secondhand through the letters of mixed-heritage Cheyenne/white George Bent, who interviewed the aging chief, as did Walter Camp, whose brief but unpublished interview is found here. Grinnell, like Campbell accomplished with the Miniconjou White Bull, gives us vivid accounts, albeit with some third-person rhetoric by White Elk and Little Wolf from his 1915 book *The Fighting Cheyennes*, as well as his interview notes, housed at the Braun Research Center of the Autry Center in Los Angeles. The Cheyenne accounts following correlate well with the accounts of the Miniconjous and Oglalas, although because of their laterally opposite position on the field prior to the ambush and tribal authority structural differences, they logically do not account for or confuse the roles between Cheyenne and Lakota leaders in the battle.

Wooden Leg

Kâhamâxéveóhtáhe, 1858–1940

Wooden Leg (b. 1858) was only eight years old at the time of the Fetterman Fight. He remained with his family in the Cheyenne Tongue River camps during the battle. His older brother Strong Wind Blowing received a mortal wound in the engagement. Wooden Leg gives us his childhood impressions of the fight thanks to Dr. Thomas B. Marquis. An agency physician on the Northern Cheyenne Indian Reservation, arriving in 1922, Marquis spent the remainder of his life in Hardin, Montana, until his death in 1935. Fascinated with finding the details of the Custer Fight from the only survivors, Marquis invited aging warriors to his home to eat at his table, smoke his tobacco, and after they realized Marquis posed no threat to their families for their role in wiping out Custer, they told him tales of the fight and their days of freedom on the plains. His most loquacious Cheyenne friend and informant for his passion was Wooden Leg. Marquis's *Wooden Leg: A Warrior Who Fought Custer* (1931) is probably his most famous book, among several books and articles. Marquis communicated in sign language and some Cheyenne with Wooden Leg. *Wooden Leg* is Marquis's interpretation of this fighting man, written in the first person as a biographical piece. Consequently, Wooden Leg gives us a brief description of his earliest childhood memories of 1866, reproduced here (including errors) from Marquis's interpretation.[1]

Another soldier fort that was being fought by the Ogallah Sioux and some of the Cheyennes was on what we called Buffalo Creek [Little Piney Creek]. Little Wolf was then our most important old man chief. Crazy Head was next

Wooden Leg.
Courtesy Wikimedia Commons.

in importance among us. Red Cloud was the leading Old Man Chief of the Ogllalas, with Crazy Horse as their principal warrior chief [*blotahunka*]. At a time when our whole tribe were in camp on Rosebud creek, just below the mouth of Lame Deer creek, and when the Ogallalas were on Tongue river, just below where Birney, Montana, is now situated, some of their people came over the divide to us and asked the Cheyennes to join them in a great attack on the Buffalo creek fort. Our chiefs considered the matter. It was decided that whatever young men of us might wish to go would be allowed to do so. Our camp then was moved to Lame Deer creek to the base of the divide, a short distance from the Ogallalas on Tongue river. Our great medicine man, Crazy Mule, showed that he could cause bullets shot at him to fall harmless at his feet. A hundred or more of our young men said that they could fight the soldiers if Crazy Mule would go with them. He agreed to go. Our second chief, Crazy Head, lead the band of warriors. Little Wolf stayed in our camp. [?]

My oldest brother, named Strong Wind Blowing, was killed in that midwinter battle with soldiers. He was about sixteen years old. Chief Little Wolf's younger brother [Big Nose] was also killed. These two were the only Cheyennes who fell that day. [?] I do not know how many Sioux may have been cut down by the soldier bullets, but I know there were not many. Our returning warriors said that more than a hundred white men lost their lives, that Crazy Mule's medicine caused them to fall down dead without need for the Indians to kill them. There was rejoicing in our camp on account of our victory. But our family and all relatives of the two dead Cheyennes were in mourning. We wept and prayed for the spirits of the lost ones.[2]

Wooden Leg's account is somewhat unique in that he claims Little Wolf, who may by this time have been Sweet Medicine Chief of the Cheyennes, remained in the Tongue River camps and did not participate directly in the fight. Certainly, as we shall see in White Elk's account, Little Wolf deferred the honor of being a decoy to his younger brother Big Nose, who then received a mortal wound in the fighting. But it is likely that Little Wolf was near the battle as were some of the Lakota chiefs, perhaps even directing activities. Of course, Wooden Leg overestimates the number killed in Fetterman's command. He also underestimates the number of Cheyenne casualties. Interestingly, however, if he remembered since childhood the tales of the returning warriors, down into the 1920s, his story to Marquis reinforces the Cheyenne belief to that time in the powerful medicine of Crazy Mule, by then imbedded in the Cheyenne cultural lexicon.

Two Moons

Éše'he Ôhnéšesêstse, 1842 or 1847–1917

Two Moons (often spelled Two Moon), a "little chief," or headman of the Kit Fox warrior society, is most famous for his participation in the Rosebud battle, the Battle of Little Big Horn, and the defeat of his band at Wolf Mountain(s) (called Belly Butte by Cheyennes), on January 8, 1877 by forces under General Nelson A. Miles. After his surrender at Fort Keogh, Montana, in April 1877, Two Moons enlisted as a scout for the army during the Nez Percé War. With the establishment of the early reserve in Montana for Northern Cheyennes, Miles appointed Two Moons "head chief" of the Northern Cheyennes following the exile of Little Wolf's and Dull Knife's bands to Indian Territory in 1877. Two Moons played a crucial role in Little Wolf's surrender at Fort Keogh in 1879, following the Cheyenne's remarkable exodus north from Indian Territory. Two Moons' grave is a frequently visited monument alongside U.S. Highway 212 west of Busby, Montana.

Two Moons' actual role in the Fetterman Fight is problematic. His story of the battle comes to us through George Bent's letters to George Hyde, William Camp, and George B. Grinnell. Two Moons recounts how he "scouted" out Fort Phil Kearny prior to December 21, 1866, determined it to be impossible to attack directly, and recommended a deception to draw troops out of the fort. Popular histories often place him in the fight, which is logical since he was certainly in the Peno Valley at the time. But Two Moons told Grinnell he did not participate directly in the fighting, although all of his accounts to Bent and Grinnell corroborate with other Indian eyewitness testimony, but only in a generalized manner as to the major events of the battle.

Two Moons.
*Photographed by Richard Throssel, c. 1910, courtesy Museum of
Photographic Arts, San Diego. Gift of Graham and Susan Nash.*

Most of Two Moons' words are from interviews with George Bent in 1904 and
1905. Bent wrote up the interviews and mailed them in letters to George Hyde, who
synthesized them in the book *Life of George Bent Written from His Letters*. Bent, the
son of trader William Bent and the Cheyenne Owl Woman, lived in Colony, Oklahoma,
during these years before his death in 1918. William Bent was the grandson of a federal
judge in St. Louis, and a great-grandson of a Massachusetts patriot who reputedly
dressed like an Indian in 1773 and participated in the Boston Tea Party. Bent was
also the son-in-law of Southern Cheyenne White Thunder, keeper of Maahotse, the
Sacred Arrows. His son George Bent received an education at private schools in St.

Louis and Westport, Missouri, and served for a short time in the Confederate army during the Civil War. Present in the village at Sand Creek during the massacre at a time when his brother Robert was forcibly impressed by Colonel John M. Chivington to help guide the Colorado Third Volunteers to Black Kettle's peaceful village, the event shaped much of the remainder of his life. Bent gives us the only detailed Cheyenne eyewitness account of the Sand Creek Massacre. After Sand Creek, Bent lived as a member of the Cheyenne Dog Men in their raids of revenge for the massacre along the overland routes.[1] Bent interviewed Two Moons at the request of George Hyde when Two Moons came south to the (Southern) Cheyenne and Arapaho Indian Reservation for visits with elderly southern Cheyenne friends.

Presented here are the original letters Bent sent to Hyde from his conversations with the aging chief, followed by Two Moons' story in Hyde's *Life of George Bent*. Sometimes, with such transferred interviews, "[a] lot can get lost in translation," states the foremost scholar of the Bent-Hyde letters, Lincoln B. Faller, "a lot can get changed. What we have in George Bent's letters is rare indeed: his own account of things in his own language—or in one of his own languages, English, for he was perfectly bilingual with both—saying just what he wanted to say with no intermediate intervention."[2] Bent translated Two Moons' spoken words into English for Hyde. Faller, however, believes that in *Life of George Bent* some of Hyde's "reordering" of the letters for book format and style led to some distortion, not the historical accuracy or truthfulness, but in allowing readers to know and appreciate Bent's unvarnished personality and passion for telling his people's "side of the story," which did not exist yet in the first decade or so of the twentieth century.[3]

George E. Hyde (1882–1968) lived in Omaha, Nebraska, for all of his life. By the turn of the twentieth century he became passionate about chronicling the Plains Indians' viewpoint of both their culture and their period of resistance to American invasion of the Great Plains. A man of modest means, Hyde put food on the table by operating a bookstore he owned in Omaha. At age eighteen he became nearly deaf and blind from the ravages of rheumatic fever. Living at the right time Hyde, through mostly written communication, befriended trusted Indian fighting men from the 1860s and 1870s. His books are classics of Indian history today. For a short time around 1908 he conducted research for George B. Grinnell. He claimed to be a ghostwriter for some of Grinnell's classic, *The Fighting Cheyennes* (1915).

We do not know how or why George Bent became fast friends through letters with Hyde beginning in 1904. None of Hyde's letters to Bent have survived. Hyde was in his early twenties and Bent in his early sixties when their correspondence began. By

December 1905, Bent quit addressing his letters to Hyde with "Dear Sir" and began opening his letters with, "My Friend." Because of his lack of academic credentials and America's involvement in the Great War in 1918, the year of Bent's death, Hyde could not find a publisher for *Life of George Bent*. The manuscript languished for half a century, until 1968, the year of Hyde's death, when historian Savoie Lottinville successfully published it with the University of Oklahoma Press. Since that time it has become the definitive original source history of the Southern Cheyennes from their point of view.[4]

Although their correspondence concerned mostly the Southern Cheyennes, Bent begins by responding to Hyde's spurned interest in Two Moons' Omisis recollections of both the Fetterman and Custer fights. Although Bent spoke fluent English, his writing is unpolished. The words, punctuation, and abbreviations are reproduced here unchanged from Bent's original cursive script.

Bent's Interviews with Two Moons in His Letters to Hyde

Colony Oklahoma Nov 16th 1904 Geo. E. Hyde Omaha Nebr
Dear Sir
Your letter of Nov 12th came to hand yesterday I will find out from Two Moons all about Fetterman's fight at Fort Phil Kearney in 1866 who was one of young Chiefs of the Northern Cheyennes and was in this fight. he came down here on visit and is now at Cantonment visit Dog Soldiers. And, will be back here in about week. and will get all the particulars right from him and also. about Custer's fight and how he was Killed and if he Knows who Killed him Two Moons took part in all these fights. and he is the best man to get particulars of all the fights up North you will find all the Writers speak of Two Moons and this is the man he is now 70 years old he is an uncle of my wife he was here few days and went up to Cantonment to see some of his old friends any thing that you wish to find out from him up North write it down and. I will get him to answer them. . . . Respectfully
Geo Bent[5]

In December 1904, Bent wrote to Hyde with Two Moons' account of the fight itself, explaining how some of the troops were a quarter mile ahead of others. These were the Second Cavalry under Lieutenant George W. Grummond, who charged ahead from slightly west of Monument Hill toward Peno Creek. Two Moons seems to be unaware of Grummond in his letter, referring instead to all the troops as "Fetterman." Two Moons identifies the Arapaho leaders in the fight and corroborates that he reconnoitered troop strength at Fort Phil Kearny prior to the principal chiefs' organization of the Indian dispositions for the intended ambush.

COLONY, OKLA., Dec 5th 1904 Geo. E. Hyde Omaha Nebr
Dear Sir
Two Moons says at Fetterman's Massacre at Fort Phil Kearney in 1866. all of Red Clouds band of Siouxs all of the Northern Cheyennes and some Northern Arapahoes were in this fight,[6] he says they all went there. purpose to draw the troops away from the Fort. he says himself and small party of Cheyennes made visit to the Fort to see if they Could take the place without losing to many Men of course you know the Indians do not want to lose any men if they can help it. so he says he seen it was best to get the Troops away from the Fort. he says Cheyennes & Sioux's had been running off stock from there and Troops was in habit of chasing the Indians. he says Jim Bridger was there as Interpreter. he says they attacked the wood train and knew that Troops would come out. when Fetterman came out few Indians with best horses went and met him and they had instructions to lead him in Hills where Indians hid behind the hills. he says some of the Troops were coming up about 1/4 mile behind Fetterman [Fetterman was a quarter mile behind Grummond at this point]. he says there were so many Indians. when they came out on the hills. Fetterman [Grummond] started to turn back but seen the Indians were all around. his men dismounted and turn their horses lose. He says Fetterman could not do any thing else only to fight he says. 14 Indians were killed in this fight 2 Cheyennes 1 Arapahoe 11 Siouxs. Strong Wolf or Brave Wolf. Dull Knife and Little Wolf were leaders of Northern Cheyennes Black. Coal and Eagle Head of the Northern Arapahoes were leaders of the Arapahoes. Most Noted Siouxs were Red Cloud. Pawnee Killer. And Blue Horse he says there were over 1.000 Siouxs in the fight not counting Cheyennes & Arapahoes. . . .
Respectfully, Geo Bent[7]

Two Moons' Story (edited by George Hyde) in *Life of George Bent*

These big Indian camps were made up of the Sioux under Red Cloud, Pawnee Killer, and Blue Horse; the Cheyennes under Strong Wolf (or Brave Wolf),

Little Wolf, and Dull Knife[?]; and the Arapahos under Black Coal and Eagle Head. The Sioux alone had over one thousand fighting men. For some time the Indians had been running off stock, making attacks on small parties near the fort, but always falling back when attacked by the soldiers. This encouraged the soldiers to chase the small raiding parties, which was just what we wanted, as the chiefs always advised us not to fight the soldiers. A small party, of which I was one sent out to spy on the fort and see if it could be taken without much loss. We saw it was too strong to take and so reported. Then the leaders decided to follow the usual plan of drawing the soldiers out by a small decoy force and then kill them all when out of reach of the fort. ("This was the plan followed at Julesburg in 1865 and at Platte Bridge later on in the same year") [Hyde's insertion]. One morning a strong body of soldiers came out with wagons to get timber for the fort. When they were about halfway to the pine woods, a small party of Indians were sent to attack them. The wagons drew up in a circle, and, as planned by our leaders, another force was sent out from the fort to help the soldiers with the wagon train. ("This relief expedition was under Lieutenant W. J. Fetterman") [Hyde]. Now a select party of warriors, mounted on the best and swiftest ponies, were sent over to the crossing of Lodgepole Creek. These men, not many in number, were ordered to draw the soldiers into the hills where the big body of Indians were hiding. The Indians attacking the wagon train rode off as the soldiers from the fort drew near, and these now turned to the right, crossing the creek, in pursuit of the Indians at Lodgepole Creek. These Indians did their work well and fell back slowly toward the Lodgepole hills. The soldiers followed fast and were well into the hills before the big body of Indians attacked them. The soldiers now turned back for the fort, but were surrounded and had to dismount. Then they turned loose their horses and fought on foot. The fight was soon over and every soldier killed. The Cheyennes had two men killed in this fight, the Arapahos one, and the Sioux eleven.[8]

Two Moons' Interview with William Camp, 1913

Researcher William Camp did not get far with Two Moons in a conversation at the Northern Cheyenne Indian Reservation in 1913. Whether Two Moons did not care for Camp or one or the other had more pressing issues at the time of the interview is not known. Still, the short interview is significant in that Two Moons by that date still relates the Cheyenne master narrative of the Fetterman Fight in generalized terms. This combined with his denial to George B. Grinnell in 1908 (interview with Grinnell below) may suggest that Two Moons was not actually in the fighting on Lodge Trail Ridge but had indeed been a spy on the fort. Transcribing the interview in passive voice, Camp leaves no clue just who the decoys were on Lodge Trail Ridge. Significantly however, Two Moons states that at the end the soldiers, although they bunched, managed to maintain some degree of tactical cohesion rather than trying to run for their lives.[9]

Fort Phil Kearny (Fetterman Massacre)
Interview with Two Moons 9/26/13
I was there. Little Wolf was leader of the Cheyennes. Most of the Inds [sic] were Sioux. The soldiers were decoyed over the ridge and Indians immediately closed in on them on all sides. The cavalry was ahead of the foot soldiers following. The cavalry got down off their horses and let them [the horses] go. The soldiers made no attempt to run back or get away. The fighting was largely at close range and mostly with spears [war lances], stone clubs and knives.[10]

Two Moons' Interview with George B. Grinnell, 1908

George Bird Grinnell's interviews give us the most important Cheyenne views of the Fetterman Fight, including those of Two Moons. Among his many natural history exploratory expeditions in the American West, and his many contributions to environmental preservation and game management, Grinnell is one of America's foremost early ethnologists of the Plains Indians, particularly the Cheyennes. His book, *The Fighting Cheyennes* (1915), remains a standard reference today. A quiet, modest man, Grinnell was a model of intellectual diversity.

During his years in the West, Grinnell spent much time on the Northern Plains Indian reservations interviewing aging fighting men about their experiences in their wars with the United States. Grinnell took prodigious notes in diaries on everything he encountered: wildlife, ecology, and Indian interviews with people he courted through the years.

Compiled between 1870 and 1923, his 568 diaries and field notebooks, housed in the Braun Research Library Collections of the Autry National Center in Los Angeles, make up the Grinnell Papers, which contain not only notes on natural history but also provide the initial written records of Grinnell's interviews among the Cheyenne,

Blackfoot, and Pawnee. These served as the basis of his numerous books and journal articles on the lives and histories of these people. His notes reveal the complexities involved with cultural transition as well as history. Grinnell's notes on reservation conditions, schools, government agents, and tribal council meetings likewise reveal some of the difficulties of cultural transition at the turn of the twentieth century. Grinnell is one the most important ethnologists of the Progressive Era to attempt to capture the experiences, perceptions, and feelings of Plains Indians. He is one of the first authors to reject dehumanizing stereotypes of Indian warriors. He realized Indians had complete cultures and histories of their own. In an excellent essay on Grinnell's contributions to Indian ethnography, historian Sherry L. Smith, paraphrasing anthropologist Margot Liberty, wrote: "He belonged to that group of 'horse and buggy ethnographers' . . . who came to the scene just after the U.S. Cavalry galloped off. Such people functioned in the 'intellectual aftermath of war' and preserved a remarkable record whose value increases geometrically as the years go by."[11] The notes remain a vast resource of original source material for historians, much of it still thoroughly untapped by researchers.

Grinnell's interview with Two Moons is the only interview with the famous chief where Two Moons expressly states that he was not part of the actual combat on Lodge Trail Ridge. Two Moons told Grinnell of the cavalry fight but does not mention the infantry engagements. Grinnell transcribed this interview in the third person.

Sunday, Sept. 6, 1908. B. 1842, now 66 yrs.

TM. Principal men at Ft. Kearny fight which known. He was not present. From each tribe of the 3, 5. ? Arap . . . & Chey . . . , a number of brave men were chosen [as decoys]. They asked old Little Wolf to go but he declined & gave his war horse to his brother Big Nose to ride. They charged on the soldiers and Big Nose was killed [later in the battle]. Then Indians retreated and soldiers followed. The Inds led them on to where the Inds were concealed behind the ridges on either side of the valley. When they had gotten far enough the Inds charged out from all sides and dismounted. The soldiers stopped to fight and finally themselves were pressed. Those who were left charged up through I's up onto ridge where there were some rocks and there dismounted and fought but at last they [the Indians] got them all. 99 men.[12]

☰ 10 ☰

White Elk

Wandering Buffalo Bull, b. 1848–1850, alive in 1914

Interviews with George B. Grinnell 1913–1914

Elkhorn Scraper warrior White Elk gives us the most complete and descriptive Omisis account of the Fetterman Fight. He gave his account to George B. Grinnell between 1913 and 1914. Grinnell spent months at a time on the northern reservations in the early twentieth century. White Elk guided Grinnell over the Fetterman battlefield. He pointed out where fighting men concealed their presence, where memorable actions happened, and where casualties occurred. Grinnell recorded White Elk's stories of the fight in several parts of a substantial portion of his field notebooks and in Diary 352, July 16, 1914, housed in the Braun Research Library at the Autry Center in Los Angeles.[1] White Elk's account forms the bulk of Grinnell's chapter of the Fetterman Fight in *The Fighting Cheyennes* (1915). White Elk's vivid memories of that winter day in 1866 are that of a youthful teenage warrior in his first major fight. Together with White Bull's account, White Elk's story forms the lengthiest eyewitness testimonies of the fighting on Lodge Trail Ridge. Since Grinnell's collected notes in Diary 352 conform well to chapter 18 in *The Fighting Cheyennes*, the edited, published book transcription is offered here for clarity.[2]

It was at the beginning of cold weather. The Cheyennes were camped on Muddy Creek, and Crazy Mule was exhibiting to them his power. Different people were shooting at him, but the bullets and the arrows did not enter his flesh.

Soon after these ceremonies were over White Elk, Plenty Camps, and Rolling Bull began to talk together about making an excursion to war, and at last determined to go, and set out toward the mountains. After leaving the camp they began to discuss the route they should follow to reach the country of the Shoshonis. They determined to go in below Fort Phil Kearny to the head of Powder River.

As they were marching along, just getting out of Tongue River Canyon, they met four Cheyennes returning to the camp, who asked: "Where are you going?" The young men said they were going to war against the Shoshonis. The four men warned them, saying: "Be careful how you go about the fort. Up to this time we have always been friendly with those people, but now they have been shooting at us. They are on the watch; so be careful."[3] The three kept on their way and stopped at Big Springs on Tongue River. After they had reached camp, Rolling Bull asked: "What do you think of this that has been said to us? Shall we go back?" Plenty Camps said: "Let us go on a little farther and see what will happen." Both these men were older than White Elk. The message given by the four Cheyennes, of course, threatened some danger from the post, and, besides this, to be warned in this way just as they were starting out on a journey was a bad omen. Plenty Camps, who seemed to be thinking, at length spoke, saying: "I believe that those four men we passed must have done some mischief up there by the fort. Let us stay here overnight and tomorrow return to the camp."

At Fort Phil Kearny something like this had perhaps happened: The Sioux had been attacking the wood trains and already had killed some people. They had thus shown their hostility. The four Cheyennes may have ventured near the fort, been recognized as Indians, and so have been fired on by the troops. To these soldiers an Indian was an Indian and so an enemy.

Next morning the three young men remained in this camp till late in the day, when Plenty Camps said: "We will not go in tonight; let us sleep here again." Next morning early, Rolling Bull said to White Elk: "Friend, get up and go down to the river and get some water." White Elk got the water, and had come halfway back to the camp when he thought he heard someone utter a yelp, and stopped to listen. As he listened closely, he heard far off a number of people singing. He carried his water to their shelter and said to the others: "I think I heard a number of people singing." As they stood there listening, all of a sudden four Sioux rode in sight. They rode up to the camp and spoke to Rolling Bull, who could talk their language. He turned and said to his companions: "These men tell me that many people are coming, some on foot and some on horseback. Women are coming with the men. They are coming up Tongue River on their way to the Cheyenne camp." The Sioux told them that this was a war party brought together for the sole purpose of fighting the soldiers who were at Fort Phil Kearny.[4]

The Indians had laid a plan to try to get the soldiers into the open. They intended to send a small party to make an attack on the post to see if they could not induce the soldiers to come out from the fort. "If we cannot get the soldiers to come out as we want them to," they said, "then we will attack the post." The four Sioux stayed there talking with the Cheyennes, and presently the whole Sioux party came in sight. Some of the older Sioux shook hands with the Cheyennes and asked them to return with the Sioux to the Cheyenne camp. The Cheyennes went with them, and that night they camped at the Big Springs near the head of the canyon. At dark an old crier went about the circle of the camp and called to all the companies of soldiers to get together, for a council was to be held.[5] The Sioux men formed in a big circle about the camp, and the chiefs and the soldier chiefs gathered in the center, where the Cheyennes too were taken. There was much talking, all of it in Sioux and so comprehended only by Rolling Bull. After they had finished talking, the Sioux came over to the Cheyennes and said to them: "Now tonight we have made our plans as to what we shall do, and we intend to ask the Cheyennes to join us.

We have chosen four men to go on ahead and notify the Cheyenne and Arapaho camp of our plans." These two camps were close together. The four men selected had got their horses and saddled them and now rode up, and the Sioux chief spoke to them and at length they rode off. The next day near sundown the four Sioux messengers returned to the war party and told the chiefs that they had reported to the Cheyennes just what the chiefs had ordered, but that the Cheyennes had said that they must have time to get ready. Nevertheless, the Cheyennes must have left their camp in the night and come part way toward the Sioux camp, for the next morning—not very early—the Cheyennes and Arapahoes charged the Sioux camp—a friendly act. Then, after the charge, the Cheyenne chiefs gathered by themselves and told their young men that the Sioux had sent for them to help fight the soldiers. They must not weaken, but every man must stand his ground and do his best. After that all the Cheyennes fell in single file and rode all around the Sioux camp and stopped on the river below the camp and dismounted. They remained there overnight.

Next morning they went as far as Crow Standing Off Creek—Prairie Dog Creek—and camped. After leaving this camp, they went up Crow Standing Off Creek beyond where it forks, keeping up the right-hand fork. Soon they came to a flat prairie and the Sioux were directed to form a line with a wide front—abreast. There were many of them. A Cheyenne chief called out to his people, saying: "Men, do not fall in line with the Sioux. We are not carrying on this war party." The Arapahoes did not form abreast like the Sioux, but stood to one side.

Soon a person, half man and half woman—Hēē mǎn ěh' with a black cloth over his head, riding a sorrel horse, pushed out from among the Sioux and passed over a hill, zigzagging one way and another as he went. He had a whistle, and as he rode off, he kept sounding it. While he was riding over the hill, some of the Cheyennes were told by the Sioux that he was looking for the enemy—soldiers. Presently he rode back, and came to where the chiefs were gathered and said: "I have ten men, five in each hand; do you want them?" The Sioux chiefs said to him: "No, we do not wish them. Look at all these people here. Do you think ten men are enough to go around?" The Hēē mǎn ěh' turned his horse and rode away again, riding in the same way as before. Soon he came back, riding a little faster than before and swaying from one side to the other on his horse. Now he said: "I have ten men in each hand, twenty in all. Do you wish them? The same man replied, saying, "No, I do not wish them; there are too many people here and too few enemies." Without a word the half-man-half-woman turned his horse and rode off. The third time he returned, he said: "I have twenty in one hand and thirty in the other. The thirty are in the hand on the side toward which I am leaning."

"No," said the Sioux, "there are too many people here. It is not worthwhile to go on for so small a number. The Hēē mǎn ěh' rode away.

On the fourth return he rode up fast and as his horse stopped, he fell off and both hands struck the ground. "Answer me quickly," he said, "I have a hundred or more," and when the Sioux and Cheyennes heard this, they all yelled. This was what they wanted. While he was on the ground, some men struck the ground near his hands, counting the coup. Then they all went back and camped on Tongue River [Prairie Dog Creek], at the mouth of the little creek they were going to follow up.

That night the names of ten young men were called out, and those called were ordered to start that night and to be ready the next morning to attack the post. There were two Cheyennes, two Arapahoes, and two from each of the three tribes of Sioux who were present. The two Cheyennes were Little Wolf and Wolf Left Hand. After he had been chosen, Little Wolf rode over to the fire at which his brother, Big Nose, was sitting. A few days before, the two brothers had quarreled with each other. Little Wolf said to his brother: "Brother, I have been called to go and attack the post; take my horse and do you go." Big Nose was still angry and said: "Take back your horse; I do not want him." Bull Hump, who wished to make the brothers friends again, said to Big Nose: "My friend, here are my moccasins and my war clothes. If you have any bad feeling you may have those clothes to lie in." ("To lie in" is to be killed in.) Big Nose accepted the clothes and agreed to go. Little Wolf and his brother Big Nose were both good men in a fight—one as good as the other.

Some time after the young men sent to the fort had gone—just as day was about to break—all the men were called and ordered to saddle their horses, and when this had been done, they moved out. They followed the stream up to the forks and there stopped. The Cheyennes kept by themselves and did not mingle with the Sioux. At the forks they stopped and a Sioux cried out, haranguing the Cheyennes, and asked them to choose which side of the ridge they wished to be on, the upper or the lower side. The Indians hoped to draw the soldiers down this ridge between their two forces hidden on either side. One of the Cheyenne chiefs said that his people would take the upper side of the ridge, and presently the order was cried out for the Cheyennes and Arapahoes to take the upper—west—side. In going up to the place selected, the people who were on foot stopped near the lower end of the ridge, not far from the stream, while those on horseback, who had the longest distance to go, went on up above. All the Cheyennes and Arapahoes were mounted. Some Sioux women who were along stayed below with the Sioux men who were on foot.[6] After the different parties had gone to their places and hidden themselves everyone kept very still. All were waiting, listening for what might be heard. After a little time a single shot was heard. Later it was said that when the young men who had been sent to the fort had charged the post, they had killed the sentry. This was the shot. A long period of silence followed during which they waited and listened; then a number of shots were heard, but the firing lasted for a few minutes only. It was afterward said that some troops came out from the fort as if to attack the decoy Indians and then turned back and went into the fort, and that someone who was with the soldiers made motions to the young Indians to go away, that the soldiers were going to eat. This was the Indian understanding of the signs, what ever they may have been.

The Sioux signed back to them that today they would get a full stomach of fighting. The soldiers re-entered the post, and the young Indians remained in sight riding about.[7] After a time a number of bugle calls were heard, and soon after a troop of cavalry marched out of the post toward these young men, and after them a company of infantry.[8] At a bugle call the cavalry charged and fired at the Indians, who, of course, ran away. This was the distant shooting heard.

It was some time before the watchers heard any more shooting. The cavalry, after firing, had stopped and would follow no longer, and the Indians were obliged to return and attack again, be shot at, and followed a little farther. In this way the infantry kept well closed up with the cavalry, which was perhaps the reason the cavalry followed slowly. After the third and fourth volleys the shooting came closer, and before long some of the Indians came riding down the ridge, and a little later another man, Big Nose, the Cheyenne, mounted on a black horse, was seen riding back and forth across the ridge before the soldiers, seeming to fight them, and they were shooting at him as hard as they could. It looked as if Big Nose was trying to fight and held back the soldiers in order to help someone ahead of him to get away. From the place where the Indians were waiting Big Nose seemed almost [alone] against the soldiers. The great body of Indians hidden along the ridge kept themselves well concealed. Not a move was made nor a sound heard.

After Big Nose, followed slowly by the soldiers, had come down off the steep ridge, the troops stopped, and Big Nose charged back and seemed to go in among the soldiers so that he was lost to sight. He went into the troops from the right and came out on the left, wheeled his horse, rode into them again and came out, and turned as if to go back.

The troops kept following, coming down the old Bozeman road which runs down the crest of the ridge. The Sioux on foot were hidden in the grass on the flat beyond the end of the ridge perhaps one and a half miles distant from the place where the troops came to it as its upper end. The mounted Sioux were hidden behind two rocky ridges on the east side of this ridge, while the Cheyennes were on the west side of it. It had been announced that a certain

Cheyenne, Little Horse, who was a Contrary (a warrior whose actions appear to be the reverse of normal, as in fighting left-handed, or opposed to fighting with the natural right hand, etc.), should give his people the word to charge, and when the proper time came, this word was to be passed on from one to another until all were notified and then all should spring up and charge.

The cavalry, who had been following the ridge down nearly to the flat by the stream, were now pretty close to the Sioux footmen, and the infantry were well within the Indians' lines. When the decoys had forded the stream beyond the end of the ridge and the cavalry had nearly come to it the decoys separated into two parties, riding away from each other, and then, turning, came back and crossed each other. This was very likely a signal, and the Indians charged. Little Horse, following the law of the Contraries, held his contrary lance in his left hand. The Cheyennes watched him, and when they saw him pass his left hand behind his neck and grasp the contrary lance with his right hand, they knew that he was about to charge, and all sprang up.

When the charge was made, the sound of many hoofs made a noise like thunder and the soldiers began to fall back. On the ridge near the place where it leaves the hill are many large, loose flat stones. The infantry took a position behind these. The cavalry moved back up the hill and stopped.

On the infantry hidden among the rocks a Sioux came charging down the old road, and the infantry stood up in sight as if about to leave the shelter. They did not do so, but let the Sioux pass through them and, after he had passed, fired at and killed him. Soon after this another man came down the road on foot and began to shoot at the infantry, and when they rose up to shoot at him, the other Indians shot at them. This young man was killed. White Elk—at that time named Wandering Buffalo Bull—was with those fighting the infantry. Soon after the second Sioux was killed, the cry was given to charge, and the Sioux and Cheyennes charged and got to the infantry about the same time, and for a little while Indians and soldiers were mixed up together in hand-to-hand fighting. Just before and in this charge a Sioux was killed and other wounded by arrows shot by their own people. The one killed was struck in the forehead just over the root of the nose, and the arrow point pierced his brain. The arrow was shot from the other side of the ridge and had passed through or over the crowd of troops.

The cavalry, who had followed the decoying party of Indians down nearly to the level of the river bottom, when they saw the Sioux charging them from the northeast, turned and retreated up to the top of a high hill toward the end of the ridge. There they halted and waited in line until the infantry were all killed at the rocks about a hundred yards north of the line of cavalry. Then the cavalry began to fall back, but slowly and in order. Some were even on foot leading their horses.

After the infantry had been killed, the Indians rushed up toward the cavalry, but the ground was slippery with ice and snow and in many places the hill was too steep for them to charge up it. Still many people crept up toward the place, and Little Horse is reported to have approached behind the rocks within forty feet of the soldiers, and fought there, yet he was not hurt in the fight. While this was going on, White Elk was a little behind, where he could see the Indians shooting at the cavalry with arrows, and the arrows flew so thickly above the troops that to him they seemed like a lot of grasshoppers flying across each other. On the hill an officer was killed, and when he fell, the troops seemed to give way and to begin to fight their way up the ridge. The weather now grew very cold, so that blood running from wounds soon froze. After the soldiers had reached the end of the ridge, they began to let go their horses, and the Indians, eager to capture the horses, began to lessen their shooting.

Up to this time Big Nose had not been hurt. Someone called out: "There are two good horses left there." Big Nose charged up toward the horses, struck them with his whip, thus taking possession of them, and then rode back and turned again, but here his horse stopped exhausted. He could not get it to move, and here Big Nose was shot off his horse. This was the only wound he had, and his horse was untouched. White Elk went to where his friend lay. He spoke to White Elk and said: "Lift my head up the hill and place me where I can breathe the fresh air." This was all he said. He breathed for a day or two after this. Big Nose was killed on the ridge in the first sag northwest of the monument, near some large rocks west of the crest of the ridge. His horse stopped as he was crossing the ridge and began to back toward the soldiers, who were west of where the monument is. While White Elk was helping Big Nose, the soldiers were shooting at them constantly.

The cavalry kept moving back to some great rocks, perhaps four hundred yards from where the infantry had been killed.[9] On the other side of the rocks there was a flat with no cover behind which the Indians could approach, and they could not get near to the soldiers. The Indians kept calling to one another to keep hidden, but to continue to creep up. They did so, and every now and then an Indian would show himself and seem to be about to charge, and when the soldiers rose to their feet to shoot, all the Indians would shoot. In this way they killed some of the soldiers. They kept calling to each other: "Be ready. Are you ready?" And others would call back: "We are ready." They were preparing for the charge—a hand-to-hand fight.

When at last the order was given to charge, they rushed in among the soldiers and a number of the Sioux were killed among the soldiers. Here they killed every one. After all were dead, a dog was seen running away, barking, and someone called out: "All are dead but the dog; let him carry the news to the fort," but someone else cried out: "No, do not let even a dog get away;" and a young man shot at it with his arrow and killed it. The last of the cavalry was killed just where the monument now stands.[10] The fight began when the sun was quite high in the heavens and ended about noon. Little Horse led the Cheyennes in the charge which had been ordered. All watched him, and when he went forward, they followed. Only two Cheyennes were killed. The Sioux were laid out side-by-side and made two long rows, perhaps fifty or sixty men. The number of Indians was very great. Of Arapahoes and Cheyennes there were a good many hundred, and there were three times as many Sioux. White Elk believes that in the Fetterman fight there were more men than in the Custer fight. Most of the Indians were armed with bows. The few who had guns had old smoothbore flintlocks. Only six of the eighty-one white men bore gunshot wounds.

Like Walter S. Campbell, Grinnell mixes his third-person rhetoric with the words of White Elk, which are written in the first person. Often it is difficult to determine which are White Elk's exact words and which are Grinnell's. As noted earlier, the White Elk–Grinnell interviews, like the stories of White Bull, and Grinnell's walks over the Fetterman battlefield with White Elk in 1914, form the most referenced eyewitness Indian accounts of the Fetterman Fight. But unlike Campbell's enduring friendship with Joseph White Bull, the Cheyenne White Elk pretty well disappears from any recognizable relationship with Grinnell after 1914. Most biographical sketches and agency census records indicate that White Elk was still living during that year. The author can find no census record for him after that time. If one studies Grinnell's prolific work with the Plains Indians he befriended, one cannot help but imagine that, although he held much respect for them, to some extent he may have "used" them to advance his work but then personally lost touch with them when he had no further need for their knowledge.

Faller suspects the same in Grinnell's relationship with George Bent. Although Bent wished to form a firm friendship with Grinnell, he instead gravitated back to George Hyde, and in his letters to Hyde, he occasionally grumbled about Grinnell's indifference. The same may be said of Grinnell's relationship with Hyde, since Hyde claimed that he had ghostwritten some of Grinnell's work.[11]

Still, White Elk's account is corroborative with other eyewitness accounts concerning the progress of the battle. But it is unique in two important ways. White Elk's is the only testimony that attributes the role of the Hēē măn ěh' in predicting the outcome of the battle and giving to history its Indian name, "Hundred in the Hand" or "Where a Hundred [Soldiers] Were Killed." Cheyenne Hēē măn ěh, or *winkte* in Lakota, or *berdache*, a half-man half-woman, are transgendered persons, often valued in Plains Indian societies as having clairvoyant powers.[12] The reader may also notice that White Elk/Grinnell presents greater detail than with any other eyewitness account of the mortal wounding of Little Wolf's brother in the battle. Most other testimonies likewise do not speak of all the infantrymen being killed before the cavalry. The relief and burial parties Carrington sent out from the fort recovered bodies of both infantrymen and cavalry troopers at the upper (south) end of the battlefield at or near the monument.[13]

Little Wolf

How much of a role might Little Wolf have personally contributed to this account? Little Wolf, Sweet Medicine Chief of all Cheyennes apparently, unlike White Elk, maintained a close friendship with Grinnell during the first decade of the twentieth century. Prior to his death in 1904, Little Wolf spent much time talking and smoking with Grinnell on the Northern Cheyenne reserve near Lame Deer, Montana. Grinnell relied heavily on Little Wolf's words in *The Fighting Cheyennes* for the seminal epic in historic Northern Cheyenne history, the exodus to their homelands from Darlington Agency, Indian Territory, in 1878–1879. But Little Wolf's personal voice is silent in all eyewitness Indian accounts of the Fetterman Fight. Little Wolf lived in self-imposed exile along the wilds of Rosebud Creek, even though others eventually came to live around him during his last years, because he had killed another Cheyenne in a drunken feud. It made no difference to Grinnell for he wrote in a letter to his friend, Robert S. Ellison, "I knew old Little Wolf almost intimately. Toward the end of his life . . . I disregarded the tribal feeling about him and used to pass him my pipe to smoke. I consider him, I think, the greatest Indian I have ever known."[14] The presence in the Fetterman Fight of Dull Knife, Little Wolf's cochief in the exodus of 1878, is unsupported by valid original sources.

Finn Burnett

A unique witness aside from the military reports, credited to the warriors who destroyed Fetterman's command, may be ascribed to a white man: Finn Burnett, a civilian contractor and teamster at Fort Phil Kearny. Burnett, who helped recover the bodies of Fetterman and his men on December 22, wrote of finding the remains of trumpeter Adolph Metzger on what is today Monument Hill. The Indians had respectfully covered Metzger's body with a buffalo robe. Burnett, an ancestor of former Wyoming senator Alan Simpson, claimed that Metzger heroically fought off his adversaries to the end with his bugle. "His heroism," Burnett wrote, "aroused the admiration of the savages, they covered his corpse with a buffalo robe as a symbol of extreme respect."[15] Metzger became somewhat of a local legend in Wyoming due to Burnett's claim. His story has not gone unnoticed in modern Indian oral tradition. But unfortunately, Burnett's claim cannot be corroborated by any of the eyewitness Lakota and Cheyenne accounts.

Despite the misty claim of Adolph Metzger's heroism related by Finn Burnett, several of the Lakota and Cheyenne testimonies presented here declare that all the men of the Second Cavalry and Second Battalion of Eighteenth Infantry who died on Lodge Trail Ridge on December 21, 1866, maintained at least some restraint from panic and attempts to disperse and escape (often called in the Civil War era "skedaddling") and, although, "bunched" at the end of the fight, maintained a semblance of tactical cohesion.

⇒ 11 ⇐

Black Bear

b. 1838

Grinnell interviewed Cheyenne warrior Black Bear on an unspecified date in 1908. The interview has been cited but not previously published. According to historian Peter John Powell, there were three Northern Cheyennes at this time named Black Bear. The man most likely to have been Grinnell's Black Bear was the youngest of the three and in 1877 served as an army scout under General Nelson A. Miles in his Nez Percé campaign. Another was a council chief in reservation years, while a third served against his own people as a sergeant of scouts for Ranald Mackenzie in the destruction of Dull Knife's village in November 1876.[1]

Black Bear spoke to Grinnell about moving down to the mouth of the Tongue River with the Cheyennes and then to the forks of Peno Creek. He designated himself as a hunter during the approach, providing buffalo meat for the camps. Black Bear's story of the fight begins when the Indians approached the broad flat where, according to the Cheyennes, the decoys were chosen. Grinnell recorded the words of Black Bear's testimony in the third person in his field notebook #348. Black Bear was likely on the south end of the west ridge along the northern bend of Peno Creek and thus was one of the warriors that attacked and chased the infantry back north toward Monument Hill. Some of his words dovetail with those of White Elk. Grinnell may have woven some of Black Bear's words with those of White Elk into the text of *The Fighting Cheyennes*. Black Bear gives one a bird's-eye view of what it was like waiting in the ravines looking south for the soldiers to come over Lodge Trail Ridge.

They stopped at a big flat covered with small box elders. Here they chose men to go and bring the enemy (i.e., to lead them into an ambuscade). After they had been chosen they were told that they must go to the post and bring the soldiers out and lead them down the main wagon road that led down the ridge toward Tongue River [Peno Creek]. After these men had gone a crier shouted to the camp saying we are to divide into two equal parties, the same number above and the same number below (the ridge). Two whom went with the party were Big Nose and Medicine Wolf. LW [Little Wolf] was called but he gave his warhorse and war shirt to his brother Big Nose.

The parties about the ridge were dispersed on either side of the ridge and some of the further Inds toward which was the S. [indistinguishable word] ridge. After a while as they stood there they could hear them, the sound of firing at first far off and then nearer. They began to close in toward the ridge, for because of the timber [along Peno Creek] they could not face the S. nor the S, the I's [Indians could not see far to the south]. At length the leaders could be seen zigzagging from side to side ahead of the soldiers whom were following them with an extended front [the Cavalry]. At last they came to a place where the ridge grew narrower and was no longer straight but about away to the [sentence not completed]. Here the soldiers, on account of the narrow way, had to fall in by 2s and here the I's [Indians] closed on them and the fight was a big one. Here the soldiers fell in single file and turned to go back. The ridge is 1½ m. long. They killed the soldiers by ones and twos and thus the soldiers made a break for some white sand rocks along the side of the road at about the beginning of the ridge. Here the soldiers dismounted and here they were killed to the last man. There was a dog along, and about the end of the fight a man called out "The only thing that is getting away is a dog" and they saw it running.

A good many [indistinguishable word] were killed but how many I don't know. Two C's [Cheyennes] were killed BN [Big Nose] and Mĭssēĕnānō (Rustling Leaf). Then C's [Cheyennes] all started home but when they looked back they could see about 90 people standing on a high hill perhaps soldiers [this was Ten Eyck's relief party]. Soldiers made a plucky fight but their bullets did not.[2]

Part 4 examines in what manner these eyewitness and contemporary secondhand accounts of the Fetterman Fight are remembered by Lakotas and Cheyennes in the years after the battle and in modern times, as well as the significance of the event in the lives of these Native peoples today.

PART FOUR

Memory and Legacy of the Fetterman Fight

Connecting the Past to the Present

Several generations of Lakotas and Cheyennes have passed away since the last of them related their vivid eyewitness memories of the Fetterman Fight. But the memories of those Lakota and Cheyenne fighting men of December 21, 1866, are told today by tribal storytellers and historians both orally and in writing. As explained in the Introduction, storytelling, usually spoken through family reminiscences, has been the favored medium for Lakotas and Cheyennes to pass down their history to present and future generations. Indians hold storytelling in deep respect to pass on their historical traditions, far more than they do strictly relying on the written word of non-Indians. Part 4 is important in honoring that memory and traditional culture of celebration.

Storytelling

Lakotas and Cheyennes were the *victors* in the Fetterman Fight and, although they ultimately lost the peace through government chicanery with the Fort Laramie Treaty of 1868, they have been perceived in white histories as the winners of Red Cloud's War. Unlike such events as the Sand Creek Massacre and the Baker Massacre, and others in which Indians were so clearly victimized, many early histories of the Fetterman battle written by non-Indians are, in fact, nationalistic histories that focus on the tragedy of the eighty-one soldiers and civilians killed in the battle. "The Fetterman Disaster" is still a commonly spoken phrase by non-Indian people. In the literature of westward expansion, the victors of this battle are still depicted as the eventual losers and the story of the Fetterman Fight is a nationalistic military history *about* Indians. The main theme in these histories is that the Indians only won because Captain Fetterman was arrogant and incompetent.

Historian Patricia Nelson Limerick argues that "Indian history is not solely *about* Indians; it is history *belonging* to Indians, in which the owners should take pride and which should make them feel better about themselves."[1] The Progressive Era of the early 1900s, though a time of reform that would lead to Indian citizenship, was not a period that witnessed movements for tribal autonomy from federal control. The aged Lakotas and Cheyennes who gave their stories to the world remembered the times of their youth when warfare was a way of life, the essence of manhood and eventually survival. Most were truly flattered, except perhaps Red Cloud, that whites were interested in learning *Indian stories* of life on the "warpath," regardless of what motivations white readers might have for learning. Although differences occur because of the storyteller's tribe and position on the battlefield, these interviews corroborate the major stages of the battle. These are tribal accepted records of their history.

In the early 1970s, historian Donald Fixico worked to revise the discipline when Indian historians recognized that inadequate means were being used to examine Indian history. Historians who study Indian history, Fixico believes, "must think in terms of culture, community, environment, and metaphysics. Ethnohistory has allowed a cross-disciplinary approach using history and anthropology to study American history."[2] Storytelling as a means of cultural celebration represents a different means of viewing history and how different cultures may define what history is. Typically, professional historians are trained in the empirical methods of Leopold von Ranke, the recognized founder of document-sourced history. Culturally celebrated history on the other hand is often regarded as community property to be shared selectively. While some Indian traditionalists believe ownership of Indian history is basically the property of the tribes, Fixico believes the story and contributions of Indian Americans should be a significant part of the national narrative of the American historical experience. "Indian history," he wrote, "should not be regarded as a special or exotic sub-field to be pushed aside or ignored."[3] Thus, Lakotas and Cheyennes today view their continued stories of the Fetterman Fight as integral to the cultural celebration of the battle.

In recent years historians have come to rely more frequently on an intersection of history and archaeology to validate or dispute both memory and archival documents. This perspective came slowly within the larger field of anthropology and not without dissonance. Historian R. David Edmonds wrote: "For years, historians had complained that although anthropologists possessed a better understanding of tribal cultures, their historical research was inadequate, their prose was jargon ridden, and they often failed to place their analysis within a broader perspective. They knew what 'was going on,' [in the specific cultural sense revealed in artifact recovery] but they did not know what 'was happening.' In rebuttal, anthropologists charged that historians were interested only in military or diplomatic affairs and were so dependent on written documents that they failed to understand the Native American viewpoint. They were writing 'white man's history' *about* [my emphasis] Native American people but they really did not know what was going on."[4]

A dramatic and controversial argument may be found in National Park Service efforts to locate the Sand Creek Massacre (November, 29, 1864) in Colorado to establish it as a National Historic Site. For almost a century the Cheyenne people have accepted the site of Black Kettle's village, at a large south bend of Sand Creek below some bluffs above the stream. The "Big Bend," mapped in the early twentieth century by mixed-heritage Southern Cheyenne and white George Bent, is still considered the spiritual holy ground of the Sand Creek Massacre. In 1997 and again in 1999, archaeological work conducted by National Park Service historical archaeologist Douglas Scott found no period artifacts at the traditional site. The core of the artifacts related to the events of November 1864 proved to be located almost a mile north of the traditional location. The fact that troops of the Colorado 1st and 3rd Cavalry deployed near or on the bluffs of the South Bend to commence their artillery attack has politically, to some degree, moderated the conundrum of oral history and archaeology. As historian Ari Kelman states, however, "Sand Creek remains a 'history front' in an ongoing 'culture war' as contested perceptions of the past reveal fault lines in the present. Each new fight over American memory," he wrote, "highlights the difficulty of agreeing on a single historical narrative within the confines of a pluralistic society."[5] This duality of thinking may seem postmodern to some historians and archaeologists but the disagreement over specific geographical locations does not extend to the meaning of events themselves. All agree that the events at Sand Creek were significant. The same holds true for the Fetterman Fight.

The eyewitness Lakota and Northern Cheyenne accounts of the Fetterman Fight are by definition, *historical memory*, oral testimony transcribed decades after the Fetterman Fight by white ethnologists and interested amateur historians. In some cases, rhetorical insertions by the white authors in a few of the accounts that were published in the first half of the twentieth century reflect their desire to present these stories to mainstream audiences. But these investigators were not intent on simply writing *about Indians* within a hegemonic narrative that celebrated martyrdom of Fetterman's lost command. The fact that these writers, if even presented in the third person, retained the Indian voices in their narratives—and those voices do not stray far except for grammatical correction from their interview notes—has provided continuity with modern oral stories of the Fetterman Fight, which are stories that do not stray far from the eyewitness stories. These stories are *oral history* of particular events that happened at a specific battle as opposed to *oral tradition*, the passing down of a broad set of behavioral expectations to sustain tribal cultural cohesion through verbal storytelling.

The stories of the Fetterman Fight, both eyewitness accounts and recent stories, also square with modern archaeological investigation. Although both official and unofficial archaeological searches of the Fetterman site have been conducted in past decades, ACR Consultants, Inc., of Sheridan, Wyoming, conducted the latest systematic search of Massacre Ridge at the Fetterman battlefield in 2002 and 2006, under the auspices of the Fort Phil Kearny/ Bozeman Trail Association. Aided by grants, ACR's chief, Kevin O'Dell, and project director Robert Wilson, of the Fort Phil Kearny Historic Site, completed a report of findings by 2007. Although the information in the final archaeological report is not for public dissemination by the Fort Phil Kearny/ Bozeman Trail Association, the author did discern from perusal in the Sheridan Fulmer Library that the western area of the battlefield is somewhat contaminated by the construction beginning in the 1910s of State Highway 87. The cumulative results of all the past archaeological activity supports the historical accounts told by Lakota and Cheyenne eyewitnesses.[6]

From the intersections of eyewitness Lakota and Northern Cheyenne testimony and archaeology, we may form a fairly reliable reconstruction of the Fetterman Fight from the time the troopers and infantrymen passed out of sight of Fort Phil Kearny. And this reconstruction is more revealing than the official military reports drafted by Colonel Henry B. Carrington, when he commanded the detail that recovered the bodies of Fetterman and his men on December 22, 1866. All of the significant Indian sources agree that as Fetterman's command crested Lodge Trail Ridge the cavalry, led by Lieutenant George W. Grummond, moved out ahead of the infantry. The Indian testimonials further state that Fetterman and the infantry hesitated at the top of a manageable low rise on Lodge Trail Ridge before descending on to Massacre Ridge.

The cavalry likely descended west of the infantry toward a brushy bend in Peno Creek, chasing decoys toward where some of the Oglala warriors were hiding. The infantry descended the eastern slope of Lodge Trail Ridge and onto the more manageable Bozeman Trail not far south of the modern monument. Once the infantry reached Massacre Ridge they tried to advance but they did not get far, although an alternative archaeological hypothesis holds that they were able to advance about halfway down the ridge not far south of where a lone tree stands today, before warriors (probably Cheyennes at that point on the trail) rose up around them from the west gullies, destroyed many or most of them, and forced the survivors to retreat south uphill on Massacre Ridge to re-assemble on the southern high point of the ridge, where the monument now stands. There they briefly maintained some semblance of tactical cohesion, however futile. Here they died in the vicinity of the rocks near the present-day monument along with retreating cavalrymen, as the Miniconjous enveloped them on the south end, preventing their escape back on the trail to the fort.

Grummond and the cavalry, meanwhile, had unwisely separated from the infantry perhaps as early as the cresting of Lodge Trail Ridge. The cavalry had maneuvered north of the infantry when they were attacked by overwhelming numbers of Indians. After an initial fierce engagement (some infantrymen ran with them by holding on to cavalry horse's tails) they tried to maintain tactical cohesion by moving as a body back north up the ridge. A few of them tried to form a small and futile perimeter on a rise on the ridge today called Cavalry Hill, probably a case of bunching or "hedgehogging," but the Indians had quickly snuffed out the brief action in that area despite the cavalrymen's repeating Spencer and Starr rifles and carbines, as few known artifacts have been found in that area. Any cohesion probably made them easy targets and did them more harm than good, although all were eventually doomed.

A few soldiers and two civilian contractors from the fort, James Wheatley and Isaac Fisher, remained near or retreated to the vicinity of the cavalry's farthest advance at the time the Indians sprung the trap. Perhaps the cavalry even penetrated a bit farther north and then retreated slightly southward to the rocks where Wheatley and Fisher, with their sixteen-shot repeating Henry Rifles, were fighting for their lives. They were no closer than about three-quarters of a mile to Fetterman's remaining troops in the rocks on Monument Hill.

Surviving cavalrymen, meanwhile, had released their horses somewhere along the line of retreat, hoping the warriors would chase the animals as the men raced as best they could up the ridge to the rocks on Monument Hill, near what was left of the infantry. Not far from the top, Indians killed and mutilated Lieutenant George W. Grummond. A relief party under Captain Tenador Ten Eyck, which arrived from the fort too late, witnessed bodies of men and horses along the ridge all the way up to the site of the future monument. The warriors captured the living horses. Likely all tactical cohesion was lost in this last desperate stampede between Cavalry Hill and Monument Hill by these few survivors and it was every man for himself. Although bunched, the troopers, once assembled within the sparse shelter of the rocks, tried to retain a semblance of order, but were soon overwhelmed by the encircling warriors. In other words, cavalrymen's remains were found all along Massacre Ridge perhaps as far away as a mile north from Monument Hill, indicating that Grummond's mounted troopers had far out run their infantry support at the time they were attacked. Given the rise in the trail at Cavalry Hill, the Lakotas and Cheyennes were able to attack the three elements of the enemy in detail, each element out of sight of the others, with the end coming against bunched survivors on Monument Hill.[7]

Today Lakotas and Cheyennes proudly remember this construction of the Fetterman Fight as an important event in their history. For the most part, stories told by second and by subsequent generation storytellers to the present day closely follow the construction derived from eyewitness accounts of their forefathers. Indigenous historians, both orally and in writing, honor their forefathers in depicting the events of the 1860s and 1870s. Second-generation transcriptions are of special importance and relevance to the history of the Fetterman Fight and Red Cloud's War because these storytellers made the acquaintance of or personally knew still-living tribesmen who had fought Fetterman's troops.

=⇒ ⇐=

Probably no second-generation memoir is as significant as that of Northern Cheyenne elder and tribal historian John Stands In Timber (b. 1882), whose stories were told to Margot Liberty of Sheridan, Wyoming, between 1956 and 1959. An edited version of the interviews appeared in Stands In Timber and Liberty's *Cheyenne Memories* (New Haven: Yale University Press, 1967). The original transcripts of the interviews are now published as John Stands In Timber and Margot Liberty, *A Cheyenne Voice: The Complete John Stands In Timber Interviews* (Norman: University of Oklahoma Press, 2013). As Raymond DeMallie states in the book's foreword: "At the time of the interviews, now more than fifty years ago, there could be no question of publishing the raw material from which *Cheyenne Memories* was written. No academic or commercial publisher would have considered such a project because of its size and limited market. It is only since the 1980s, with the increased interest of . . . anthropologists [and in Native American history] that attention has become focused on the sources of significant published works."[8]

John Stands In Timber told Liberty in Interview no. 311, "You know a white man when he gets these things puts it in a file and writes it down; sometimes if he forgets it he can find it. But an Indian has to keep it in his head."[9] Stands In Timber was told the story of the Fetterman Fight by White Elk (Grinnell's storyteller) and his grandfather Wolf Tooth, among others who were still living when John heard their stories. Stands In Timber corroborates the idea there may have been three separate attempts to lure troops out of Fort Phil Kearny: a feint on the fort itself, the feint on the wood train, and the decoy maneuver on Lodge Trail Ridge once Fetterman's command came out of the fort. Each of these feints can be viewed as a decoy attempt to lure soldiers out of the fort and bring them over Lodge Trail Ridge.

Stands In Timber also refers to the ravine where troops came down on the north side of the ridge to Peno Creek. This ravine is on the west side of the Bozeman Trail and is the likely route of Grummond's Second Cavalry troopers after separation from

Indian view of the retreat of Fetterman survivors; looking south
to Monument Hill, where the last stand was made.
Photo by author.

the infantry. Stands In Timber incorrectly states that Little Wolf's brother Big Nose, killed in action in the Fetterman Fight, was still living shortly before his interviews with Liberty. Big Nose's death in battle is described in detail by White Elk in Grinnell's *The Fighting Cheyennes*. Although some of John's understanding of a few episodes, primarily dealing with Southern Cheyenne history is confused, his recollections of eyewitness storytellers of the Fetterman Fight are mostly reliable in dovetailing with the eyewitness accounts in this study. His account is particularly detailed in its descriptions of Plains Indian fighting tactics. John Stands In Timber's original interviews with Liberty, nos. 205 and 210 are offered here in their entirety.

John Stands In Timber (1882–1967)

Interview No. 205

There is a certain clan the Sioux had, a man dressed in woman's clothes; they believe whatever he does they could find out about the battle, through that ceremony, how many would be killed or scalped. He threw down on the

Margot Liberty and John Stands In Timber, circa 1956.
Photograph by Robert Pringle courtesy of Margot Liberty.

ground so many times; the last time they wished to kill so many, and he gets up and says I have so many on this hand and so many on the other hand. But they want more. So he did it again. Sometimes they get off the horse and throw themselves on the ground. He jumped up and announced it. When they got there they sent a courier to the fort—they attacked it before and they came out and fought them outside, but this time they sent just a few to go out there and charge by. I think the soldiers were prepared to go out and fight. They went in there close, and they came out and followed these. Once or twice they stopped but they would go back and charge on them, and kept coming over the hill from Tepee Pole Creek they call it. Over the hill there is a gap there; that's the one we want to see. They came down through this gap to another creek. The Sioux were on the right-hand side as you come this way, and the Cheyennes were on this side. White Elk used to say they gave us the poorest place, there is not much shelter there, and they had the other side with high hills and some down in the creek quite a ways. These decoys came out through; they did not come all the way into the trap, but the Sioux charged on them and that pushed the soldiers back toward the hills. They retreated back and climbed up there where they were all killed.

White Elk says they had mostly bows and arrows. After they got them all killed several had arrows still on their bodies. And they had dogs too—some say there were two dogs and some only one, but they killed them. It was real cold weather, after mid-winter. Several Sioux were wounded in this battle, and White Elk says one Cheyenne was wounded—I think two or three Sioux were killed that he saw, but he did not know how many altogether. There was too much open space where the Sioux came back on the other side. After they retreated up the hill they had a better place, they were closer shooting at the soldiers. Some Sioux came around shooting from the top of the hill. It took some time but they got them all killed. There were only three left, and those three they ran down that way and they were killed down at the bottom. And the dog came out—they caught it and killed it.

I thought we had that story. Seems to me I took down notes on it. White Elk was Eddy Gray's father. And Wolf Tooth was there too. Little Sun too.

These three said they were on the other side where the Sioux were standing behind them—they claim these last three or four they did not kill them, they shot themselves. But I don't know, it looked like they kept on fighting until they were killed, but White Elk said they saw them shoot themselves. But they did the best shooting back that way on this side. The Cheyennes were on this side and more Sioux the other side came around top; it is high land but not even with the other side, but low place gap where they came on over through this divide between there and that little Piney Creek they call it. The Cheyennes call Tepee Pole Creek.

Somebody wrote a letter to me from Santa Fe describing that fight and asking about Fetterman. No, that half-and-half one. Grinnell did not mention those last few that shot themselves but he asked that too.

Interview No. 210

The story of the Fetterman massacre, quite a few Cheyennes took part. My grandfather Wolf Tooth, Big Foot, Black Horse, White Elk, Sap, Magpie Eagle—those that I remember when I heard these stories. They had been fighting the soldiers there once, and this time they had planned to bring them out and lead them into a trap, laid just over the ridge from the fort. They tried it three times and tried to bring them out; they would start to chase them and then stop and go back in. And then they would come back again. The last time they brought them across a divide; here they stopped. Wolf Tooth says they could hear the sound of the guns a long distance; it was not too far from where the monument is today to the old fort. And Wolf Tooth says the guns sounded clearer and louder, and pretty soon the soldiers came on top. The cause [?] came out on the bottom and they started charging back on them, and then they started down. They stood there quite a while and they thought they would go back again, and pretty soon the infantry came out. Then all came down again. From there the soldiers charged on them; they gone pretty rapidly that the horses run, but they didn't keep up, they stopped.

What they were doing, the infantry came and mount down behind them. Then they got there they stood quite a while again, and started to follow planned to give signals and there's a man that died here not long ago, Big Nose; and was one of the decoys and he got used to it. He must have been pretty lucky not to get hit. He would turn around and go back. But one was killed; he got wounded—hit after the battle started. And two Sioux were killed right there before they attacked the soldiers.

The signal was given and another Cheyenne came along and passed the word before the soldiers approached that place he was to go up on top and keep watching; then the Sioux gave the signal he would come out, and use his war club and raise it in the air then charge. This man must have seen the Sioux on the other side, maybe both sides; he was on top of the hill. Wolf Tooth said he saw that man come out and hold that war club like he said he would on the left hand, and next time he came out again he came in plain sight. He must have seen the Sioux start charging; he took the war club in his right hand and waved it in the air—that means everybody charge.

He said he noticed the infantry retreated back up a little ways, half ways from where the monument stands now, and took a stand behind some big flat rocks laying here and there on the side hill. The infantry went back up on a little bench like, and of course the Indians surrounded them and the way the Indians fight they do not stand still and shoot but keep moving—one time on one side, next on the other side, keeping from getting hit. Each time they got closer. One side the Indians would charge up to the soldiers, and when they started shooting that way they would come up on the other side behind them—kept coming that way. These infantry on foot behind the rocks, those Sioux on the north side of the big hill all got off and when those on the other side charged at the soldiers they started shooting the other way; these would start running a little ways, then sometimes all drop and shoot from there and keep crawling up the side hill. By doing this some Sioux were killed, and Wolf Tooth said when he came close to behind the line those Sioux on foot, the line down in a little low place, and they were up two or three hundred yards. They could see on top after they killed all the soldiers on foot; they came up on them by hand-to-hand and quite a few Sioux were killed by doing it. Then the infantry started to retreat up, but the Sioux came up around behind it and they were going back up toward the fort, and they came up close—Wolf Tooth was there. And he said he could see the arrows almost reach to where they were from the Sioux on the other side.

Them days they made bows you don't see any more, real good ones of part of the buffalo horn tied, on each end of the bow, and they shot a long way. Several of the Sioux were wounded, hit by arrows from the other side. There were too many using a bow and arrow not far from where the soldiers took a stand.

Wolf Tooth said he was pretty near hit by one himself. He was talking to Sap—he run out of arrows, and he gave him a few of his own, and he was better shooting with a bow because it was bitter cold. It took time when some of those still had muzzleloaders. They claimed they were the last few that shot themselves; soldiers left on top of the hill three or four tried to get away but were killed. Then they saw the dog come running around and barking, and the man—Big Rascal—says don't let the dog go. The Sioux started to catch it and take it home, and somebody went and took a shot at it with an arrow and killed it. They did not wait there long after they were all killed, but took what they wanted—most of the ammunition was picked up and from that time they had quite a bit.

They came back down to camp. They did not mind about the cold weather; they built big fires and had a victory dance. But there were no scalps—all the soldiers had haircuts, and anyway the Cheyennes didn't count white scalps. The Sioux adopted the Cheyenne way too, and did not count clipped scalps, but criticized a man instead of praising him for scalping a white man. But some maybe scalped them because they were avenging the killing of relatives at Sand Creek or other places. They say the white man never used to scalp an Indian but I guess they caught on; when somebody scalped them, they scalped all the ones they killed, like in the Chivington Massacre in Colorado and other places too.

Maybe some of the tribes counted white man's scalps as much as Indian ones with braids on. The Cheyenne law was it had to be a scalp with braids or loose hair and it was taken to the Hat tepee and kept there; they would not accept a white man's scalp. That is why they didn't use them. All the scalps in their possession today have long hair. I don't know how many they have but there are five special ones for ceremonies.

In this Fetterman battle I heard many different stories. Each would tell what they saw and what they done. Like Wolf Tooth and his friend Big Foot were down at the bottom, next time they were on one side—they saw what they could see from there.

White Elk told quite a bit too. They all told stories like that—the Sioux scattered after battle was over, took them down to the big rocks at another place and brought the dead together. They covered them with buffalo hides and then stones; they said they could be found there. They said there were two or three Cheyennes; one died after. Quite a few Sioux were killed. They attacked the soldiers by coming close a little at a time. But if there were suicide warriors they went right in, or behind them; that way they kill enemies, or scare them away. If nobody is a suicide vow, it takes time; like this one early in the morning to the middle of the day, and they outnumbered the soldiers. If there had been suicide warriors even a small group of Indians might have won the victory. They all followed in among the enemy and got them excited and they would start to run.

The Cheyenne rule instructed each member of the warrior band not to wait for anybody or orders, not to try to do like the rest; he should do all he could for himself, and fight privately. He can retreat if he wants to but he would be criticized by many people who watched the battle. So they kept going in, took care of themselves that way; but they were anxious to count coup, and that caused them to get down close.

I used to hear those warriors, White Elk, and others, say the white man has a poor way of fighting; they all listen to one man to say shoot. And sometimes the warriors could come up behind them that way before they had time to turn around. Now the white man has adopted many ways of the Indian fights, and goes in smaller groups.

The other stories, like Black Horse and White Elk and Sap maybe came close to each other, going together.

≡ ≡

Oral stories from later generations are mostly faithful also to the original eyewitness testimonies. The late Bill Tallbull (Wolf Feathers, Northern Cheyenne), former board member of the Fort Phil Kearny/Bozeman Trail Association and member of the President's Council on Historic Preservation, related the Cheyenne accounts of the Battle of 100 in the Hand. Bill's grandfather, Blue Feather (1834–1938), fought in the battle and provided family history of the engagement. Blue Feather was an arrow maker and according to Tallbull made many of the arrows for warriors in the fight. Tallbull corroborates the Cheyenne eyewitness testimonies of Two Moons' reconnaissance of Fort Phil Kearny prior to the ambush. Above all, Bill Tallbull stresses that both Cheyennes and Lakotas were fighting for their families and their future, emphasizing that when Northern Cheyennes made decisions about the future they did so for all the people, not just individuals. They cared most for the "survival of their culture" and held to the primary belief that the northern plains were their eternal home.[10]

Jennie Littlehawk Gardner (Oglala/Inuit) in school projects proudly told of her Lakota ancestral family at the Fetterman Fight and how they retrieved hundreds of fired arrows in the grass and amongst the rocks after the battle; she displayed several that are still in her family's possession as war mementos.[11] Michael Badhand (mixed heritage), an American Indian artist, film actor, historian, living history model presenter, and horseman, has given demonstrations riding his beloved horse, Apache Warhorse, at the speed with which the Indians, waiting in ambush for Fetterman's infantry to march into the trap, would have ridden to the top of Massacre Ridge and to engage the enemy.[12] College students in the tribal college system still learn of their history of resistance to American conquest. At Chief Dull Knife College in Lame Deer, Montana, Cheyenne students, for years before his retirement, learned of the Battle of 100 In The Hand in the Cheyenne culture and history courses of

Dr. Alonzo Spang (Northern Cheyenne). A student literary quarterly at the college publishes student essays on Plains Indian history, including Two Moons and White Elk's versions of the Fetterman fight. In 2003, the journal published an edition saluting "Our Cheyenne Warriors and all Military Troops for their Courage, Honor, and Love for Their Country."[13] Today, Terry Richards (Oglala) interprets the Lakota stories of the Fetterman Fight for the public on Massacre Ridge each December 21, during the anniversary commemorations of the fight by the Fort Phil Kearny/ Bozeman Trail Association; in the summer, at the location of the 1867 actions, he interprets the Lakota accounts of the Wagon Box Fight.[14]

Today, both Lakota and Cheyenne storytellers as well as tribal academic historians are using family stories and the published and unpublished accounts from earlier times as an educational outreach effort for their own people as well as the wider world. They view this as an expression of pride and veneration for their heroes of the past, especially during the resistance era. Much emphasis today is placed on remembering individual chiefs and military heroes from that time. Lakotas, especially those who trace their lineage to him, tell the story of Crazy Horse. One of the most impressive outreach efforts is *The Authorized Biography of Crazy Horse and His Family*, a four-part DVD video series on the great Oglala warrior developed in part by descendants of Ṫhašúnke Witcó. Despite the lack of eyewitness testimony of Crazy Horse's exact role in decoying Fetterman's troops over Lodge Trail Ridge, Part 4 of the series, "Defending the Homeland Prior to the 1868 Treaty," is an excellent and convincing story by great-grandsons of his acknowledged leadership in the fight as well as "providing further personal insight into the cultural and spiritual values of Crazy Horse and Lakota interpretive methodology."[15]

For wider audiences, best-selling storyteller, novelist, and historian Joseph Marshall's (Oglala) *Hundred in the Hand: A Novel* advances the aura of Crazy Horse. Not to be outdone, other tribes keep their people and others mindful of Miniconjou chiefs and *blotahunkas* like White Bull and High Backbone (Hump).[16] Alfred Red Cloud (Oglala), great-grandson of Red Cloud, confirms through family history that Red Cloud and others observed the action from a hill west of the Bozeman Trail with binoculars acquired in 1865. Alfred Red Cloud also disputes that American Horse killed Captain Fetterman. While taking to task American Horse's later claims to the contrary, Alfred Red Cloud states that according to his family history, American Horse fought on the north end of Massacre Ridge where he killed an officer that he later claimed as being Fetterman but whom Alfred says "was not."[17] Johnson Holy Rock (Oglala), grandson of Holy Bald Eagle or Holy Bull, likewise questions American Horse's role in killing Fetterman, while confirming Red Cloud's role as a "general" observing the battle. He also touts the oral stories of Crazy Horse's courageous leadership with the young Oglala warriors.[18] Wilmer Mesteth (Oglala), descendant of Chief Red Shirt, acknowledges the role of the *winkte* in foretelling the outcome of the Battle of 100 in the Hand.[19] Although no known publicly available eyewitness Arapaho accounts of the Fetterman Fight exist, Leona Buckman, descendent of Chief Sharp Nose, relates that her family history asserts Eagle Head and Black Coal were members of the decoy party, a claim corroborated by the eyewitness White Bull (Part 1).[20]

Finn Burnett's story of finding the unmutilated body of Corporal Adolph Metzger, Second Cavalry bugler, covered by a buffalo robe due to his bravery on Lodge Trail Ridge is today incorporated into the storytelling of both Lakotas and Cheyennes. A Crazy Horse descendant gave a most interesting account (including his personal rough sketch of the fight) to Lieutenant Colonel Edward Saunders (Ret.), of Billings, Montana, who is seeking evidence to have Metzger awarded a posthumous Congressional Medal of Honor. Saunders shared with the author the storyteller is Douglas War Eagle (Oglala/Miniconjou) of Dupree, South Dakota. Mr. War Eagle understandably credits his ancestor Crazy Horse with much bravery. His oral family history declares that Metzger came into the fight unarmed, with only his bugle, and was honored for such bravery. War Eagle also corroborates that about forty women (Cheyennes) had accompanied the warriors and it was they who mutilated the bodies of the soldier dead. American Horse (chapter 4) and the autopsy reports at Fort Phil Kearny confirm that Mr. War Eagle's assertion that Fetterman and Brown killed each other in an act of suicide is incorrect. War Eagle's story—despite some known contradictions—is illustrative of how Crazy Horse's bravery is woven into current storytelling of the Fetterman Fight.

Our oral story of the Fetterman Fight of this soldier Second U.S. Cavalry: Corporal Adolph Metzger; Bugler, Second U.S. Cavalry.

Our Great Grandfathers who fought in this battle (six war leaders) (4) Lakota (1) Cheyenne, (1) Arapahoe.

Crazy Horse & five others decoy Fetterman over the ridge and Crazy Horse stay in sight of soldiers acting he was wounded and five other Lakotas went down right side ridge to the people waiting by the river creek. The infantry that was on foot followed five Lakota right ridge and calvary [sic] under Fetterman to chase after our great-grandfather Crazy Horse the warrior on hills left side ridge and would get off his horse and check his horse and shoot around at the head officer taunted Fetterman to decoy to our main warriors in waiting east creek and west ridge and northern river creek where the women of Cheyenne decoy in the open for Fetterman men to see them.

East Creek, over 600 warriors

West Ridge 200 to 300 Cheyenne under Little Wolf, Spotted Elk

North River Creeks of over 40 women, Roman Nose & children that can move fast. 300 mix Cheyenne and Lakota teen and adult. Some Cheyenne women seek revenge for massacres of Cheyenne camp south, lost [sic] of loved ones. (Black Kettle, camp massacre.) 40 Cheyenne women painted with husbands' paint and mark of Cheyenne warrior would ID the soldier & mutilate of what was done to their family members.

Fetterman gave chase and was decoy to our people in north river creek area seen by Fetterman calvary gave chase to northern river creek and Crazy Horse would shoot a round at the solders give the warriors in waiting his position and soldier position passed warrior in waiting for soldiers cannot retreat back to fort. Warriors cut the soldiers' retreat back up ridge to south; back to Lodge Trail Ridge. Infantry had set an [sic] line of defense and Fetterman met full force of Lakota & Cheyenne & Arapahoe decoy down creek and then over run retreat back up to infantry defense.

Every time Crazy Horse shot a round reveal his and soldiers [sic] position when passed main warriors in waiting surrounded & squeezed them into open ridge of infantry line & retreat of calvary back up ridge to south of north river creek and infantry defense line and complete surrounded and Fetterman and Brown faced each other executed [sic] save last bullet for yourself and didn't want to be mutilated by the warriors but it was of Cheyenne women warriors widows whom familys [sic] was mutilated by soldiers earlier committed to see revenge for the families and did the mutilating of Fetterman soldiers.

(Oral) One of officers excuted [sic] Corporal Metzger he carried no weapon but his bugler [sic] to carry out last order from being over run and officer shot himself after Corporal Adolph Metzger was excuted and when all was defeated the women came seek revenge of their loved one butcher [sic] at Cheyenne camp to south. The war leaders over looked the soldiers and officers and while the women getting revenge for loved one butcher did the same to soldiers.

Warriors taking weapons and supplies of soldiers that the warrior killed and came upon Corporal A. Metzger. War leader was Crazy Horse Uncle Cakuhu (Hump) and Cheyenne leader stopped Cheyenne women of mutilate Corporal Metzger. This earthman came into our fight with no weapon but a noisemaker that the soldiers act upon its music. This man be respected to come into battle with no weapon and was excuted by his own officer stayed to die with his men. Gave his last call of bugle then was excuted and warrior seen this and honor this man he is brave and wish to die with his men and followed to last order of his commanding officer. Corporal Adolph Metzger was left alone and bravery was seen by our people. No weapon and under order stayed till the end. This a [*sic*] earthman lies here honor & respect for this brave man; wrap him by our people of buffalo people (Buffalo robe offer).

Great-grandson of Tasunke Witko family

Douglas A. War Eagle.[21]

The Cheyennes also honor Metzger. Bill Tallbull relates that Metzger fought "like a lion" with "whatever he could use as a weapon" and warriors found his body filled with arrows and covered his body with a buffalo robe because he had fought so bravely.[22] The late Ted Risingsun, Cheyenne elder, tribal historian, and great-grandson of Chief Dull Knife and Pawnee Woman, lamented during his lifetime that most young Cheyennes know little about their history. Risingsun and Richard Littlebear, Alonzo Spang, Conrad Fisher, Leo Killsback, and others have done much to change that situation in recent years in public forums and at Chief Dull Knife College, Lame Deer, Montana. Risingsun declared that his great-grandfather Dull Knife participated in the Battle of 100 in the Hand and possibly served as a decoy.[23]

Professor Leo Killsback of Arizona State University likewise states: "While growing up in southeastern Montana, I rarely heard about the 'old-time' warriors of our people in the classroom, on television, or in any other form of media," he wrote. "When I encountered Indians in history," he continued, "they were simple, one-dimensional creatures that arrived only to battle. Time is due for the stories of the old-time warriors, and it is time that our humanity is written back into history." Killsback brings Sweet Medicine Chief Little Wolf back into the lives of the Northern Cheyenne people, historians, and others through his scholarly efforts. Little Wolf is most revered for bringing his people home from exile in Indian Territory (Oklahoma), 1878–1879, but who is also remembered for deferring his selection as a decoy in the Battle of 100 in the Hand to his brother Big Nose, who was killed in the battle. Not only does Killsback refresh the story of Little Wolf as a great warrior but also as a farsighted chief and leader of his people in all matters, who today has songs composed in his name. In a conversation with Little Wolf's descendant, Little Coyote, president of the Northern Cheyenne Tribe, 2004–2007, Killsback recalls that Little Coyote thought that Little Wolf "should be used as an example [symbol] of decolonization, and that his style of leadership should be applied to today's struggles. 'I believe,' Little Coyote said, 'that would be truly amazing.'"[24]

Legacy and the Treaty of 1868

The Fetterman Fight was a pyrrhic victory for Lakotas and Northern Cheyennes. What they may have won in war they lost in peace, through a peace treaty they did not understand that was designed by the government to make them reservation Indians and end their way of life. Anger today is manifest by Lakotas and Cheyennes as a platform for restitution for violations of the Treaty of 1868 and especially later clandestine seizure by the government of the Black Hills. Some still view popular outrage over Fetterman's annihilation, followed by Custer's annihilation, as the reason for the loss of the Black Hills.

Sometime during the later days of August 1868, after the fighting ended and the peace treaty concluded, a disgruntled group of Omisis warriors with their chief, Little Wolf, nevertheless rode into an abandoned Fort Phil Kearny and burned it to the ground. Some of his people wanted to occupy the fort but Little Wolf rejected the idea. John Stands In Timber remembered the old stories told of Little Wolf's anger: "He tried two or three days, trying to talk to the people. Then he got mad and burned the fort. The soldiers were already out of it—it was supposed to be an agency there. In that session they told Little Wolf let the fort stay there this winter, next year they would move out; and they did move out, but Little Wolf was mad and he went over and burned it."[1]

Little Wolf and his followers who burned the fort likely realized that any vestige of physical evidence of Vehoé/Wasicu occupation of their lands, so hard-won a decade previous from the Crows, would corrupt the way of life of the people. The circumstances were somewhat ironic. On August 1st and 2nd of 1867, respectively, soldiers of the old Second Battalion of the Eighteenth Infantry, now the Twenty-Seventh Infantry, held off superior numbers of Lakota and Cheyenne warriors at the Hayfield Fight near Fort C. F. Smith, and at the Wagon Box Fight in the wood-cutting area west of Fort Phil Kearny. The soldiers now were armed with .50-70 Allin-modified breech-loading cartridge Springfield rifles, which had replaced the old .58-caliber muzzle-loading weapons. The Springfields were faster-loading guns that caught the Lakotas and Cheyennes off guard in these fights and drove them from the fields with casualties.[2]

Yet, during the time following the Fetterman Fight and the abandonment of the hated forts, Fort Phil Kearny was practically in a continuous state of siege. The army relieved Colonel Henry Carrington of his command in January 1867, as well as relieving General Philip St. George Cooke of command of the military's Department of the Platte. The government closed the Bozeman Trail to civilian traffic for good in January 1867, excepting military supply contractors. Meanwhile, the Union Pacific Railroad to the south of the Powder River Country in the Platte Valley had pushed westward past Fort Laramie and the Bozeman Road. This made the route north to Montana's gold country west of the Bighorn Mountains safer, faster, and more feasible. The troops at the Bozeman Trail forts Reno, Phil Kearny, and C. F. Smith found themselves protecting no one except their own garrisons. The government had no further use for the posts and decided to close them. Then they sued for peace with the Lakotas and Cheyennes with a new treaty that would appear to the chiefs that they had won "Red Cloud's War," when in fact the Fort Laramie Treaty of 1868 was purposefully obfuscated in its design to win for the government in peace what it could not win in war.

Following the Treaties of Medicine Lodge with the southern tribes in October of 1867, the United States government sent a "Blue Ribbon Peace Commission" to Fort Laramie, after previous efforts to end the war, to conclude a new treaty with chiefs whom they considered to be the most important among the warring Lakotas and Cheyennes in the Powder River Country. The commissioners were Generals William T. Sherman, the aged William S. Harney, Alfred H. Terry, C. C. Augur, John B. Sanborn, and politicos Nathaniel G. Taylor, commissioner of Indian Affairs, reform-minded Senator John B. Henderson, and Indian agent Samuel F. Tappan. The Treaty of 1868 that resulted is otherwise known as the Second Treaty of Fort Laramie. Although Dee Brown has contended that the Indians got everything they asked for and the United States received nothing in return, this was far from the case.[3] In reality the treaty is ambiguous, riddled with legalistic language that the Indians could scarcely understand, and was purposefully designed to end the traditional life ways of the Plains tribes. Historian Colin G. Calloway states that the Treaty of 1868 was "one of the most significant and controversial treaties in the history of Indian–U.S. relations. It ended the war, planted the seeds for another war, and provided the legal foundation for Sioux claims to the Black Hills for more than a hundred years."[4]

The treaty not only ended hostilities by removing the forts on the Bozeman Trail, a measure that had actually become expedient for the government by making one-dimensional concessions to the tribesmen, it also consolidated the Indians on reservations. Although the government agreed to close the Bozeman Trail forever, articles of the treaty gave the government the right to build new roads through hunting grounds. The treaty placed Indians under the jurisdiction of civil courts for individual crimes even though they were not citizens of the United States. It included provisions to force re-education of Indian children in the ways of the white man.[5]

The Treaty of 1868 created the Great Sioux Reservation, all of present-day South Dakota west of the Missouri River, but ambiguously confirmed the hunting grounds north of the Platte and east of the Bighorns as "unceded territory." But Article 11 stipulated that, at some future time, the Indians "will relinquish all right to occupy permanently the territory outside the reservation."[6] Although the treaty appeared to cede all the northern plains except for Montana to the Lakotas, the government created Wyoming Territory the same year, indicating its intent to settle the Powder River Country and surrounding lands below Montana with white settlers. The next year, 1869, General Philip Sheridan issued a general order that all Indians off the reservation, essentially those persons in the unceded territory, "as a rule will [could] be considered hostile." Military historian John Gray contended that the Treaty of 1868 might be viewed as "exclusively a white man's device . . . that it served primarily as an instrument of chicanery and a weapon of aggression that was designed to obtain from the Indians in peace what the army had been unable to seize in war."[7]

Most of all, the treaty guaranteed to the Lakotas, Paha Sapa, the sacred Black Hills forever. Discovery of gold in the Hills, however, would precipitate the Great Sioux War in 1876 and 1877. As a result the government confiscated the Black Hills with a contrived sale to a few sycophant chiefs in what was the most blatant violation of the Treaty of 1868. The sale was supposed to require a two-thirds vote of the male population on the new Great Sioux Reservation. Today the legal challenges to return the Black Hills still dominates federal relations with Lakotas and are some of the most visible concerns. Charlotte A. Black Elk, the granddaughter of Nicholas Black

Elk, confidant of John G. Neihardt, dedicated her life and career to a reclamation of the Black Hills by the Lakotas: "It is occupied Territory," she said, "and it would do the hearts good of every American to give it back to the Lakota people."[8] In essence the Treaty of 1868 created far more problems for both the Indians and the federal government than it solved and became one of the biggest failures of President Ulysses S. Grant's so-called Peace Policy. It cost the government millions and strengthened the Quaker-led Indian reform movement. For the Lakotas it set in motion conditions and infrastructure that would lead directly to renewed war, impoverishment on the reservation, the misguided boarding school experience, disillusionment, the Ghost Dance movement, and the tragic massacre at Wounded Knee in 1890. The Indians did not foresee the long-range provisions of the treaty. Unlike their Dakota cousins in Minnesota, the Lakotas in 1868 had no previous experience with the reservation system. Bear in the Grass later said: "These words of the treaty were never explained. It was said that the treaty was for peace and friendship among the whites. When we took hold of the pen they said they would take the troops away so we could raise our children." And Red Cloud, among the last to sign, stated in a speech at Cooper Union, New York in 1870, "We thought the treaty was [just] to remove the forts and for us to cease from fighting."[9]

The Brûlés met with the commissioners in April at Spotted Tail agency and signed the treaty. Arapaho chiefs also signed. Little Wolf, Dull Knife, and others signed for the Northern Cheyennes and were allowed to "attach themselves" to the Great Sioux Reservation. Other Northern Cheyennes were furious with Little Wolf for signing the treaty without meeting with the forty-four council chiefs. Many rejected it.[10]

The Oglalas proved to be far more recalcitrant. During deliberations between May 24 and May 25, 1868, Oglala chief Kills the Bear stated, "I will sign the treaty provided that the commissioners promise they will remove the posts and give us a big present. I am a rascal, and if the whites don't fulfill this treaty I will show myself [to be] one."[11] American Horse was more specific: "I would like to have my friends here to sign the treaty. I will sign, and if there is anything wrong afterwards I will watch the commissioners, and they will be the first one[s] that I will whip."[12] Many Hunkpapas, including Sitting Bull, rejected the treaty, as did Bad Face Oglala Crazy Horse. But already, on May 19, General Augur had ordered the abandonment of the posts on the Bozeman Trail. Red Cloud would not come in to Fort Laramie, however, until the forts actually were vacated He contended: "We are on the mountains looking down on the soldiers and the forts. When we see the soldiers moving away and the forts abandoned, then I will come down and talk.[13]

The army began to dismantle the forts in early summer. Sometime around August 18–20, 1868, the last wagons rolled out of Fort Phil Kearny. But not until November 4 would Red Cloud, possibly by then recognized as a de facto *itancan*, come in to Fort Laramie with a contingent of warriors to sign the treaty. Red Cloud's War was over. Red Cloud would keep the treaty but the United States would not. During his long life, Red Cloud became a grand statesman fighting for his people's rights as a diplomat. He would travel to Washington, D.C., in 1870 to confer with President Grant. His influence would be felt with the Dawes Committee and the Edmunds Commission. He worked for reform not only between Indian and white but among his own people as well. But throughout his life he continued to believe that the government, with the Treaty of 1868, had tricked him.[14] But Red Cloud never would go to war again.

In later years he became a culture broker fighting for his people's rights. Red Cloud did not speak for all of the Lakotas. By the 1870s, many of the younger generation of resisters like Crazy Horse disavowed Red Cloud's posture of peace. Little did the Lakotas and Cheyennes realize that the government framed the Fort Laramie Treaty of 1868 not only to remove them from lands guaranteed them in the Treaty of 1851, but also to transform their lives through forced assimilation to farming and ranching, and, arguably, Christian conversion on reservations designed for those purposes. The "Non-Treaty" Indians who had refused to sign or accept the new treaty continued to live in their traditional ways in the unceded lands of the Powder River Country—a recipe for further armed conflict with the government. In the autumn of 1875 a large contingent of Lakotas and Cheyennes refused an order to return to the Great Sioux Reservation by January 1, 1876, which led directly to the Great Sioux War, 1876–1877. In addition, the government wished to speed assimilation and open Dakota and Wyoming. With the end of Reconstruction, political fears were looming among northern Republicans. These politicians were concerned with advancing statehood to loyal western territories by attracting white settlers with *free land* under the Homestead Act. Added to that were promises of good eastern agricultural markets with land-grant railroads, all of which abetted speedy assimilation efforts following the tribes' defeat in the Great Sioux War, despite their great victory at Little Big Horn on June 25, 1876.

Subsequent to the Great Sioux War the Manypenny Commission figuratively "stole" the Black Hills and the unceded territory from the tribesmen. With the government cutting food rations to the reservation, the commission secured the consent of a few *persuaded* chiefs and that of about 10 percent of the adult male population of the reservation—about 65 percent short of the number required by the 1868 treaty to "purchase" Paha Sapa and the Powder River Country. Throughout the remainder of the nineteenth century several more constitutionally questionable acts, including the First Sioux Act, of 1888, invoked the Dawes Allotment Act of the same year to open unused reservation lands to white settlement. This policy of "allotment" essentially applied the homestead principle to Indians and thus became another instrument of forced assimilation. In 1889 the Crook Commission, under the authorization of the 2nd Sioux Act, began the process of fracturing the Great Sioux Reservation into six smaller reservations. In the span of twenty-two years, the Lakotas had by 1890 lost millions of acres from the Treaty of 1868 and had been reduced from 134 million acres recognized by the original Treaty of 1851 to 15 million acres by 1890.[15]

The Lakotas never accepted the loss of the Black Hills and consider them today to be stolen property. Beginning in 1923, they began an arduous process of regaining Paha Sapa. Federal courts dismissed each attempt until 1980. In 1942, 1954, 1974, and after a government appeal in 1978, the Supreme Court of the United States ruled the Annexation Act of 1877 unconstitutional and upheld a Court of Claims 1974 award of $17.5 million plus 5 percent interest, for a total of $122.5 million. After their fifty-seven year struggle the Lakotas had won a legal monetary claim to the Black Hills. Their response came almost immediately: "The Black Hills are not for sale." At this writing the proud Lakotas, despite what the infusion of what today would be around $1 billion (counting interest) would do to help the people, are still attempting to regain their most sacred land from the federal government.[16]

The Indian Bureau authorized the exile of many of the Northern Cheyennes to Darlington Agency in Indian Territory (Oklahoma) in 1877, essentially for their participation in the Great Sioux War. The decision to move them appears arbitrary. They would not go so easily. The band of Two Moons, along with Lakotas including Crazy Horse, fought Nelson A. Miles's force to a standstill at the Battle of Belly Butte (Wolf Mountain to Lakotas) on January 8, 1877. They then enlisted as scouts with Miles at Fort Keogh against the Nez Percé and were thus allowed to remain in Montana. But the followers of Little Wolf and Morning Star (Dull Knife), defeated by Ranald S. McKenzie in the Bighorn Mountains on November 26, 1876 were, upon their surrender by the spring of 1877, strongly persuaded by General George Crook to remove to Indian Territory to live with the Southern Cheyennes after he promised them they could return to the northern plains should they not like Darlington Agency—a promise Crook had no authority to make unilaterally, and a promise the government had no intention to keep. The influx of almost a thousand Omisis at Darlington Agency stretched resources to the limit during the lean winter of 1877–78. Quite a few died of disease. In July of 1878 Little Wolf and Morning Star, with about 353 of their people, left the reservation for their homelands in the north. Pursued by federal troops of three military departments, aided by railroad support, the Omisis traveled 1,200 miles in one of the most incredible exoduses in American history. Fighting troops along the way, needing to raid settlements in northwest Kansas after losing horses and all their provisions at the Battle of Punished Woman Fork on September 27, 1878, in order to survive, the bands of Morning Star and Little Wolf divided in the Nebraska Sand Hills.

Troops from Fort Robinson captured Morning Star's band and on the night of January 9–10 his people made a dramatic escape from a barracks prison at the fort rather than be forced to return to Indian Territory. Many perished in the ensuing weeks. Meanwhile Little Wolf's followers wintered in the Sand Hills but surrendered at Fort Keogh, Montana, by April 1, 1879. Eastern public opinion that spring turned in favor of the Northern Cheyennes and the Interior Department allowed them to remain in Montana. They are living there today on their own reservation of 460,000 acres centered at Lame Deer.[17]

Today, much of the land where the tribes roamed freely is no longer Indian land, mostly in Wyoming, the site of the Fetterman Fight. Montana lands north and west of the Northern Cheyenne Indian Reservation is now Crow land, as it had been by the original terms of the Treaty of 1851. The beloved Powder River Country at the base of the Bighorns is privately owned or held by the government. The city of Sheridan, Wyoming, sits on favored village sites of both Lakotas and Cheyennes. The two tribes strive for de-colonization, sovereignty, and self-determination over their economic affairs. Having tried agriculture and ranching through the twentieth century, diversification is now common. The birth in 1969 of the Tribal College and University System is now placing Indian physicians and nurses in tribal hospitals, Indian attorneys in American courts where oral history is utilized in claims cases, and Indian professors in graduate schools and colleges, and all of their voices are starting to be heard in public forums. These endeavors are still shadowed by injustice on the reservations. Disease and addiction have not disappeared. In addition, long criticized by many non-Indians for living, going to school, and working on government subsidies and programs, the indigenous stewards of Lakota and Cheyenne lands have faced over a century of corporate exploitation, colonization, and crime by extractive natural resource interests. Even among their own people arguments between "traditionalists" of the Medicine Way who wish to keep the lands unaltered and "progressives" wishing to utilize, benefit, and profit from development can become heated, as in the days of Red Cloud and his militant detractors following the 1868 Treaty of Fort Laramie. Still, despite anger and resentment of government and industry, both tribes, through good times and bad, remember and honor their ancestors and their heroes, who fought for the freedom, dignity, and integrity of their people and families.

In conclusion, this study has sought to provide a glimpse to the wider world of some of the heroes of the Lakotas and Northern Cheyennes in one specific but highly remembered episode in American Indian history. The eyewitness testimonies that have been presented in this book are recorded and edited in the written word of the English language by non-Indians, who intended to flesh out the complete history of the Fetterman Fight for wider audiences enamored with the nostalgia of the recent passing of the frontier in the early twentieth century. They are stories of war and manhood. But, again, they are not simply Lakota and Cheyenne eyewitness accounts *about* Indians. Rather they are spoken words in Native tongues, telling firsthand Indian history. Although these stories are about the sequences of a single battle, today they serve transitional purposes recognized finally by scholars. Since the 1970s, according to historian John Southard, military historians have increasingly amalgamated "social, cultural, economic, and political themes with war-related topics," thus adapting military history to the evolving nature of the history discipline as a whole. This has created "a much more diverse and dynamic field," taking the sub-discipline beyond unoriginal traditional narrative military history of "day by day and in some cases hour-by-hour accounts of battles and operations . . . drums and trumpets." Historic battles and victories have become symbols of decolonization, and today, the heroes of those battles are viewed as leadership style models for efforts to achieve sovereignty and restitution within the tribes' legal and political platforms and with the mainstream community.[18]

Lakotas, Cheyennes, and Arapahos have never forgotten the victories and the heroes. Their military history is still relevant in a broader cultural sense than ever before. Indigenous peoples across all hemispheres today remind the wider world they are still here, their past is present—they are growing in greater numbers than ever before since invasion and conquest. They have command of their history—and they too are a relevant part of the large American story.[19] Their voices suggest not so much to forgive and forget as they do to continue on and remember.

Afterword

Captain William J. Fetterman

This book focuses on the eyewitness testimonies of Lakota and Cheyenne participants in the Fetterman Fight, December 21, 1866. This is their story and presents their points of view. But students of the Fetterman Fight, mostly non-Indians, have always first been anxious to know a writer's take on the two most important enemy leaders in this battle, Captain William Judd Fetterman and his commanding officer, Colonel Henry Beebe Carrington. Did the Indians win the battle or did Fetterman lose it through arrogance, stupidity, and hate for his commanding officer? The question seems unavoidable. Is Captain William Judd Fetterman solely culpable for what is a monumental achievement by Plains Indians in their history of resistance to conquest? Can Indian views of the Fetterman Fight be fully appreciated until this question, irrelevant to them, is put to rest? Are there cultural ramifications regarding this question? Indian perspectives do not place any importance on *why* Fetterman came over Lodge Trail Ridge. But non-Indian students of the battle have historically fixated on casting blame on a white officer in order to explain an important Indian victory. The result is to focus on blaming non-Indians rather than crediting Indians who fought there that day.

A greatly admired anthropologist, writing a review of a newer traditional chronological narrative history of Red Cloud's War largely from the military perspective, asserts that the question of Fetterman's disobedience "has been hotly debated" and that the book's author "has resolved this question that has dogged the literature. He shows clearly, for example, that Fetterman disobeyed Carrington's orders."[1] In fact, no such question should dog the literature or be "hotly debated." No historian ever wrote with any factual certainly that Fetterman did *not* disobey his commander's orders. Only J. W. Vaughn, nearly a half century ago, speculated on this, but his supposition is unsupported by definitive primary sources or conclusive logic. Vaughn's suggestion is not seriously debated by scholars and is largely dismissed today.[2] Without question, the overwhelming evidence from 1866 illustrates that Captain William J. Fetterman disobeyed his orders. In my 2008 reexamination of the Fetterman Fight, I wrote: "The question of course remains: did Fetterman disobey orders, the results being the annihilation of his entire command, regardless of who committed the tactical blunder that sealed the fate of eighty-one men? If we are to assume that [Lieutenant George W.] Grummond [leading the Second Cavalry element with Fetterman's infantry] had been instructed not to cross Lodge Trail Ridge [which he *was* so ordered and several eyewitnesses heard those orders], we must assume that Fetterman's earlier orders had been the same, then certainly, Fetterman disobeyed orders."[3]

In government investigations following the fight, several enlisted men at Fort Phil Kearny testified, or were prepared to testify, that Fetterman disobeyed orders.[4] Does arrogance, ethnocentrism, or lack of respect for Colonel Carrington alone explain his disobedience? If so, then all junior officers at Fort Phil Kearny share his blame, for such were their feelings toward the inexperienced Carrington, and they also had a naïve estimation of Plains Indian fighting abilities. But army officers understood obedience to orders.

So the important question is: *why* did Fetterman disobey his orders? Much of the confusion is derived from the nature of Carrington's directive to Fetterman and his subordinate, Lieutenant Grummond, to relieve a wood-cutting detail being attacked a mile and a half to four miles, depending on the source, *west* of the fort and to not cross Lodge Trail Ridge, which would then obscure Fort Phil Kearny from Fetterman's view. Upon leaving the fort under these orders, Fetterman proceeded instead *northeast* avoiding the ridge road that went west to the pineries, skirted Sullivant Hill at the east end, and then moved up to a manageable crest on Lodge Trail Ridge. After a brief pause, the command pushed over the ridge, chasing Lakota and Cheyenne decoys that lured them north. Was Fetterman insubordinate by proceeding in the opposite direction from the wood train, or was he insubordinate only when he actually crossed over Lodge Trail Ridge and thus out of sight of the stockade? We may debate the interpretations of formal codes of military conduct forever, but Fetterman unquestionably proceeded away from the location of the wood train.

Technically speaking, Fetterman disobeyed his orders the minute his command came around to the north in front of the stockade. From that point Fetterman proceeded around Sullivant Hill and then up and over Lodge Trail Ridge, following the ten decoys whose obvious intentions were not a secret to the command. Why? There is little doubt that many junior officers at Fort Phil Kearny thought Colonel Carrington incompetent to wage war against the Lakotas and Cheyennes. Until a fight on December 6, when Carrington ordered a flanking movement over Lodge Trail Ridge to intercept warriors that had attacked a wood-cutting detail, he had ordered nothing resembling aggressive maneuvers against the Indians. So was this simply a case of Fetterman disrespecting the judgment of his commander, risking the lives of his men, courts-martial for himself, and inviting a ruined career? In just two weeks Fetterman would have become part of the newly authorized Twenty-Seventh Infantry under the 1866 Army Reorganization Act, thus severing his ties with Carrington. Would he risk his future simply to infuriate his commanding officer with an act of contemptuous insubordination? Or was he so chauvinistic toward the fighting skills of the Plains Indians that he was unconcerned with what he might find on the northern slopes of Lodge Trail Ridge and thought only to enhance his career?

The first argument––that he was impulsive simply to defy Carrington––is illogical given that Fetterman was a "short-timer." He survived the Civil War in a regiment that suffered one of the highest casualty rates of any regular army infantry regiment. Such illogic also is not likely, given Fetterman's combat experience and his tempered professional interactions with other senior officers in the Army of the Cumberland. During the campaigns in middle Tennessee for example, rather than demonstrate rashness and causing trouble for a new, universally disliked brigade commander, Brigadier General Robert S. Granger, Fetterman simply and quietly requested and received a transfer to recruiting duty. Nor did he exhibit rashness in the killing fields of Stone's River in December of 1862, when he shrewdly ordered his company to fall back no less than three times in the face of superior enemy firepower.[5]

As for Fetterman's arrogance about the fighting abilities of the Plains Indians, all junior officers at Fort Phil Kearny in 1866 held chauvinistic views toward the Lakotas and Cheyennes prior to actually meeting them in combat. After the tenuous fight of December 6, 1866, in which Lieutenant Horatio Bingham lost his life, Margaret Carrington remembered Captain Fetterman coming to headquarters at the fort and addressing her husband. She wrote: "Captain Fetterman has been in, and says 'he has learned a lesson, and that this Indian war has become a hand-to-hand fight, requiring the utmost caution,' and he wants no more such risks." In his official report of the fight, Henry Carrington praised Fetterman and stated that the captain "carried out his orders promptly."[6]

So again, why did Fetterman so dramatically disobey orders to relieve the wood-cutting detail on December 21? Disobeying orders was not that uncommon among both junior and senior officers of the Civil War culture when they perceived changing battle scenarios that presented possible tactical advantages, especially in the heat of a fight, but also in expansive troop movements. John Pelham at Fredericksburg, refusing to withdraw his artillery, and J. E. B. Stuart's tardiness against orders to reunite with Lee's army at Gettysburg, are but two of many such examples.[7] Unstated in any nineteenth-century manual of arms is the rule that if an officer's disobedience results in victory, little or nothing is said regarding his disobedience, but if his decision results in defeat, he often would be charged with insubordination. In Fetterman's case two factors come into play that are not immediately obvious in the official reports and hearings but must be pieced together by comparing all of Fort Phil Kearny officers' reports and testimonies of the fight and by examining the time and motion of the action.

First, within minutes of Fetterman's egress form the fort (about 11:15 a.m.), the tactical situation abruptly changed. Lookouts on a hill behind the fort (on Pilot Knob), who had a clear view of the wood train to the west, signaled that the warriors attacking it had broken off their assault and were retreating east behind the ridges lying north of the fort, and that the wood cutters were out of danger and proceeding unimpeded west toward the wood-cutting pineries. Fetterman, judging from his next actions, saw the signal and so did Carrington, for Carrington wrote in his report that he "entertained no further thought of danger."[8] At this point Fetterman likely seized an initiative to move east along the southern slope of the ridges parallel with the retreating warriors who were moving below the north side of the ridges, and then head up the Bozeman Trail and over Lodge Trail Ridge in order to intercept the warriors' retreat before they spread out and evaporated in the broad Peno Valley. This tactical shift apparently seemed proper to Colonel Carrington, who wrote in his report that Fetterman was "moving *wisely* [emphasis mine] up the creek and along the southern slope of the ridge with good promise of cutting off the warriors as they should withdraw."[9] Two years later, in her book, Margaret Carrington also wrote that Fetterman maneuvered to cut off the warriors' retreat.[10]

Lieutenant W. F. Arnold, observing Fetterman's movements from the fort, later testified that after Fetterman moved up and over Lodge Trail Ridge, "[i]t did not alarm anybody, as it was the largest force that had ever been sent out from the garrison."[11] Arnold's statement is critical corroboration, as Carrington apparently felt the same way. Had he been concerned at that moment with Fetterman's obvious disobedience of his orders, he had plenty of time to send out a courier, at least for the record, to officially order Fetterman to return to the fort. But he did not. Instead he went in and ate breakfast until reports of gunfire alerted him that things were amiss.[12] The author has briskly hiked from Fort Phil Kearny to the lower crest of Lodge Trail Ridge that Fetterman ascended, and then hiked down to Monument Hill. The "quick march" took in excess of forty-five minutes. Arnold's testimony, and Carrington's inaction to try to retrieve the "wayward" Fetterman, also reveals that no one at the fort on that morning realized 1,500 or more warriors could be waiting with a well-set ambush on the north side of the ridge. Surely eighty-one men were sufficient to combat the retreating wood train attackers plus perhaps an *expected* sixty to one hundred more warriors covering their retreat north of Lodge Trail Ridge.

Despite reports earlier in the fall of 1,500 lodges in the Tongue River Valley, the Indians were yet to muster war parties exceeding 100–150 warriors. The troops at Fort Phil Kearny had not previously encountered more than that and never met disaster given the numbers they did encounter. Little did they realize that many more Lakotas and Cheyennes had arrived in the warring camps along the Tongue River during the previous week, intent on staging a massive ambush. Fetterman's responses to large numbers of the enemy at Stone's River logically indicate he was not the type of officer to rashly commit men to battle against known impossible odds such as twenty to one. Only when the truth of Indian numbers became known after the fight did Carrington, as the senior officer responsible for the garrison at Fort Phil Kearny, begin to cast all blame for the disaster on the dead Fetterman because of his disobedience of orders, alleged arrogance, and disrespect for his commanding officer. Carrington would hold onto this position for the remainder of his life.[13]

Emphasis on the officers at Fort Phil Kearny continues to persist. By focusing through the years so intensively on the Fetterman/Carrington conflict historians have cast an ethnocentric net over the Fetterman Fight. In searching for culpability for a disastrous tactical military decision among junior and senior officers at Fort Phil Kearny and in the Department of the Platte, much past literature raises culturally biased inferences, which also engulf the literature of George Armstrong Custer and the Battle of Little Big Horn a decade later––that no overwhelming force of "aboriginal" people could defeat a smaller element of the U.S. Army unless some army officer made disastrous mistakes, disobeyed orders, or was madly arrogant.

When one examines the eyewitness accounts of the "victors" it becomes obvious that the planning and execution of the ambush of Fetterman's command was nothing less than spectacular for its tactical success. The significance of Fetterman's actions and Carrington's reactions on December 21 clearly illustrates how successfully the Indians conceived and executed their ambush plan. By demonstrating in front of the fort, then feigning attack on the wood train, and purposefully breaking off that engagement to retreat behind the ridges toward Peno Creek where it makes a southward upstream bend, the allure of cutting off the Indians' retreat now that the wood cutters were out of danger was too much for Fetterman and Grummond to resist, especially if they did not anticipate the great numbers of enemy awaiting them over Lodge Trail Ridge. The presence of the ten decoys on Lodge Trail Ridge was nothing new. All three officers had witnessed decoy maneuvers before. Fetterman was not *tricked* into crossing the ridge. He did so on purpose to support Grummond's cavalry advance, and was undoubtedly convinced that the anticipated number of warriors waiting to engage him on the other side were manageable for his command of eighty-one men. It is highly unlikely that an officer of Fetterman's caliber and experience would have crossed the ridge if he knew an enemy of 1,500 awaited him. Coming to the support of the impetuous Grummond, who had charged ahead with the cavalry, however, was another matter, a matter of the tactical commander's responsibility.

In essence, the Indians' plan to create a feint, and then lure troops into a well-staged ambush out of sight of the fort with a large fighting force—which they reasoned, correctly, would be unanticipated—worked. Given this realization, the Native testimonies examined in the previous sections are critical to understanding the nature of their achievement and the complexity of nineteenth-century Plains Indian strategy and tactics. Scholars should recognize and conduct further research accordingly in ways that transcend a simple minute-by-minute rehash of guns and trumpets.

Appendixes

Appendix A

*Claimed Indian Warriors Killed or Mortally Wounded
on December 21, 1866 near Fort Phil Kearny*

Name	Tribal Designation	Source
Lone Bear	Oglala Lakota	American Horse; White Bull
Yellow White Man	" "	American Horse; White Bull
Horse Looking	" "	American Horse
Little Bear	" "	American Horse
Eats-Meat	Miniconjou Lakota	White Bull
Charging-Crow	" "	White Bull
Flying Hawk	" "	White Bull
Bear Ears	Probable Miniconjou	White Bull
Little Crow	" "	White Bull
Clown Horse	" "	White Bull
Male Eagle	" "	White Bull
He Dog[1]	" "	White Bull
Fine Weather	" "	White Bull
Eagle-Stays-In-The-Air	" "	White Bull
Broken Hand	" "	White Bull
Eats-Pemmican	" "	White Bull
Porcupine Hash	" "	White Bull

Name	Tribal Designation	Source
Bird Head	Arapaho	American Horse
Good Shield	"	American Horse
Strong Wind Blowing	Cheyenne	Wooden Leg
Big Nose	"	White Elk, Two Moons,[2] B. Bear
Rustling Leaf	"	Black Bear
Bear Robe	"	American Horse; White Elk; W. Leg; Two Moons

Appendix B

Wasicu/Vehoé Casualties

Although the names of all the enemy soldiers and civilians killed by the Lakotas, Cheyennes, and Arapahos at the Fetterman Fight on December 21, 1866 in Dakota Territory are well known, they are listed here for readers' convenience.

List of Men Killed in Action near Fort Philip Kearny, D. T., on the 21st day of December 1866

(Source: Margaret Carrington, Absaraka: Home of the Crows, 282–84)

No.	Name	Rank	Company	Battalion and Regiment
1.	Augustus Lang	1st Sgt.	A	2/18th Inf.
2.	Hugh Murphy	Sgt.	"	"
3.	Robert Lennon	Crpl.	"	"
4.	William Dule	"	"	"
5.	Frederick Acherman	Pvt.	"	"
6.	William Betzler	"	"	"
7.	Thomas Burk	"	"	"
8.	Henry Buchannan	"	"	"
9.	George E. R. Goodall	"	"	"
10.	Michael Harlen	"	"	"
11.	Martin Kelley	"	"	"
12.	Patrick Shannon	"	"	"
13.	Charles N. Taylor	"	"	"

No.	Name	Rank	Company	Battalion and Regiment
14.	Joseph D. Thomas	Pvt.	A	2/18th Inf.
15.	David Thorey	"	"	"
16.	John Timson	"	"	"
17.	Albert H. Walter	"	"	"
18.	John M. Weaver	"	"	"
19.	Maximillian Dehring	"	"	"
20.	Francis S. Gordon	"	"	"
21.	John Woodruff	"	"	"
22.	Francis Raymond	Sgt.	C	"
23.	Patrick Rooney	"	"	"
24.	Gustave A. Bauer	Crpl.	"	"
25.	Patrick Gallagher	"	"	"
26.	Henry E. Aarons	Pvt.	"	"
27.	Michael O'Gara	"	"	"
28.	Jacob Rosenberg	"	"	"
29.	Frank P. Sullivan	"	"	"
30.	Patrick Smith	"	"	"
31.	William Morgan	Sgt.	E	"
32.	John Quinn	Crpl.	"	"
33.	George W. Burrell	Pvt.	"	"
34.	Timothy Cullinans	"	"	"
35.	John Maher	"	"	"
36.	George N. Waterbury	"	"	"
37.	Alexander Smith	1st Sgt. H	"	
38.	Ephraim C. Bissell	Sgt.	"	"
39.	George Philip	Crpl.	"	"
40.	Michael Sharkey	"	"	"
41.	Frank Karston	"	"	"
42.	George Davis	Pvt.	"	"
43.	Pierre F. Doland	"	"	"
44.	Asa H. Griffin	"	"	"
45.	Herman Keil	"	"	"
46.	James Kean	"	"	"
47.	Michael Kinney	"	"	"
48.	Delos Reed	"	"	"
49.	Thomas M. Madden	Recruit	unassigned	"

No.	Name	Rank	Company	Battalion and Regiment
50.	James Baker	Sgt.	C	2d Cavalry
51.	James Kelley	Crpl.	"	"
52.	Thomas F. Honigan	"	"	"
53.	Adolph Metzger	Bugler	"	"
54.	John McCarty	Artificer	"	"
55.	Thos. Amberson	Private	"	"
56.	Thos. Broglan	"	"	"
57.	William Bugbee	"	"	"
58.	William Cornog	"	"	"
59.	Charles Cuddy	"	"	"
60.	Patrick Clancey	"	"	"
61.	Harry S. Deming	"	"	"
62.	Hugh B. Doran	"	"	"
63.	Robert Daniel	"	"	"
64.	Nathan Foreman	"	"	"
65.	Andrew M. Fitzgerald	"	"	"
66.	Daniel Greene	"	"	"
67.	Charles Gamford	"	"	"
68.	John Giller	"	"	"
69.	Ferdinand Houser	"	"	"
70.	Frank Jones	"	"	"
71.	James B. McGuire	"	"	"
72.	John McColley	"	"	"
73.	George W. Nugent	"	"	"
74.	Franklin Payne	"	"	"
75.	James Ryan	"	"	"
76.	Oliver Williams	"	"	"
77.	James Wheatley	Citizen		
78.	Isaac Fisher	"		

Enlisted Men 18th U.S. Infantry	49
Enlisted Men 2d U. S. Cavalry	27
Citizens	2
Total	78

Names of Officers of the 18th U.S. Infantry Killed in the Same Action

Captain William Judd Fetterman
Captain Frederick H. Brown
Lieutenant George W. Grummond

Recapitulation

Officers	Officers	Sgts.	Crpls.	Pvts.	Citizens	Aggregate
2d/18th Inf.	2	7	8	34	0	51
2d Cavalry	1	1	2	24	0	28
Citizens	0	0	0	0	2	2
Total	3	8	10	58	2	81

Appendix C

Margaret Carrington's Views of Indians

(Source: Margaret Carrington, *Absaraka: Home of the Crows*, 187–93.)

Many older studies of the Fetterman Fight declare that the military personnel at Fort Phil Kearny were ignorant of Plains Indian customs, culture, and methods of warfare. By the time of the Fetterman Fight on December 21, 1866, they had learned much. Although she was ultimately provincial and condescending, when Margaret Carrington wrote and published her memoir, *Absaraka, Home of the Crows* (1868), she gave to history a vivid, if limited, picture of the material culture, as Victorian-era whites viewed it, of tribes in the Powder River Country of the 1860s. Below is her description from chapter 22 of her memoir.

Popular opinion has regarded the Indian bow and arrow as something primitive and well enough for the pursuit of game, but quite useless in a contest with the white man. This idea would be excellent if the Indian warriors would calmly march up in line of battle and risk their masses so armed against others armed with the rifle. But the Indian comes as the hornet comes, in clouds or singly, yet never trying to sting until his ascendancy is assured and his own exposure is slight.

At fifty yards a well-shapen [*sic*], iron-pointed arrow is dangerous and very sure. A handful drawn from the quiver and discharged successively will make a more rapid fire than that of the revolver, and at very short range will farther penetrate a piece of plank or timber than the ball of an ordinary Colt's navy pistol.

The arrow-head varies in length and shape, and the shaft itself slightly changes, according to the tastes of different bands or tribes; and yet so constantly are arrows exchanged in gambling or barter that the character of the arrow used does not invariably determine the tribe engaged. Such were many of the arrows taken from the bodies of Captains Fetterman, Brown, Lieutenant Grummond, and others, after the massacre of December 1866. All the peculiarities there found have been seen in the quivers of the Kittekehas, Chowees, Petropowetaws, and other Pawnees, all of whom are friendly, and some of whom are now, as in the winter of 1865–6, in the employ of the United States. The head is often barbed, but not generally, and is from two to three and a half inches in length, made of iron, and ground to a double edge. The shaft, which is about twenty-five inches in length, is winged by three feathers of the eagle, sage-hen, or wild-goose, and from the sinew wrapping of the head to that which binds the feathers is deeply marked by three grooves or blood seams, so that when the flesh of man or beast closes about the shaft, these seams act as conduits and gradually bleed the victim to death. These grooves are, with some Indians straight, and with others are zigzag or winding from midway down to the feathers.

The bows of Ogillalla [sic], and Brûlé Sioux, Arapahoes, Cheyennes, and most of the Indians east of the Rocky Mountains, are from thirty-two to forty inches long, of great elasticity and tension, so that they easily drive an arrow through a two-inch plank, and even through a man or buffalo.

The hatchet is generally that which is furnished by Indian agents or traders, often having the head and handle hollow and connected for use as a pipe; and, when possible, the handle itself is profusely studded with brass nails such has once distinguished parlor sofas and chairs.

Rifles, both English and American, abound. The "Hawkins" is a favorite, carrying what is called the "trade ball," and requiring a patch; but many of the old guides, trappers, and half-breeds still cling to their use as in the days of Pathfinder and other heroes of Cooper.

The quiver and bow-case are made of deerskin, bearskin, otter and other hides, or furs; and the armament of Hawkeye, which now hangs before the writer, is elaborate with tassels and pendants from well-dressed beaver.

The shield is worn by many of the leading braves, and is formed of several thicknesses of hide fastened through and through about the edge with sinew, and studded with brass nails, or ornamented with silver and other bright metal.

The spear varies from five and a half to seven feet in length, having a head nearly eighteen inches long, with a small pennon; and the heel of the shaft is balanced with eagle feathers, while others are caught along the shaft, giving steadiness to the flight, and suiting the diversified tastes of the owner.

The right and left hair of the warrior or braves brought before the ear, braided or twisted, and wrapped with strings or ribbons, and falling upon the breast; while a third braid, falling behind and below the scalp-lock or tuft, often is covered with a succession of silver medallions hammered from coin, gradually diminishing in size from four inches to one inch as the series approaches the ground.

Earrings, necklaces, bracelets, and armlets are of brass, beads, bears' claws, or silver, but more generally of beautiful combinations of shells from the Pacific, seventy-five of which have been the price of a pony, and show the close relations of trade maintained between the tribes of the opposite slopes of the Rocky Mountains.

Moccasins, leggings, breechcloth, and a buffalo robe belted about the waist, leaving the breast bare, is the sole dress of the majority. Others have jackets more or less fancifully decorated with small bullet buttons, and every article of dress that an American soldier uses is at once assumed when its possession is acquired. Trowsers [sic] are, however, cut off at the hip, as their own style of protection is habitually preferred. Gifts of clothing are quickly put on; and a present of gentlemen's underclothes once given to a Pawnee was so quickly substituted for his original garments as barely to allow escape from the room during the process.

The women vary little in costume except in a wrapping something like a petticoat or skirt, but wear less paint. The hair parting is, however, invariably painted vermilion when visiting or in full dress, and cheeks, chin, and arms have their share of brilliant tints. Warriors, squaws, and children alike use the bow and arrow, but the Women are peculiarly apt with knife and hatchet. The youngsters have a javelin exercise which is admirably fitted to prepare them for their future life. A small hoop is held by the thumb and forefinger of the right hand, while within the hand is the spear. The hoop is thrown forward on the ground, and the javelin is sent after and through the ring with great dexterity and success. This, with the cast of the hatchet and play of the knife, takes the place of the white boy's baseball or marbles; and the blunt-headed arrow brings down birds and small game that would be spoiled by the keener shaft.

The revolver is becoming quite common, and is used with more dexterity and skill than is the rifle. The following instance will illustrate a remarkable failure in rifle firing. Soon after Captain Fetterman arrived, he rode to the Pinery with Lieutenant Bisbee, Captain Ten Eyck, and one or two other officers who had just arrived, to see the locality. They descended to Pine Island just after the last timber-wagon had come out on the road, and in advance of their escort. They were received by a volley of from fifteen to twenty rifle shots, which were fired from a rest upon a fallen tree, at a distance of only fifty paces, as actually measured, without injury to anybody. A second volley equally failed to touch a man. A little bugle-boy brought word to the garrison that all were killed, for he saw the Indians as they fired and the officers as they disappeared. They were compelled to skirmish down the island before they could extricate themselves from the dilemma. A supporting party went out, but met them returning, and thus relieved the anxiety of the garrison.

The Indians not only use mirrors and flags for signal purposes, but many carry with them good field and spy-glasses, some of English styles, procured from Canada, and others are supplied by traders on the frontier.

The domestic life of the Indian, with the barbarity of the sun-dance and the filth of his home, have been often described; but the plenitude of furs in the land of Absaraka have furnished peculiar facilities for adornment and somewhat better wardrobes than are usual nearer the Lower Missouri and Mississippi waters. Their tepah (tepee, or lodge) is the model from which the Sibley tent was derived, and will accommodate several families; but nothing else on the face of the earth will furnish a more curious medley of contents than does a tepah where two or three families, of all ages and sizes, with all their worldly goods and hopes are huddled, piled, and crammed about its fire, and where the fitful wind and lazy squaws are combined in the effort to smoke buffalo tongues, strips of meat, and *Injun* all together. The picture is complete, by way of contrast, if a kettle of boiling water over the fire has received a fat dog just after his throat felt the knife, and a white officer, on a pile of furs, is doing his best to show how gracefully he can endure the honors and dinner specially designed for his presence. All this, too, while other officers and ladies are cheerfully waiting outside in the glad consciousness of escape from the hospitality of a chief.

Bells, triangles, and common horns have found their way among these Indians, and they eagerly adopt from the white man whatever makes noise or show.

Appendix D

Indian Speeches Made Regarding the 1868 Fort Laramie Peace Treaty

One Horn (Miniconjou)

Speech Made to Commissioners at Fort Laramie, May 27, 1868
(Taken from Miniconjou Council proceedings)

You and ourselves all wish for peace. I am the last to have a talk with you. I have not much to say to you. This Indian country we all [the Sioux Nation] claim as ours. I have never lost the place from my view. It is our home to come back to. I like to be able to trade here, although I will not give away my land. I don't ever remember ceding any of my land to anyone. If the whites had listened to me in times back, we should never have had any of this war. But they would not. Instead they established forts and drove away the game. I am fifty-three-years-old and do not remember ever having treated the whites wrongly [but] The whites kept coming more and more through our country. I see that the whites blame the Indians, but it is you that acted wrong in the beginning. The Indians never went to your country and did wrong. This is our land, and yet you blame us for fighting for it. I remember your word that you told me. You told me whenever any wrong was done to tell you and you would make it right. I have told you that I did not like the military posts in my country, and that is what brought me over here. I would like the soldiers to leave as soon as possible that we may have plenty of game again.

You have come here in earnest to make peace, I believe. . . . There have been great lies told before you came, and it is often the fault of the interpreters. When you do send us interpreters, send good, honest men.

Iron Shell (Brûlé Sioux)

"We want you to take away the forts from the country."

Brûlé Council, Fort Laramie (April 28,1868)

Although no known Brûlés left accounts of the Fetterman Fight they were a factor in Red Cloud's War, often active in the vicinity of Fort Reno. At the 1868 Fort Laramie Treaty talks Iron Shell gave testimony to the grievances of all Lakotas.

I am getting to be an old man. . . . My father and grandfather used to be with the whites, and I have been with them, too. We used to treat them well. I do not recollect that there was any war while we were with the whites. We used to take pity on one another and did nothing bad to each other while we were together. I know that the whites are like the grass on the prairie. Anybody that takes anything from the whites must pay for it. You have come into my country without my consent and spread your soldiers all over it. I have looked around for the cause of the trouble and I cannot see that my young men were the cause of it. All the bad things that have been done, you have made the road for it. That is the truth. I love the whites. You whites went all over my country, killing my young men, and disturbing everything in my country. My heart is not made out of rock, but of flesh, but I have a strong heart. All the bad deeds that have been done I have had no hand in, neither have any of our young men. I want to hear you give us good advice. I came here for that purpose. We helped you to stop this war between us and the whites. You have put us in misery; also these old traders whom the war has stopped. We want you to set us all right and put us back the same as in old times.

We want you to take away the forts from the country. That will leave big room for the Indians to live in. If you succeed about the forests all the game will come back and we will have plenty to eat. If you want the Indian to live do that and we will have a chance to live. One above us has created all of us, the whites the same as the Indians, and he will take pity on us. Our God has put us on earth to live in the way we do, to live on game. Our great father we depend on at Washington. We do not deliberate for ourselves, and we want him to take pity on us. Do you think that our God is for us the same as for the whites? I have prayed to God and asked him to make me succeed, and He has allowed it to me. I succeeded often. Your commissioners want to make peace and take pity on the Indians. Take away all these things if you intend to make peace, and we will live happy and be at peace. All we have is the land and the sky above. This war has set an example to our young men to make war on the whites. If it had not been for that we should have been at peace all the time.

You generally pick on bad white men to give them office , which is the cause of our being put in trouble. From this our young men have learned all these bad things and we are in misery and have a hard time. Me and some others of the sensible men have been put in trouble by you. I have listened to your advice, General Sanborn, and I told the others to listen to you. You sent messengers to us last winter and we have come in to you. A few of us are inclined to do well out of way of those that are for war, and we have pushed for them to make peace with you. The Single Horn [a chief, probably Lone Horn or One Horn] went to the Missouri. I brought a chief of the Sans Arcs to you, and I want you to send word by him to the Sans Arcs when he goes away.

You are passing over the foolish acts of our young men, and we are pleased at that. Try to get all the Indians in and give them good advice and it will be all right. Push, push as hard as you can, and in that way you will take great pity on me. I want to live. It goes slow, and there are a great many Indians who are pushing for peace. Go slow yourselves and you will succeed. Get through with the Brûlés at once. I want to go home. You will have plenty of Indians in and will have enough to do. You will hear pretty much the same from the different tribes of Indians as you have heard from me. Three moons is too long in which to move the forts. I would like them to be moved before. Winter will come before that time. . . .

Those forts are all that is in the way—wagons coming backward and forward. You have taken Spotted Tail away from me and have him to go around with you. That is good. I expect you will listen to him when he talks with you. You are right in bringing him here. There are a very few who are out yet. Often when you are persecuting me and the Indians with papers we do not get well thought of. I have one recommendation, which I take good care of. I always talk to the whites in a good way and they generally listen to me. Today you tell us you will take pity on us. I have listened to it all. I will recollect all you have to say.

Our country is filling up with whites. Our great father has no sense; he lets our country be filled up. That is the way I think sometimes. Our great father is shutting up on us and making us a very small country. That is bad. For all that I have a strong heart. I have patience and pass over it, although you come over here and get all our gold, minerals, and skins. I pass over it all and do not get mad. I have always given the whites more than they have given me.

Yesterday you tell us we would have a council and last night I did not sleep; I was so glad. Now I would like you to pick some good sensible young men, from one to four, and send them men who can be depended upon. I name Blue Horse, myself, and I want him to pick the others. We have been speaking very well together, and I am glad we get along so smoothly. The last thing I have to ask you about are the forts. This is sufficient and all right. We have got through talking. Give us our share of the goods and send them over to our village. We want to get back immediately as our children are crying for food. What you are doing with the Brûlés will be a good example to the others. It will encourage them. We do not want to stay here and loaf upon you. . . .

I will always sign any treaty you ask me to do, but you have always made away with them, broke them. The whites always break them, and that is the way that war has come up.

Red Cloud

Interview with Eli S. Ricker, 1906

Three years prior to his death Red Cloud remembered the injustices of the Fort Laramie Treaty of 1868. Although he rarely spoke in detail about war with the whites, he seemed explicit in doing so regarding the treaties of his people and the Black Hills in this edited interview with Ricker. (Source: Ricker, *Voices of the American West*, 1:344–49.)

[Tablet 25]

Interview with Chief Red Cloud at Pine Ridge (in his home)

November 24, 1906. Aged 86. Clarence Three Stars, Interpreter

According to our understanding the south line of the Reservation was to be along the Niobrara River clear to the mouth, under the treaty of 1868. It has been a puzzle to me and to the Indian people how the line came to be where it has been put. They always settle questions by the treaty, and the treaty does not mention. The agreement when made was that the line was to run from the headwaters of the Niobrara to the mouth.

The first treaty that I heard of was the treaty of 1851; at that time the south line of our great Sioux Reservation was the Platte River.

Under these two treaties the first line of our great Sioux Reservation was the Platte River, and the next one was the Niobrara River.

As the line is to today we never knew how it came so to be because it is not mentioned in the treaty of 1868. The treaty does not say that we shall cede the part between the Platte River and the present line for a given sum, and we do not understand how we lost it.

The treaties of 1876 and 1888 provide that all the land not within the boundaries fixed by these treaties for our Reservation belongs to the government. In the agreement of 1876 the boundary line of the great Sioux Reservation was never fully explained to us. They told us the line was to start at the old temporary Whetstone Agency on the Missouri River, and from there to run straight due west to run parallel with the Niobrara River and twelve miles north of it, striking somewhere near Crow Butte, and from there to run to the head waters of the Cheyenne River, and then follow this stream to its mouth striking somewhere near Crow Butte, and from there right on west to the old line of the reservation as previously established; thence to the line now between the two Dakotas, striking what the Indians call Great River but called by the whites Grand River, thence down the Missouri River to the place of beginning. The Indians did not understand the white man's way of bounding tracts; they cannot understand except by landmarks like hills and streams. They did intend to sell the Black Hills, and they were not mentioned in the agreement or in any treaty as being sold to the government. I told the commissioners in the council of 1876 that I would not sell the Black Hills unless they gave me money enough to last seven generations. The commissioners did not accept this, and so we made up our minds that the Hills were not sold; but a few years afterwards we discovered that the Hills were outside the line that the government recognized as the boundary of the Sioux Reservation. The interpreters at that council were not good, and I believe they made the mistake of interpreting my proposition for money for seven generations to seven millions. The commissioners thought this was too much and so we stopped counseling with them. We never sold the Black Hills to the government.

I have been in Washington about twenty times [more like 10 times]. I understood that the white people went all the time to the Hills; it seemed that they wanted the Hills; and the Great Father sent commissioners out to talk with us about the Black Hills. The first thing they said was that the Great Father wanted to borrow the Hills for fifteen years for so much a year, but I do not remember the amount. But we did not at that time even think of loaning the Hills and we quit counseling with them and they went home. This was in 1875. Then they came out again in 1876 and they wanted to buy the Hills.

The reason we say we never sold the Hills to the government is that the value between the Hills and other land is different and so great that we never had in contemplation the sale of the Hills which were of such value, at so insignificant a price.

After I made my talk in the council Spotted Tail [Brûlé] stood up and said that as long as the earth remains as it is we will not let anybody have the Black Hills. This is all that was said and done in 1875.

I tell you these freely the things I plainly remember. There are other things not now so clear in my mind and these I do not try to speak. I try hard to remember what you want to know.

Appendix E

The Treaty of 1868
(as ratified by Congress)

Articles of a treaty made and concluded by and between Lieutenant-General William
T. Sherman, General William S. Harney, General Alfred H. Terry, General C. C.
Augur, J. B. Henderson, Nathaniel G. Taylor, John B. Sanborn, and Samuel F. Tappan,
duly appointed commissioners on the part of the United States, and the different
bands of the Sioux Nation of Indians, by their chiefs and head-men, whose names
are hereto subscribed, they being duly authorized to act in the premises.

ARTICLE 1. From this day forward all war between the parties to this agreement
shall forever cease. The Government of the United States desires peace, and its honor
is hereby pledged to keep it. The Indians desire peace, and they now pledge their
honor to maintain it.

If bad men among the whites, or among other people subject to the authority
of the United States, shall commit any wrong upon the person or property of the
Indians, the United States will, upon proof made to the agent and forwarded to the
Commissioner of Indian Affairs at Washington City, proceed at once to cause the
offender to be arrested and punished according to the laws of the United States, and
also re-imburse the injured person for the loss sustained.

If bad men among the Indians shall commit a wrong or depredation upon the
person or property of any one, white, black, or Indian, subject to the authority of the
United States, and at peace therewith, the Indians herein named solemnly agree
that they will, upon proof made to their agent and notice by him, deliver up the
wrong-doer to the United States, to be tried and punished according to its laws; and
in case they wilfully refuse so to do, the person injured shall be re-imbursed for his

loss from the annuities or other moneys due or to become due to them under this or other treaties made with the United States. And the President, on advising with the Commissioner of Indian Affairs, shall prescribe such rules and regulations for ascertaining damages under the provisions of this article as in his judgment may be proper. But no one sustaining loss while violating the provisions of this treaty or the laws of the United States shall be re-imbursed therefor.

ARTICLE 2. The United States agrees that the following district of country, to wit, viz: commencing on the east bank of the Missouri River where the forty-sixth parallel of north latitude crosses the same, thence along low-water mark down said east bank to a point opposite where the northern line of the State of Nebraska strikes the river, thence west across said river, and along the northern line of Nebraska to the one hundred and fourth degree of longitude west from Greenwich, thence north on said meridian to a point where the forty-sixth parallel of north latitude intercepts the same, thence due east along said parallel to the place of beginning; and in addition thereto, all existing reservations on the east bank of said river shall be, and the same is, set apart for the absolute and undisturbed use and occupation of the Indians herein named, and for such other friendly tribes or individual Indians as from time to time they may be willing, with the consent of the United States, to admit amongst them; and the United States now solemnly agrees that no persons except those herein designated and authorized so to do, and except such officers, agents, and employes of the Government as may be authorized to enter upon Indian reservations in discharge of duties enjoined by law, shall ever be permitted to pass over, settle upon, or reside in the territory described in this article, or in such territory as may be added to this reservation for the use of said Indians, and henceforth they will and do hereby relinquish all claims or right in and to any portion of the United States or Territories, except such as is embraced within the limits aforesaid, and except as hereinafter provided.

ARTICLE 3. If it should appear from actual survey or other satisfactory examination of said tract of land that it contains less than one hundred and sixty acres of tillable land for each person who, at the time, may be authorized to reside on it under the provisions of this treaty, and a very considerable number of such persons shall be disposed to commence cultivating the soil as farmers, the United States agrees to set apart, for the use of said Indians, as herein provided, such additional quantity of arable land, adjoining to said reservation, or as near to the same as it can be obtained, as may be required to provide the necessary amount.

ARTICLE 4. The United States agrees, at its own proper expense, to construct at some place on the Missouri River, near the center of said reservation, where timber and water may be convenient, the following buildings, to wit: a warehouse, a store-room for the use of the agent in storing goods belonging to the Indians, to cost not less than twenty-five hundred dollars; an agency-building for the residence of the agent, to cost not exceeding three thousand dollars; a residence for the physician, to cost not more than three thousand dollars; and five other buildings, for a carpenter, farmer, blacksmith, miller, and engineer, each to cost not exceeding two thousand dollars; also a schoolhouse or mission-building, so soon as a sufficient number of children can be induced by the agent to attend school, which shall not cost exceeding five thousand dollars.

The United States agrees further to cause to be erected on said reservation, near the other buildings herein authorized, a good steam circular-saw mill, with a grist-mill and shingle-machine attached to the same, to cost not exceeding eight thousand dollars.

ARTICLE 5. The United States agrees that the agent for said Indians shall in the future make his home at the agency-building; that he shall reside among them, and keep an office open at all times for the purpose of prompt and diligent inquiry into such matters of complaint by and against the Indians as may be presented for investigation under the provisions of their treaty stipulations, as also for the faithful discharge of other duties enjoined on him by law. In all cases of depredation on person or property he shall cause the evidence to be taken in writing and forwarded, together with his findings, to the Commissioner of Indian Affairs, whose decision, subject to the revision of the Secretary of the Interior, shall be binding on the parties to this treaty.

ARTICLE 6. if any individual belonging to said tribes of Indians, or legally incorporated with them, being the head of a family, shall desire to commence farming, he shall have the privilege to select, in the presence and with the assistance of the agent then in charge, a tract of land within said reservation, not exceeding three hundred and twenty acres in extent, which tract, when so selected, certified, and recorded in the "land-book," as herein directed, shall cease to be held in common, but the same may be occupied and held in the exclusive possession of the person selecting it, and of his family, so long as he or they may continue to cultivate it.

Any person over eighteen years of age, not being the head of a family, may in like manner select and cause to be certified to him or her, for purposes of cultivation, a quantity of land not exceeding eighty acres in extent, and thereupon be entitled to the exclusive possession of the same as above directed.

For each tract of land so selected a certificate, containing a description thereof and the name of the person selecting it, with a certificate endorsed thereon that the same has been recorded, shall be delivered to the party entitled to it, by the agent, after the same shall have been recorded by him in a book to be kept in his office, subject to inspection, which said book shall be known as the "Sioux Land-Book."

The President may, at any time, order a survey of the reservation, and, when so surveyed, Congress shall provide for protecting the rights of said settlers in their improvements, and may fix the character of the title held by each. The United States may pass such laws on the subject of alienation and descent of property between the Indians and their descendants as may be thought proper. And it is further stipulated that any male Indians, over eighteen years of age, of any band or tribe that is or shall hereafter become a party to this treaty, who now is or who shall hereafter become a resident or occupant of any reservation or Territory not included in the tract of country designated and described in this treaty for the permanent home of the Indians, which is not mineral land, nor reserved by the United States for special purposes other than Indian occupation, and who shall have made improvements thereon of the value of two hundred dollars or more, and continuously occupied the same as a homestead for the term of three years, shall be entitled to receive from the United States a patent for one hundred and sixty acres of land including his said improvements, the same to be in the form of the legal subdivisions of the surveys of the public lands. Upon application in writing, sustained by the proof of two disinterested witnesses, made to the register of the local land-office when the land sought to be entered is within a land district, and when the tract sought to be entered is not in any land district, then upon said application and proof being made to the Commissioner of the General Land-Office, and the right of such Indian or Indians to enter such tract or tracts of land shall accrue and be perfect from the date of his first improvements thereon, and shall continue as long as he continues his residence and improvements, and no longer. And any Indian or Indians receiving a patent for land under the foregoing provisions, shall thereby and from thenceforth become and be a citizen of the United States, and be entitled to all the privileges and immunities of such citizens, and shall, at the same time, retain all his rights to benefits accruing to Indians under this treaty.

ARTICLE 7. In order to insure the civilization of the Indians entering into this treaty, the necessity of education is admitted, especially of such of them as are or may be settled on said agricultural reservations, and they therefore pledge themselves to compel their children, male and female, between the ages of six and sixteen years, to attend school; and it is hereby made the duty of the agent for said Indians to see that this stipulation is strictly complied with; and the United States agrees that for every thirty children between said ages who can be induced or compelled to attend school, a house shall be provided and a teacher competent to teach the elementary branches of an English education shall be furnished, who will reside among said Indians, and faithfully discharge his or her duties as a teacher. The provisions of this article to continue for not less than twenty years.

ARTICLE 8. When the head of a family or lodge shall have selected lands and received his certificate as above directed, and the agent shall be satisfied that he intends in good faith to commence cultivating the soil for a living, he shall be entitled to receive seeds and agricultural implements for the first year, not exceeding in value one hundred dollars, and for each succeeding year he shall continue to farm, for a period of three years more, he shall be entitled to receive seeds and implements as aforesaid, not exceeding in value twenty-five dollars.

And it is further stipulated that such persons as commence farming shall receive instruction from the farmer herein provided for, and whenever more than one hundred persons shall enter upon the cultivation of the soil, a second blacksmith shall be provided, with such iron, steel, and other material as may be needed.

ARTICLE 9. At any time after ten years from the making of this treaty, the United States shall have the privilege of withdrawing the physician, farmer, blacksmith, carpenter, engineer, and miller herein provided for, but in case of such withdrawal, an additional sum thereafter of ten thousand dollars per annum shall be devoted to the education of said Indians, and the Commissioner of Indian Affairs shall, upon careful inquiry into their condition, make such rules and regulations for the expenditure of said sum as will best promote the educational and moral improvement of said tribes.

ARTICLE 10. In lieu of all sums of money or other annuities provided to be paid to the Indians herein named, under any treaty or treaties heretofore made, the United States agrees to deliver at the agency-house on the reservation herein named, on or before the first day of August of each year, for thirty years, the following articles, to wit:

For each male person over fourteen years of age, a suit of good substantial woolen clothing, consisting of coat, pantaloons, flannel shirt, hat, and a pair of home-made socks.

For each female over twelve years of age, a flannel skirt, or the goods necessary to make it, a pair of woolen hose, twelve yards of calico, and twelve yards of cotton domestics.

For the boys and girls under the ages named, such flannel and cotton goods as may be needed to make each a suit as aforesaid, together with a pair of woolen hose for each.

And in order that the Commissioner of Indian Affairs may be able to estimate properly for the articles herein named, it shall be the duty of the agent each year to forward to him a full and exact census of the Indians, on which the estimate from year to year can be based.

And in addition to the clothing herein named, the sum of ten dollars for each person entitled to the beneficial effects of this treaty shall be annually appropriated for a period of thirty years, while such persons roam and hunt, and twenty dollars for each person who engages in farming, to be used by the Secretary of the Interior in the purchase of such articles as from time to time the condition and necessities of the Indians may indicate to be proper. And if within the thirty years, at any time, it shall appear that the amount of money needed for clothing under this article can be appropriated to better uses for the Indians named herein, Congress may, by law, change the appropriation to other purposes; but in no event shall the amount of this appropriation be withdrawn or discontinued for the period named. And the President shall annually detail an officer of the Army to be present and attest the delivery of all the goods herein named to the Indians, and he shall inspect and report on the quantity and quality of the goods and the manner of their delivery. And it is hereby expressly stipulated that each Indian over the age of four years, who shall have removed to and settled permanently upon said reservation and complied with the stipulations of this treaty, shall be entitled to receive from the United States, for the period of four years after he shall have settled upon said reservation, one pound of meat and one pound of flour per day, provided the Indians cannot furnish their own subsistence at an earlier date. And it is further stipulated that the United States will furnish and deliver to each lodge of Indians or family of persons legally incorporated with them, who shall remove to the reservation herein described and commence farming, one good American cow, and one good well-broken pair of American oxen within sixty days after such lodge or family shall have so settled upon said reservation.

ARTICLE 11. In consideration of the advantages and benefits conferred by this treaty, and the many pledges of friendship by the United States, the tribes who are parties to this agreement hereby stipulate that they will relinquish all right to occupy permanently the territory outside their reservation as herein defined, but yet reserve the right to hunt on any lands north of North Platte, and on the Republican Fork of the Smoky Hill River, so long as the buffalo may range thereon in such numbers as to justify the chase. And they, the said Indians, further expressly agree:

1st. That they will withdraw all opposition to the construction of the railroads now being built on the plains.

2d. That they will permit the peaceful construction of any railroad not passing over their reservation as herein defined.

3d. That they will not attack any persons at home, or travelling, nor molest or disturb any wagon-trains, coaches, mules, or cattle belonging to the people of the United States, or to persons friendly therewith.

4th. They will never capture, or carry off from the settlements, white women or children.

5th. They will never kill or scalp white men, nor attempt to do them harm.

6th. They withdraw all pretence of opposition to the construction of the railroad now being built along the Platte River and westward to the Pacific Ocean, and they will not in future object to the construction of railroads, wagon-roads, mail-stations, or other works of utility or necessity, which may be ordered or permitted by the laws of the United States. But should such roads or other works be constructed on the lands of their reservation, the Government will pay the tribe whatever amount of damage may be assessed by three disinterested commissioners to be appointed by the President for that purpose, one of said commissioners to be a chief or head-man of the tribe.

7th. They agree to withdraw all opposition to the military posts or roads now established south of the North Platte River, or that may be established, not in violation of treaties heretofore made or hereafter to be made with any of the Indian tribes.

ARTICLE 12. No treaty for the cession of any portion or part of the reservation herein described which may be held in common shall be of any validity or force as against the said Indians, unless executed and signed by at least three-fourths of all the adult male Indians, occupying or interested in the same; and no cession by the tribe shall be understood or construed in such manner as to deprive, without his consent, any individual member of the tribe of his rights to any tract of land selected by him, as provided in article 6 of this treaty.

ARTICLE 13. The United States hereby agrees to furnish annually to the Indians the physician, teachers, carpenter, miller, engineer, farmer, and blacksmiths as herein contemplated, and that such appropriations shall be made from time to time, on the estimates of the Secretary of the Interior, as will be sufficient to employ such persons.

ARTICLE 14. it is agreed that the sum of five hundred dollars annually, for three years from date, shall be expended in presents to the ten persons of said tribe who in the judgment of the agent may grow the most valuable crops for the respective year.

ARTICLE 15. The Indians herein named agree that when the agency-house or other buildings shall be constructed on the reservation named, they will regard said reservation their permanent home, and they will make no permanent settlement elsewhere; but they shall have the right, subject to the conditions and modifications of this treaty, to hunt, as stipulated in Article 11 hereof.

ARTICLE 16. The United States hereby agrees and stipulates that the country north of the North Platte River and east of the summits of the Big Horn Mountains shall be held and considered to be unceded Indian territory, and also stipulates and agrees that no white person or persons shall be permitted to settle upon or occupy any portion of the same; or without the consent of the Indians first had and obtained, to pass through the same; and it is further agreed by the United States that within ninety days after the conclusion of peace with all the bands of the Sioux Nation, the military posts now established in the territory in this article named shall be abandoned, and that the road leading to them and by them to the settlements in the Territory of Montana shall be closed.

ARTICLE 17. It is hereby expressly understood and agreed by and between the respective parties to this treaty that the execution of this treaty and its ratification by the United States Senate shall have the effect, and shall be construed as abrogating and annulling all treaties and agreements heretofore entered into between the respective parties hereto, so far as such treaties and agreements obligate the United States to furnish and provide money, clothing, or other articles of property to such Indians and bands of Indians as become parties to this treaty, but no further.

In testimony of all which, we, the said commissioners, and we, the chiefs and headmen of the Brûlé band of the Sioux nation, have hereunto set our hands and seals at Fort Laramie, Dakota Territory, this twenty-ninth day of April, in the year one thousand eight hundred and sixty-eight.

N. G. Taylor, [SEAL]
W. T. Sherman, [SEAL]
Lieutenant-General.
Wm. S. Harney, [SEAL]
Brevet Major-General, U.S. Army.
John B. Sanborn, [SEAL]
S. F. Tappan, [SEAL]
C. C. Augur, [SEAL]
Brevet Major-General
Alfred H. Terry, [SEAL]
Brevet Major-General, U.S. Army.

Appendix F

Red Cloud's Speech at Cooper Union, New York, July 16, 1870

In 1870 Red Cloud visited the East, at which time he gave the following speech at a reception in his honor at Cooper Union in New York on July 16. Though a persistent critic of the government and of its Indian agents, whom he charged with graft and corruption, Red Cloud opposed agitation for further wars that, he knew, would only result in losses for his people.

MY BRETHREN AND MY FRIENDS who are here before me this day, God Almighty has made us all, and He is here to bless what I have to say to you today. The Good Spirit made us both. He gave you lands and He gave us lands; He gave us these lands; you came in here, and we respected you as brothers. God Almighty made you but made you all white and clothed you; when He made us He made us with red skins and poor; now you have come.

When you first came we were very many, and you were few; now you are many, and we are getting very few, and we are poor. You do not know who appears before you today to speak. I am a representative of the original American race, the first people of this continent. We are good and not bad. The reports that you hear concerning us are all on one side. We are always well disposed to them. You are here told that we are traders and thieves, and it is not so. We have given you nearly all our lands, and if we had any more land to give we would be very glad to give it. We have nothing more. We are driven into a very little land, and we want you now, as our dear friends, to help us with the government of the United States.

The Great Father made us poor and ignorant—made you rich and wise and more skillful in these things that we know nothing about. The Great Father, the Good

Father in Heaven, made you all to eat tame food—made us to eat wild food—gives us the wild food. You ask anybody who has gone through our country to California; ask those who have settled there and in Utah, and you will find that we have treated them always well. You have children; we have children. You want to raise your children and make them happy and prosperous; we want to raise [our children] and make them happy and prosperous. We ask you to help us to do it.

At the mouth of the Horse Creek, in 1852 [1851], the Great Father made a treaty with us by whom we agreed to let all that country open for fifty-five years for the transit of those who were going through. We kept this treaty; we never treated any man wrong; we never committed any murder or depredation until afterward the troops were sent into that country, and the troops killed our people and ill-treated them, and thus war and trouble arose; but before the troops were sent there we were quiet and peaceable, and there was no disturbance. Since that time there have been various goods sent from time to time to us, the only ones that ever reached us, and then after they reached us (very soon after) the government took them away. You, as good men, ought to help us to these goods.

Colonel Fitzpatrick of the government said we must all go to farm, and some of the people went to Fort Laramie and were badly treated. I only want to do that which is peaceful, and the Great Fathers know it, and also the Great Father who made us both. I came to Washington to see the Great Father in order to have peace and in order to have peace continue. That is all we want, and that is the reason why we are here now.

In 1868 men came out and brought papers. We are ignorant and do not read papers, and they did not tell us right what was in these papers. We wanted them to take away their forts, leave our country, would not make war, and give our traders something. They said we had bound ourselves to trade on the Missouri, and we said, no, we did not want that. The interpreters deceived us. When I went to Washington I saw the Great Father. The Great Father showed me what the treaties were; he showed me all these points and showed me that the interpreters had deceived me and did not let me know what the right side of the treaty was. All I want is right and justice. I represent the Sioux Nation; they will be governed by what I say and what I represent.

Look at me. I am poor and naked, but I am the Chief of the Nation. We do not want riches, we do not ask for riches, but we want our children properly trained and brought up. We look to you for your sympathy. Our riches will . . . do us no good; we cannot take away into the other world anything we have—we want to have love and peace. . . . We would like to know why commissioners are sent out there to do nothing but rob [us] and get the riches of this world away from us?

I was brought up among the traders and those who came out there in those early times. I had a good time for they treated us nicely and well. They taught me how to wear clothes and use tobacco, and to use firearms and ammunition, and all went on very well until the Great Father sent out another kind of men—men who drank whisky. He sent out whisky-men, men who drank and quarreled, men who were so bad that he could not keep them at home, and so he sent them out there. I have sent a great many words to the Great Father, but I don't know that they ever reach the Great Father. They were drowned on the way; therefore I was a little offended with it. The words I told the Great Father lately would never come to him, so I thought I would come and tell you myself.

And I am going to leave you today, and I am going back to my home. I want to tell the people that we cannot trust his agents and superintendents. I don't want strange people that we know nothing about. I am very glad that you belong to us. I am very glad that we have come here and found you and that we can understand one another. I don't want any more such men sent out there; who is so poor that when they come out there their first thoughts are how they can fill their own pockets.

We want preserves in our reserves. We want honest men, and we want you to help to keep us in the lands that belong to us so that we may not be a prey to those who are viciously disposed. I am going back home. I am very glad that you have listened to me, and I wish you good-bye and give you an affectionate farewell.

Notes

Introduction

1. Not to be confused with Fort Kearny II, est. June 1848 in Nebraska. Named for General Stephen Watts Kearny, this post's name is often misspelled "Kearney" in early literature, and still retains that spelling in some modern venues. Fort Phil Kearny is named for the general's nephew, Major General Philip Kearny, who was killed in Chantilly, Virginia, on September 1, 1862. See Robert W. Frazer, *Forts of the West: Military Forts and Presidios and Posts Commonly Called Forts West of the Mississippi River to 1898* (Norman: University of Oklahoma Press, 1965), 87, 183.

2. John H. Monnett, *Where a Hundred Soldiers Were Killed: The Struggle for the Powder River Country in 1866* (Albuquerque: University of New Mexico Press, 2008), xxix–xxx; Adjutant General's Office, *Chronological List of Actions, e'tc [sic] With Indians from January 15, 1837 to January 1891*, facsimile copy (Fort Collins, CO: Old Army Press, 1979), 25. Quotes are from Sgt. F. M. Fessenden to Grace R. Hebard and E. A. Brininstool, *The Bozeman Trail* (Cleveland, Ohio: Arthur H. Clark Co., 1922), 2:101–102; and Nicholas Black Elk and John G. Neihardt, *Black Elk Speaks* (Lincoln: University of Nebraska Press, Bison Books, 2000), 11. A warrior named Spotted Blue Belly (Miniconjou) claimed that three Crow warriors were among the Indians that ambushed Fetterman, but the tale cannot be corroborated with other sources. "Special Commission to Investigate the Fetterman Massacre," National Archives and Records Administration (hereafter referred to as NA), M740, May 9, 1867.

3. Margaret Irving Carrington, *Absaraka, Home of the Crows* (Philadelphia: Lippincott, 1868); Frances C. Carrington, *My Army Life: A Soldier's Wife at Fort Phil Kearny* (Philadelphia: Lippincott, 1910).

4. For example, see Stephen E. Ambrose, *Crazy Horse and Custer: The Parallel Lives of Two American Warriors* (New York: Doubleday, 1975), and Larry McMurtry, *Boone's Lick* (New York: Simon and Schuster, 2000).

5. Thanks to researcher Billy Markland of Overland Park, Kansas, many of the original military documents pertaining to the Fetterman Fight and Fort Phil Kearny are available on the Internet at http://freepages.history.rootsweb. com/-familyinformation/#fpk.

6. Although some Northern Arapahos fought Fetterman's command, none later would give interviews or otherwise state testimonies outside their own families.

7. Annual precipitation would drop 30 percent over nine of the years in the decade following 1846. See Dan Flores, *The Natural West: Environmental History of the Great Plains and Rocky Mountains* (Norman: University of Oklahoma Press, 2001), 66; G. J. Wiche, R. M. Lent, and W. F. Rannie, "Little Ice Age: Aridity in the North American Great Plains," *The Holocene* 6, no. 4 (2004). For an abstract of this article, see http://nd.water.usgs.gov/pubs/abs/abs429.html. Archaeologist Brian Fagan argues that while assessing aboriginal changes centuries ago during the early stages of the Little Ice Age may be intellectually bankrupt, the evidence shows that climate change is not gradual. It comes in sudden and dramatic shifts that bring about corresponding adaptations by human societies. Thus the changes to a drier climate occurring on the northern plains beginning circa 1846 would be sufficient to cause concern among converging populations of peoples suddenly stressing diminishing resources. See Brian Fagan, *The Little Ice Age: How Climate Made History, 1300–1850* (New York: Basic Books/ Persons, 2000), xviii. An overview of the environmental history of the Powder River Country is considered in Monnett, *Where a Hundred Soldiers Were Killed*, 12–19.

8. Pictorial comparisons of Oglala Lakota Sioux battles with Crows and whites are found in Amos Bad Heart Bull, *A Pictographic History of the Oglala Sioux*, text by Helen H. Bliss (Lincoln: University of Nebraska Press), 1967.

9. James C. Olson, *Red Cloud and the Sioux Problem* (Lincoln: University of Nebraska Press, 1965), 32–33.

Note on American Indian Testimony

1. Portions of this introduction appear in Monnett, *Where a Hundred Soldiers Were Killed*, xix–xxiv.

2. An excellent study of these ethnological concerns in Indians who remembered free life on the Plains is Sherry L. Smith, *Reimagining Indians: Native Americans through Anglo Eyes, 1880–1940* (New York: Oxford University Press, 2002).

3. Ned Blackhawk, *Violence Over the Land: Indians and Empires in the Early American West* (Cambridge, MA: Harvard University Press, 2006), 11.

4. The original Ledger at Harvard (MS AM 2337) may be viewed at the Harvard Library website at http://pds.lib.harvard.edu/pds/view/12151780. The drawings have recently been published as Castle McLaughlin, *A Lakota War Book from the Little Bighorn* (Cambridge, MA: Peabody Museum Press, 2013). For Northern Nation see Kingsley Bray, *Crazy Horse: A Lakota Life* (Norman: University of Oklahoma Press, 2006), 162.

5. Lee H. Whittlesey, *Storytelling in Yellowstone: Horse and Buggy Tour Guides* (Albuquerque: University of New Mexico Press, 2007), 15, 20. Since the 1940s many stories regarding the great Oglala warrior Crazy Horse have entered both oral and written testimony.

6. For example, General John B. Sanborn reported to the commission charged with investigating the Fetterman Fight that where the infantry were killed, "[t]here were no indications of a severe struggle . . . all the bodies lay within a space not exceeding thirty-five feet in diameter. No empty cartridge shells were about and there were some full cartridges." Sanborn's report is not corroborated by either the eyewitness Indian accounts or the archaeology at the site over the years. His report is for an army general unbelievably discredited by his apparent ignorance of army ordnance in 1866. If Sanborn was speaking of an infantry position, of course there were no "shell casings" as the infantry utilized .58-caliber Springfield *muzzleloaders* that had no shell casings. Paper pouches with powder were tied in manufacturing to "Minnie balls" and the ball and pouch were rammed down the barrel with the pouch breaking open by ramrod and serving as a "wad" for the charge. Archaeology has proven that many Minnie balls have been recovered over the years between the monument and a hundred yards down range from the monument. If there were indeed unfired "shells" at the site these were from the Spencer rifles of the cavalry, which used copper and brass cartridges, indicating, like the Indians claim, that some cavalry retreated south to the monument where infantry fought fiercely but certainly left no ballistic evidence around the position. Unfired bullets of any variety, the Indians indicate, were picked and taken by warriors as there was a significant amount for their use (see Part 3). Officer reports are from *Records of the Special Commission to Investigate the Fetterman Massacre and the State of Indian Affairs, 1867*, NA, RG 75, M740. Cited also in John D. McDermott, *Red Cloud's War: The Bozeman Trail, 1866–1868* (Norman: Arthur H. Clark, 2010), 1:226n31. For distributions of ballistic artifacts: information is from a conversation

with Robert Wilson, curator, Fort Phil Kearny State Historic Site, June 29, 2014. At this writing, artifact maps are copyrighted and unavailable to the public.

7. *Records of the Special Commission to Investigate the Fetterman Massacre and the State of Indian Affairs, 1867.*

8. Jerome A. Greene, ed., *Lakota and Cheyenne: Indian Views of the Great Sioux War* (Norman: University of Oklahoma Press, 1994), xxi–xxiv.

9. Ibid.

10. Lydia Whirlwind Soldier, review of *The Journey of Crazy Horse*, by Joseph Marshall III: Ebsco Host Research Databases, Bibliography of Native North Americans, #10525505 (Summer 2005).

11. Bernard Fontana, "American Indian Oral History: An Anthropologists Note," *History and Theory* 8, no. 3 (1969): 367.

12. Gordon M. Day, "Oral History as Complement," *Ethnohistory* 19, no. 2 (Spring 1972): 99n55.

13. Joyce Ann Kievit, "A Discussion of Scholarly Responsibilities to Indigenous Communities," *American Indian Quarterly* 27, nos. 1 and 2 (Winter and Spring 2003): 3–45.

Part One

1. For this dubious claim that White Bull personally slayed Custer, see James H. Howard, ed., *The Warrior Who Killed Custer: The Personal Narrative of Chief Joseph White Bull* (Lincoln: University of Nebraska Press, 1968).

2. Stanley Vestal, *Warpath: The True Story of the Fighting Sioux Told in a Biography of Chief White Bull* (1934; repr., Lincoln: University of Nebraska Press, Bison Book edition, 1984), 50–69.

Chapter 1

1. Walter S. Campbell Papers, *Oklahoma Federation of Labor Collection*, M 452, Box 106, Folder 53 (Norman: Western History Collections, University of Oklahoma Libraries), 17–27.

2. The Indian accounts vary, giving the number of decoys as being from six to ten.

3. This verbatim irony was not uttered by Fetterman in 1866 but rather appears in the work of writer Cyrus Townsend Brady in 1904. Fetterman's actual boast, "[A] company of regulars could whip a thousand, and a regiment could whip the whole array of hostile tribes," was common parlor rhetoric among a majority of officers without experience fighting Indians on the frontier and does not carry the irony of the number 80. That was the number of men Fetterman died with,

and that would stereotype him for more than a century to come. For the actual boast see Margaret Carrington, *Absaraka*, 171.

4. John Collier was superintendent of Indian Affairs under Franklin Roosevelt. For the Indian Reorganization Act and subsequent legislation stemming from it, see William C. Canby, *American Indian Law in a Nutshell* (Eagan, MN: West Publishing, 1994).

5. For the campaigns of 1865, see John D. McDermott, *Circle of Fire: The Indian War of 1865* (Mechanicsburg, PA: Stackpole Books, 2003); David E. Wagner, *Powder River Odyssey: Nelson Cole's Western Campaign of 1865* (Norman: Arthur H. Clark, 2009), and David E. Wagner, *Patrick Connor's War: The 1865 Powder River Indian Expedition* (Norman: Arthur H. Clark, 2010).

6. Campbell's information for Fetterman's actions is taken from "Records of the Special Commission to Investigate the Fetterman Massacre and the State of Indian Affairs, 1867," M740, RG 75, Records of the Bureau of Indian Affairs, NA. The surgeon's report for the autopsy on the bodies of the officers is also found in this record. The report clearly states that a war club crushed Fetterman's head and then the assailant cut his throat to the cervical spine. Captain Brown's body showed a gunshot wound to the temple. The two officers did not commit "joint" suicide but Brown may have done so. Fetterman's body had no gunshot wounds.

7. Royal B. Hassrick, *The Sioux: Life and Customs of a Warrior Society* (Norman: University of Oklahoma Press, 1964), 72–94.

8. Campbell's notes are exclusively of White Bull's personal experiences. Military accounts are interjected in between White Bull's statements in the manuscript but not in the field notes. A sense of time, motion, distance, and direction is occasionally missing in both. For comparison, see Oklahoma Foundation of Labor Collection, Walter S. Campbell Papers, M452, Box 5, Folder 2, notes 17–21, Western History Collections, University of Oklahoma, Norman, Oklahoma.

9. Conversation with Fort Phil Kearny State Historic Site curator Robert C. Wilson, June 29, 2014.

10. In Campbell's second book (writing as Stanley Vestal), *Warpath and Council Fire: The Plains Indians Struggle for Survival in War and Diplomacy* (New York: Random House, 1948), 89–106, the sequence and geography becomes more generalized. Strangely, much of Campbell's commentary is close to undocumented narrative and draws heavily on paraphrases from Grinnell's interviews with the Cheyenne White Elk rather than his friend White Bull. White Bull died in 1937. In addition to Carrington's and others reports from RG 75, M740, the most recent synthesized reconstructions of the fight are found in Monnett, *Where A Hundred Soldiers Were Killed*, Smith, *Give Me Eighty Men*, and McDermott, *Red Cloud's War*. White Bull and Campbell are in denial regarding the subject of mutilation.

The mutilations of enemies killed in battle were "insult wounds" to strike fear in still living enemies. Mutilation for purposes of inflicting handicaps in the afterlife is largely a myth. See Richard J. Chacon and David H. Dye, eds., *The Taking and Displaying of Human Body Parts as Trophies by Amerindians* (New York: Springer, 2007); and Hassrick, *The Sioux*, 171–72.

11. Raymond DeMallie, introduction to Vestal, *Warpath: The True Story of the Fighting Sioux*, v.

Part Two

1. Bad Heart Bull/Bliss, *A Pictographic History of the Oglala Sioux*, 117–87. Amos Bad Heart Bull, although born in 1869, rendered his drawings of battles that predated his birth from descriptions and with the approval of Oglalas who participated in the fights. For the Crow War of 1856–59 see Brian L. Keefe, *Red Was the Blood of Our Forefathers: Episodes from Crow Indian Intertribal Warfare* (Caldwell, ID: Caxton Press), 220–302. See also Brian L. Keefe, "The Battle of Rainy Butte: A Significant Sioux-Crow Encounter of 1858," *The Brand Book* 39, nos. 1–2, English Westerners Society (2006). The statement of Black Horse is cited as being in a microfilm file titled "Margaret Carrington," in the University of Michigan Libraries, 1979; Keefe, "The Battle of Rainy Butte," 223. The ecological history of the Powder River Country prior to Red Cloud's War is covered in Monnett, *Where a Hundred Soldiers Were Killed*, 12–21.

2. Likely, Crazy Horse, George Sword, American Horse, and Young Man Afraid of His Horses were the last Oglala shirtwearers in American history.

3. An excellent scholarly source for understanding the political organization and operation of Oglala society is Catherine Price, *The Oglala People, 1841–1879* (Lincoln: University of Oklahoma Press, 1996), and Catherine Price, "Lakotas and Euroamericans: Contrasted Concepts of 'Chieftainship' and Decision Making," *Ethnohistory* 41, no. 3 (Summer 1994): 447–463. See also the works of ethnohistorian, Raymond J. DeMallie, including "Sioux Ethnohistory: A Methodological Critique," *Journal of Ethnic Studies* 4 (Fall 1976): 77–84, and "American Indian Treaty Making," *American Indian Journal* 3 (January 1977): 2–10.

4. Price, *Oglala People*, 61–62.

Chapter 2

1. This story told by Black Elk of his earliest subconscious memory is excerpted from John G. Neihardt and Black Elk, *Black Elk Speaks as told through John G. Neihardt (Flaming Rainbow) by Nicholas Black Elk* (Lincoln: University of Nebraska Press, Bison Books edition, 1979), 6–8, 11.

2. For the exodus from the Tongue River Camps see Monnett, *Where a Hundred Soldiers Were Killed*, 181–82.

3. Red Cloud was a *blotahunka* at this time, not an *itancan*.

4. Black Elk, as told through John G. Neihardt (Flaming Rainbow), *Black Elk Speaks: Being the Life Story of a Holy man of the Oglala Sioux*, Premier edition (Albany, NY: State University of New York Press, Excelsior Editions, 2008), 7–10.

Chapter 3

1. John G. Neihardt Collection, Western History Collections, University of Missouri, Columbia.

2. Oglalas mostly took up positions at the north end of Massacre Ridge in the shrubbery along Peno Creek while Cheyennes and Arapahos, and some Oglalas, staged in the gullies farther up on the west side of the road, and Miniconjous gathered in the ravines on the east side of the Bozeman road.

3. John G. Neihardt Collection, Western History Collections, University of Missouri, Columbia. Neihardt's original transcriptions are in the Neihardt Collection, University of Missouri, Columbia. In 1984 ethnohistorian/anthropologist Raymond J. DeMallie published these transcriptions in *The Sixth Grandfather: Black Elk's Teachings Given to John G. Neihardt* (Lincoln: University of Nebraska Press, 1984), which DeMallie edited. "Red Cloud was over all of us" refers to Red Cloud being the main *blotahunka* of the Oglalas in the fight.

4. Again, Fire Thunder means Red Cloud was the principle *blotahunka* of the Oglalas at this battle, not an *itancan*. This account from Black Elk/Neihardt, *Black Elk Speaks*, Premier ed., 10–11.

Chapter 4

1. For a good overview of the life and career of American Horse, see Elbert D. Belish, "American Horse (Washechun-Tashunka): The Man Who Killed Fetterman," *Annals of Wyoming* 63, no.2 (Spring 1991): 54–67.

2. Federal Bureau of Ethnology, "Pictographs of North American Indians," *Fourth Annual Report* (Washington, D.C.: Government Printing office, 1886), 140.

3. Josephine Waggoner, *Witness: A Hunkpapha Historian's Strong-Heart Song of the Lakotas*, edited and with an introduction by Emily Levine (Lincoln: University of Nebraska Press, 2013), 460.

4. American Horse Winter Count, Ms. 12, book 08746923–0874993, National Anthropological Archives, Smithsonian, Washington, D.C.

5. Eli S. Ricker, interview with American Horse, June 16, 1905, "Eli S. Ricker Papers, Tablet 16," Nebraska State Historical Society. Today, the entire interview may

conveniently be found in *Voices of the American West*, vol. 1, *The Indian Interviews of Eli S. Ricker, 1903–1919*, edited by Richard E. Jensen (Lincoln: University of Nebraska Press, 2005), 277–83.

6. For example, see Carrington's statement in Dee Brown, *Fort Phil Kearny, An American Saga* (later renamed, *The Fetterman Massacre* over Brown's objection) (Lincoln: University of Nebraska Press, Bison Books edition, 1971), 189.

7. Testimony of Assistant Surgeon Horton, "Records Relating to the Investigations of the Ft. Philip Kearney [*sic*] (or Fetterman Massacre)," July 25, 1866, RG 75, M740, roll 1 of 1, NA.

8. See also Belish, "American Horse, The Man Who Killed Fetterman," 54–67.

9. Sheldon Papers, Box 59, *American Horse*.

10. Sidney Sheldon Papers, Box 59, MS 2039, *American Horse*, Nebraska State Historical Society.

11. For the narrative of this demonstration in front of the fort described by the Cheyenne White Elk, see Monnett, *Where a Hundred Soldiers Were Killed*, 124–25.

12. Ricker, interview with George Sword, June 29, 1906, Tablet 16, and Interview with George Colhoff, undated, 1906, Tablet 17, Ricker Papers, Nebraska State Historical Society.

Chapter 5

1. All the short interviews are from the Sidney Sheldon Papers, Box 59, MS 2039, Folder 2, Nebraska State Historical Society.

2. For example, Little Wolf's Crooked Lance warrior society, following the Fetterman Fight, wore the uniforms taken from the bodies of Fetterman's men when fighting after 1866. They rode in formations emulating American cavalry formations. Military uniforms, especially officers' uniforms, were worn often in battle by men of many tribes, uniforms either taken from the dead or given out as presents in treaty talks. Indians also valued bugles, using them in battles in imitation of American cavalry. The photographic record is profuse with important Indian male warriors wearing uniform coats and even hats. See George B. Grinnell, *The Cheyenne Indians: Their History and Ways of Life* (New Haven: Yale University Press, 1923), 2:59.

3. A reporter for the *Rapid City Journal* on July 7, 1907, told of Crazy Horse and others being "sent by Red Cloud" to feint on the fort by riding around it to lure the soldiers out and then led them over Lodge Trail Ridge. The military reports concur that Indians appeared around the fort near Piney Creek but a howitzer shot dispersed them. In any event, the demonstration in front of the fort, the feint on the wood train, and the decoys on Lodge Trail Ridge may all be viewed as

separate decoy movements to draw the soldiers out of the fort. But Rocky Bear's statement forty-one years after the battle is the only verifiable eyewitness account in a warrior's exact words mentioning Crazy Horse as being one member of the group demonstrating in front of the fort. Certainly this statement is an example of what Crazy Horse might do but it is uncorroborated and unverified by other eyewitnesses, which is unusual given his reputation by 1907.

Chapter 6

1. R. Eli Paul, ed., *Autobiography of Red Cloud, War Leader of the Oglalas* (Helena: Montana Historical Society Press, 1997).
2. The best Red Cloud Biography remains Robert W. Larson's *Red Cloud: Warrior Statesman of the Lakota Sioux* (Norman: University of Oklahoma Press, 1997). For the traditional sources on Red Cloud, see George E. Hyde, *Red Cloud's Folk* (Norman: University of Oklahoma Press, 1937) and James C. Olson, *Red Cloud and the Sioux Problem* (Lincoln: University of Nebraska Press, Bison Books edition, 1965). For his warrior society affiliation see McLaughlin, *A Lakota War Book*, 84–85.
3. Paul, *Autobiography of Red Cloud*, 32.
4. Larson, *Red Cloud*, 135.
5. M. Carrington, *Absaraka*, 79.
6. F. Carrington, *My Army Life*, 291–92. The second Mrs. Carrington's book is, in general, largely a paraphrase of that of the first Mrs. Carrington's book.
7. Ibid., 46–47.
8. M. Carrington, *Absaraka*, 171. For a discussion of the boast and its ironic impact, see Monnett, *Where a Hundred Soldiers Were Killed*, 231–36.
9. Cyrus Townsend Brady, *Indian Fights and Fighters* (New York: McClure Phillips, 1904), 27.
10. Doane Robinson, *A History of the Dakota or Sioux Indians* (Minneapolis: Ross & Hague, 1956, reprint), 536–37.
11. A good example is a recent millennial quasi-biography written for the mass trade market purporting to be the "Untold Story of Red Cloud," by authors Bob Drury and Tom Clavin. Nothing previously "untold" is offered and much of the substance is misleading. The book is scantily documented with endnotes consisting of trailing phrases. The danger inherent in the book is that the authors attribute to Red Cloud too much centralized power and leadership exercised over the entire coalition of Indians in the Fetterman Fight. Certainly, they capture Red Cloud's mood in 1866, but for the sake of writing a lively story for mass-market consumption, they take far too many liberties with assertions that cannot be

substantiated or logically argued with the weight of known evidence. See Bob Drury and Tom Clavin, *The Heart of Everything That Is: The Untold Story of Red Cloud, An American Legend.* (New York: Simon and Schuster, 2013).

12. Walter S. Campbell Papers, M452, Box 106, Folder 45, Western History Collections, University of Oklahoma, Norman, Oklahoma.

13. Sheldon Papers, Box 59, *George Sword.*

14. Hyde, *Red Cloud's Folk*, 146.

15. Price, *Oglala People*, 101.

16. Ibid.

17. Clearly, Cook remembered Red Cloud relating a story of his leadership in the Fetterman Fight. James H. Cook, *Fifty Years on the Old Frontier* (New Haven: Yale University Press, 1923), 184–85, 198.

18. Grace Raymond Hebard and E. A. Brininstool, *The Bozeman Trail* (Lincoln: University of Nebraska Press, Bison Books edition, 1990), 1:342–43. Also see Post Returns, Fort Phil Kearny, December 1866, RG 94, NA.

19. Sheldon Papers, Box 59 White Horse Account, July 30, 1903.

20. Sheldon Papers, Box 59, Rocky Bear Account, no date.

21. Sheldon Papers, Box 59, Red Fly Account, July 30, 1903.

22. Sheldon Papers, Box 59, American Horse Account, July 30, 1903.

23. Charles Eastman (Ohiyesa), *Indian Heroes and Great Chieftains* (Boston: Little, Brown and Company, 1918), 7. Scholars through the years have questioned the precise wording of Eastman's historical memory. But in this quote he captures the angry thoughts that must have been going through Red Cloud's mind in 1866.

24. Sheldon Papers, Box 59, Red Cloud Account, June 18, 1903.

25. Eli Ricker, interview with Chief Red Cloud at Pine Ridge (in his home), November 24, 1906, Clarence Three Stars, interpreter, Ricker Interviews, Tablet 25, Nebraska State Historical Society; *Voices of the American West*, 1: 344–47. Other parts of the Ricker interview with Red Cloud concerning the Treaty of Fort Laramie are located in Appendix D.

26. Dorothy M. Johnson, *The Bloody Bozeman: The Perilous Trail to Montana's Gold* (New York: McGraw-Hill, 1971), 309. This author does not wish to risk crediting any "first author" who may have used the term "Red Cloud's War" originally in a published work.

27. Rocky Bear's account, Sheldon Papers, Box 59, Item 2.3; Bray, *Crazy Horse*, 102; Monnett, *Where a Hundred Soldiers Were Killed*, 144.

28. For an excellent photographic history of Red Cloud's most important years as a diplomat, see Frank H. Goodyear III, *Red Cloud: Photographs of A Lakota Chief* (Lincoln: University of Nebraska Press, 2003).

29. An "unnamed Indian" spoke these words to Reverend William J. Cleveland at a meeting of the Indian Rights Association in 1891. See *Ninth Annual Report of the Indian Rights Association, 1891*, 29. See also Robert M. Utley, *The Indian Frontier, 1846–1890*, rev. ed. (Albuquerque: University of New Mexico Press, 2003), 283n15. Utley ascribes the statement to "an old Sioux man" (Utley, 239). See also *Records of the Indian Rights Association*, Collection 1523, State Historical Society of Pennsylvania, "Ninth Annual Report," 29.

Chapter 7

1. Earlier versions of this essay appeared in John H. Monnett, "Prelude to Little Bighorn: Crazy Horse and the Fetterman Fight," *Greasy Grass* 24 (May 2008): 3–14, and in Monnett, *Where a Hundred Soldiers Were Killed*, 209–219. In both these versions I questioned the authenticity and veracity of early sources attesting to Crazy Horse's very presence in the battle. In this specific regard, I am mistaken.
2. A good example of the exploits of Crazy Horse based almost solely on oral tradition is Joseph Marshall, *The Journey of Crazy Horse: A Lakota History* (New York: Viking, 2004).
3. Bridger makes no mention of Crazy Horse at this time in print sources.
4. Biographer Kingsley Bray gives Crazy Horse's birth year as 1840, making him twenty-six in 1866. Black Elk claims he was nineteen. See Bray, *Crazy Horse*, 5–6, and Black Elk/Neihardt, *Black Elk Speaks*, 8. Crazy Horse's close friend Chips told Eli S. Ricker that Crazy Horse was born in 1840. Chips interview, February 14, 1907, Ricker Papers, Nebraska State Historical Society, Tablet 18.
5. Vestal (Walter Campbell), *Warpath: The True Story of the Fighting Sioux*, 68. Some readers may find it surprising that Campbell did not make more of White Bull's brief mention of Crazy Horse in 1866, given that he tried his best to convince his readers that White Bull was the warrior to personally kill Custer a decade later. James H. Howard made the same claim when he translated and edited White Bull's drawings in *The Warrior Who Killed Custer*. Ethnohistorian Raymond DeMallie, in his introduction to the Bison Books edition of Vestal's *Warpath: The True Story of the Fighting Sioux*, discredited Campbell's assertion that White Bull killed Custer. There are no references to such in the Campbell Papers. See Campbell Papers, Western History Collection, University of Oklahoma Library, Norman, Oklahoma, Box 105 (White Bull notes). Stanley Vestal, "The Man Who Killed Custer," *American Heritage* 8, no. 2 (Feb. 1957): 4–9, 90–91; James H. Howard, "The White Bull Manuscript," *Plains Anthropologist* 6, no. 12, part 2 (1961): 115–16; Raymond Bucko in James H. Howard, ed. *Lakota Warrior: Joseph White Bull* (Lincoln: University of Nebraska Press, Bison Book Edition, 1998),

v–xix. For a short overview see Charles Vollan, "White Bull, Joseph (1849–1947)" in David J. Wishart, ed. *Encyclopedia of Great Plains Indians* (Lincoln: University of Nebraska Press, 2007), 218–19. Campbell's lack of concern for the stature of Crazy Horse at the Fetterman Fight, while placing so much fame on White Bull at Little Big Horn, only furthers the question as to Crazy Horse's presence as a decoy on Lodge Trail Ridge.

6. Robinson, *A History of the Dakota*, 361n603. This author has been unable to find any reference to a warrior named White Bear as having participated in the Fetterman Fight. Could Robinson have meant White Bull? Roman Nose was a ubiquitous name among the Cheyennes and other Plains Indians. But the famous Crooked Lance warrior was more prominent than any other individual of that name prior to his death at Beecher Island in 1868. Robinson could not have meant any other.

7. For a thorough examination of Crazy Horse as a shirtwearer see, Bray, *Crazy Horse*, 119–40.

8. Thomas B. Marquis, *Wooden Leg, a Warrior Who Fought Custer* (Lincoln: University of Nebraska Press, Bison Books edition, 1986), 14–15.

9. Joe De Barthe, ed., *Life and Adventures of Frank Grouard* (Norman: University of Oklahoma Press, 1958), 181. See also Frank Grouard, "An Indian Scout's Recollections of Crazy Horse," *Nebraska History Magazine* 12 (Jan.–Mar., 1929): 72; and White Bull's account in Vestal, *Warpath: The True Story of the Fighting Sioux*, 54.

10. George B. Grinnell, *The Fighting Cheyennes* (Norman: University of Oklahoma Press, 1982), 234–44.

11. Bent to Hyde, December 5, 1904, April 19, 1912, May 20, 1913 (Coe Collection, Yale University Libraries); June 7, 1913 (Bent Collection, Denver Public Library); Bent in George F. Hyde, *Life of George Bent Written from His Letters* (Norman: University of Oklahoma Press, 1968), 343–46; Hyde, *Red Cloud's Folk*, 146.

12. Hyde, *Red Cloud's Folk*, 146–47. Hyde wrote: "White Bull of the Miniconjous was present, and he states that Crazy Horse led." Two Moons' account in Hyde, *Life of George Bent*, 343–46, makes no mention of Crazy Horse being in the fight. Two Moons' earlier account, which makes no mention of Crazy Horse, is from Bent to Hyde, December 5, 1904. Two Moons denied personally being in the fight in a statement to Grinnell, September 6, 1908. See Peter John Powell, *People of the Sacred Mountain: A History of the Northern Cheyenne Chiefs and Warrior Societies, 1830–1879, With an Epilog, 1969–1974* (San Francisco: Harper & Row, 1981), 1:666n8. For Hyde's claim that Crazy Horse made his reputation in the 1870s in *Life of George Bent*, see p. 347.

13. Chips interview, 1907, Ricker Papers, Nebraska State Historical Society, Tablet 18.

14. Colhoff to Ricker, interview, 1906, Ricker Papers, Nebraska State Historical Society, Tablet 17.

15. George Sword (Hunts the Enemy) (Owns Sword) interview, 1907, Tablet 16; American Horse Interview, 1906, Tablet 16; George W. Colhoff interview, circa 1906, Tablet 17; all are to be found in the Ricker Papers, Nebraska State Historical Society. American Horse told Ricker that some Oglalas viewed Crazy Horse as dangerous in 1877. Certainly there was rivalry and jealousy of Crazy Horse at that time. This might account for American Horse's lack of detail about Crazy Horse at the Fetterman Fight in his interview with Ricker.

16. For easy access to the Hinman interviews as well as most other early interviews pertaining to Crazy Horse, see Richard G. Hardorff, *The Death of Crazy Horse: A Tragic Episode in Lakota History* (Lincoln: University of Nebraska Press, Bison Books Edition, 2001), or see R. Eli Paul, *The Nebraska Indian Wars Reader, 1865–1877* (Lincoln: University of Nebraska Press, 1998), 180–216.

17. Robinson, *A History of the Dakota*, 361n603; Vestal, *Warpath: The True Story of the Fighting Sioux*, 68; Hyde, *Red Cloud's Folk*, 146.

18. Other glaring examples are Marshall, *Journey of Crazy Horse*, 145–152; Members of the Fort Phil Kearny Bozeman Trail Association, *Portraits of Fort Phil Kearny* (Banner, WY: Fort Phil Kearny/Bozeman Trail Association, 1993), 74–79; and Hardorff, *Death of Crazy Horse*, 34n16.

19. Mari Sandoz, *Crazy Horse: Strange Man of the Oglalas* (Lincoln: University of Nebraska Press, 1942), 199–201.

20. Ibid., 199–200; Mari Sandoz, *Hostiles and Friendlies: Selected Short Writings of Mari Sandoz* (Lincoln: University of Nebraska Press, Bison Books edition, 1992), 79; Mari Sandoz Papers, Nebraska State Historical Society.

21. M452, Box 5, Folder 2, Campbell Papers, University of Oklahoma Libraries.

22. Dee Brown, *Fort Phil Kearny: An American Saga* (Lincoln: University of Nebraska Press, Bison Books edition, 1962), 78.

23. Stephen Ambrose, *Crazy Horse and Custer: The Parallel Lives of Two American Warriors* (New York: Doubleday, 1975), 223, 462n14. Drury and Clavin, *The Heart of Everything That Is*, 329. There is no previous secondary source, oral source told to the author, and certainly no eyewitness sources attesting to Crazy Horse "mooning" on Lodge Trail Ridge. This author has found no evidence of American Indians "mooning" U.S. soldiers in combat, although the practice does have origins in the ancient world. By the time Fetterman committed to turning away from the wood road he did not need to "lured" over Lodge Trail Ridge.

24. Powell, *People of the Sacred Mountain*, 1:456.
25. Larry McMurtry, *Crazy Horse: A Life* (New York: Viking, 1999), 59.
26. Mike Sajna, *Crazy Horse: The Life behind the Legend* (New York: John Wiley, 2000), 200.
27. Marshall's convictions of the explicit validity of latter generation oral tradition passed down through tribal elders are admirable. But trade market published oral histories are perhaps unfortunately ahead of their time in gaining acceptance with wider audiences outside Indian country. Although Marshall lists tribal storytellers in his credits, he does not footnote specific events as to the individual oral source. See Marshall, *The Journey of Crazy Horse*, 145–71, 295–98. Another source of modern oral tradition presented to the general public by descendants of Crazy Horse is *The Authorized Biography of Crazy Horse and His Family*, a DVD in four parts produced by William Matson and Mark Frethem, in association with Tȟašúŋke Witcó Tiwahe (Reel Contact, 2007). Part Two, "Defending the Homeland Prior to the 1868 Treaty," portrays Crazy Horse's exploits at the Fetterman Fight vis-à-vis vintage Sandoz.
28. Bray's closest sources for Crazy Horse being chosen as leader of the decoys, and the role of the decoys in general, are the previously examined Ricker 1906 and 1907 interviews with American Horse and George Sword (Hunts the Enemy) (Owns Sword). Neither of these Oglalas mentions anything about Crazy Horse being in the Fetterman Fight in their interviews with Ricker. The third source Bray cites is a secondary account, an un-footnoted statement by Powell in *People of the Sacred Mountain*, 1: 456, that Lakota chiefs chose Crazy Horse to lead the decoys. Powell later on the same page cites Grinnell, *The Fighting Cheyennes*, 238–39, claiming that Crazy Horse rode off with the decoys. Grinnell makes no such statement in his book or in his papers and correspondence in the Southwest Museum. Again, there are simply no solid original testimonies available to the public or to historians establishing Crazy Horse as a decoy, and certainly there are no original testimonies ascribing any long, detailed exploits to him in the battle save Grouard's secondhand claim that Lone Bear died in his arms following the fight. The dramatic differential between Crazy Horse's *assumed* actions given a general knowledge of Lakota culture and what details can actually be verified is an example of some of the differences of viewpoint experienced today between ethnohistorians and academic historians. See Bray, *Crazy Horse*, 97–102, 419n44.
29. Interviews with Eagle Hawk, American Horse, Rocky Bear, and Red Fly. Sheldon Papers, Nebraska State Historical Society, Box 59.
30. *Rapid City Journal*, July 7, 1907.

31. Robert Wilson, on-site historian and curator at the Fort Phil Kearny State Historic Site, believes that numerous warriors down Lodge Trail Ridge made taunting feints after the trap was sprung. Conversation with the author, June 10, 2014.

32. Eastman, *Indian Heroes*, 94.

33. Francis Taunton of the English Westerners Society strongly suggested this possibility in a review of Bray's *Crazy Horse*, "The Crow's Nest," *The Journal of the Custer Association of Great Britain* 9, no.1 (2009).

34. The more recent being Thomas Powers, *The Killing of Crazy Horse* (New York: Alfred A. Knopf, 2010) and Drury and Clavin, *The Heart of Everything That Is*.

35. The alleged presence of all but a few important warriors at the Fetterman Fight is another example of the differences between historical versus ethnohistorical methodologies for evaluating sources. But rather than detract from historical interpretation and dialog, such comparisons serve rather to stimulate debate. Who *was* there? Who was *not* there? Who did what? As with Little Big Horn, such mysteries surround events like the Fetterman Fight more pervasively, it seems, than many other topics in American history that are much greater and more significant. And that form of scholarly debate is what keeps the military frontiers of the West and the story of Native American resistance to colonialism one of the most intriguing topics in the American mind.

36. Testimony of Mitch Bouyer, *Records of the Special Commission to Investigate the Fetterman Massacre*, NA, RG 75, M740, Records of the Bureau of Indian Affairs, 1867, Exhibit F, 3–4.

PART THREE

1. E. Adamson Hoebel, *The Cheyennes: Indians of the Great Plains* (New York: Holt, Rinehart and Winston, 1960), 1–2.

2. Ibid.

3. Ibid., 37.

4. These names are the designations translated by Grinnell, *The Cheyenne Indians*, 2:48. Some of the military society names differ among ethnologists and historians. Bent/Hyde recognize the Pointed-Lance Men, often called Crooked Lances, while Dorsey in 1905 recognizes the Hoof-Rattle Warriors and Coyote Warriors. See Hyde, *Life of George Bent*, 22n2, and George A. Dorsey, *The Cheyenne: Ceremonial Organization* (Chicago: Field Columbian Museum, Publication 99, Anthropological Series 9, no. 1), 18–20.

5. Following the tribal split between Northern and Southern Cheyennes, especially beginning in 1864, the southern bands became very factionalized between war

and peace. Meanwhile, the Dog Men, who were for war with whites, became almost a completely southern military society that attracted other southern, and even, northern allies to their cause in Kansas, Nebraska, and Colorado. Some ethnologists consider them a completely separate patrilineal "band" by the 1860s, since their members and other followers brought wives to the society's camps and villages year-round. Traditionally, a warrior might raid with his military society during summer then customarily return to his matrilineal band during the winter. This custom caused confusion in the south during the 1860s at such places as Washita, where so-called "hostiles" would return to their wives' villages and mix with peace-faction Cheyennes, thus making problematic winter attacks on those villages by white soldiers.

6. John Monnett, *Tell Them We Are Going Home: The Odyssey of the Northern Cheyennes* (Norman: University of Oklahoma Press, 2001), 12.

7. Early Cheyenne trade relations are examined in Joseph Jablow, *The Cheyenne in Indian Trade Relations, 1795–1840* (Lincoln: University of Nebraska Press, Bison Books edition, 1984).

8. Powell, *People of the Sacred Mountain*, xxxviii.

9. Elliot West, "Called out People," *Montana: The Magazine of Western History* 48 (Summer 1998): 2–15.

10. Two of the original arrows were eventually returned to the Cheyennes through trade with the Pawnees.

11. For an examination of the environmental impact on Cheyennes in the central and northern plains of the 1860s, see Monnett, *Where a Hundred Soldiers Were Killed*, 12–19.

12. For the story of Roman Nose and his death at Beecher Island, see John H. Monnett, *The Battle of Beecher Island and the Indian War of 1867–1869* (Niwot, CO: University Press of Colorado, 1992).

13. Thomas B. Marquis, interview of "A Cheyenne Old Man," in *The Cheyennes of Montana, with an Introduction and a Biography of the Author by Thomas D. Weist* (Algonac, MI: Reference Publications, 1978), 94. Marquis communicated with his Cheyenne friends almost exclusively through sign language and the Cheyenne tongue. Crazy Mule received a scalp wound at the Wagon Box Fight, August 2, 1867.

Chapter 8

1. Marquis' original notes on Wooden Leg and others are in Marquis, MD, MSC 308, series 3, "Indian Diaries, 1919–1934," National Library of Medicine, Bethesda,

Maryland. Wooden Leg's story in the Marquis notes is almost identical to the book copy, reproduced here, sans grammatical corrections. Thomas B. Marquis, *Wooden Leg: A Warrior Who Fought Custer* (Lincoln: University of Nebraska Press, Bison Books edition, undated), 14–15.

2. Ibid.

Chapter 9

1. Silas Bent to George B. Grinnell, February 15, 1910, Grinnell Papers, Sterling Memorial Library, Yale University; Lincoln B. Faller, "Making Medicine against 'White Man's Side of the Story': George Bent's Letters to George Hyde," *American Indian Quarterly* 24, no. 1 (Winter 2000): 64. Faller is the foremost scholar today studying the Bent-Hyde Letters in the archives of Yale, Colorado Historical Society, and the Denver Public Library.

2. Faller, "Making Medicine," 67.

3. Ibid., 72.

4. Ibid., 68. Hyde's other classics are: *Red Cloud's Folk: A History of the Oglala Sioux Indians* (1937, revised, 1957); *The Pawnee Indians* (1951); *A Sioux Chronicle* (1956); *Indians of the High Plains: From the Prehistoric Period to the Coming of Europeans* (1959); *Spotted Tail's Folk: A History of the Brûlé Sioux Indians* (1961); *Indians of the Woodlands: From Prehistoric Times to 1725* (1962); and finally, *Life of George Bent: Written From His Letters* (1968).

5. Bent to Hyde, November 16, 1904, Bent Papers, Colorado Historical Society, Denver, Colorado.

6. Not all Northern Cheyennes chose to participate in this fight. Some chose to remain in winter camps. Dull Knife went to Fort Laramie in October to sign Carrington's peace agreement but according to some of the Indian accounts presented here returned and participated in the Fetterman Fight.

7. Bent to Hyde, December 5, 1904, Bent Papers, Yale University, New Haven, Connecticut.

8. Hyde, *Life of George Bent*, 344–46.

9. Bunching is often the first sign of a breakdown of tactical cohesion but prior to panic.

10. Walter Mason Camp, Box 5, Envelope 69, Camp Papers, Lilly Library, Indiana University, Bloomington, Indiana.

11. Smith, *Reimagining Indians*, 46, 47, and 65–66.

12. George B. Grinnell, MS. 5, Grinnell Papers, Notebook #348, 1908, Los Angeles: Southwest Museum, Braun Research Library, 50–51.

Chapter 10

1. Grinnell, Notebook #352, 1914.
2. Grinnell, *The Fighting Cheyennes*, 234–44.
3. These young men were possibly members of Dull Knife's band.
4. These were most likely the Miniconjous.
5. Grinnell, *The Fighting Cheyennes*, 236. Here again, as with some Lakota accounts like that of Rocky Bear, both Lakotas and Cheyennes often referred to their fighting men as "soldiers" rather than warriors. See chapter 5, Sidney Sheldon Short Interviews: Rocky Bear.
6. Some modern oral accounts (Part 4) assert the women who came with the warriors were Cheyennes wishing to avenge the mutilation of relatives at Sand Creek two years previous.
7. This action may have been the first feint on the fort as a decoy action. Compare with Rocky Bear's Oglala account.
8. White Elk was in the Cheyenne position half-way down Massacre Hill on the west side and would have seen the cavalry charge in advance at this point. He could not have known that the infantry had left the fort ahead of Grummond's cavalry, because the fort was far out of White Elk's view from below Lodge Trail Ridge. This part of his account is from his general knowledge of the decoy maneuver. He likely heard the advancing cavalry shooting at the decoys above him on the ridge.
9. Grinnell refers here to the advance infantry position where White Elk had been fighting prior to their retreat to Monument Hill where they were joined by surviving cavalrymen.
10. The last of the cavalry were killed along with Fetterman and Brown, who had been mounted, and whatever infantrymen were left and had managed to fight their way to the rocks on Monument Hill. Private Murphy, part of Ten Eyck's relief force that gathered forty-nine bodies around Monument Hill on the evening of December 21, noted body parts of both infantrymen and cavalrymen. Since there were only twenty-seven cavalrymen in Fetterman's command, obviously both infantry and cavalry died on or in the vicinity of Monument Hill.
11. See Faller, "Making Medicine," 68–71.
12. For more on the roles of transgendered persons in all manners of Indian culture, including warfare, see Will Roscoe, *Changing Ones: Third and Fourth Genders in Native North America* (New York: St. Martin's Griffin, 2000); and Sabine Lang, *Men as Women, Women as Men: Changing Gender in Native American Cultures* (Austin: University of Texas Press, 1998). See also Grinnell, *The Cheyenne Indians*, 2:39–44; Hassrick, *The Sioux*, 133–35; and Hoebel, *The Cheyennes*, 77. Hyde talked about this ceremony with several unnamed Oglalas, who claimed

that the *winkte*, whose name is unknown, was a Miniconjou. See Hyde, *Red Cloud's Folk*, 147n6.

13. John Guthrie, "The Fetterman Massacre," *Annals of Wyoming* 9 (1932): 717.

14. George B. Grinnell to R. S. Ellison, October 1, 1925, Ellison Collection, Denver Public Library, doc. 29.

15. Robert B. David, ed., *Finn Burnett, Frontiersman* (Glendale, CA: Arthur H. Clark, 1937), 127.

Chapter 11

1. Powell, *People of the Sacred Mountain*, 2:1381n11.

2. Interview with Black Bear, 1908, Grinnell Papers, Notebook #348, 53–55.

Part Four
Chapter 12

1. Patricia Nelson Limerick, *The Legacy of Conquest: The Unbroken Past of the American West* (New York: W. W. Norton, 1987), 219–20. For an excellent essay on the conundrums illuminated by national history vs. Indian history, see Limerick, *Something in the Soil: Legacies and Reckonings in the New West* (New York: W. W. Norton, 2000), 33–73. For the difficulty of doing justice to both these histories see *Something in the Soil*, 70. One scholar has defined conquest and land dispossession as "ethnic cleansing," while genocide is taken to mean outright attempts at extermination by death of entire groups or ethnicities of people, thus differentiating conquest of Indian lands from something like the Nazi Holocaust, although the threat of and term "extermination" is often found in U.S. government documents and military reports. Gary Clayton Anderson, *Ethnic Cleansing and the Indian: The Crime That Should Haunt America* (Norman: University of Oklahoma Press, 2014).

2. Donald L. Fixico, "Ethics, and Responsibilities in Writing American Indian History," *American Indian Quarterly* 20, no. 1, Special Issue: Writing About (Writing about) American Indians (Winter 1996): 30–31.

3. Leopold von Ranke, *Historicism*, Ranke Papers, Syracuse University Library, Syracuse, New York.

4. R. David Edmonds, "New Voices: American Indian History, 1895–1995," *The American Historical Review* 100, no. 3 (June 1995): 724.

5. Ronald K. Wetherington, et al., *Battles and Massacres on the Southwestern Frontier: Historical and Archaeological Perspectives* (Norman: University of Oklahoma Press, 2014), 130. The definitive study on the problems faced in establishing

the Sand Creek National Historic Site, including the divide between oral history and archaeology, is Ari S. Kelman, *A Misplaced Massacre: Struggling Over The Memory of Sand Creek* (Cambridge: Harvard University Press, 2013).

6. AFBPP Grants, GA 2255–01–005 and GA 2255–03–004: Fetterman Battlefield Survey: Final Technical Report, ACR Consultants, Inc., Sheridan, Wyo., 2000s (report not for public dissemination). Robert Wilson, curator at Fort Phil Kearny State Historic Site, during a fact-finding tour of the battlefield suggested quite convincingly that Fetterman's infantry may have succeeded in advancing farther north down the ridge behind the cavalry than originally suspected, before warriors sprung the trap by rising up through somewhat deeper ravines that exist farther north, down the ridge. According to earlier archaeology circa 1960s conducted by L. C. Bishop and J. W. Vaughn, percussion caps, Minnie balls, and a Spencer cartridge or two were found on or around Monument Hill, indicating that both cavalry and infantry were trying to take shelter in the boulders where Fetterman and Brown died. Vaughn doubts from that archaeology that many cavalrymen (there were only twenty-seven, plus three officers) made it all the way to the rocks; he believes most were killed near Cavalry Hill. He insightfully claims that some of the Indian confusion over troop disposition was due to the three positions of the soldiers and civilians on the ridge, who were out of sight of each other, and probably also out of sight of many of the Indians who were fighting on the south end and those fighting on the north end of the ridge. See J. W. Vaughn, *Indian Fights: New Facts on Seven Encounters* (Norman: University of Oklahoma Press, 1966), 71–74.

7. Vaughn, *Indian Fights*, 71–74.

8. Raymond DeMallie, foreword to *A Cheyenne Voice: The Complete John Stands In Timber Interviews*, by John Stands In Timber and Margot Liberty (Norman: University of Oklahoma Press, 2013), xxvi.

9. Ibid.

10. Publication rights to Bill Tall Bull's complete story are the sole property of the Fort Phil Kearny/Bozeman Trail Association, Story, Wyoming and "may not be copied and sold by anyone else," at the request of the Tall Bull family. The story, with this disclaimer, is, however, available for viewing on the Fort Phil Kearny/ Bozeman Trail association website: http://www.philkearny.ven.com/fpk-tallbull.htm.

11. Jennifer Gardner was an upper-division student in the author's "Native Americans in American History" class at Metropolitan State College (now University) of Denver in 2002.

12. Badhand is part Seminole. He did not time his ride up from the west ridges to the Bozeman Trail, but remembered that it was "fast." Set of correspondence with the author, May 2014.

13. *Lame Deer Literary Journal* (Spring 2003), Chief Dull Knife College, Lame Deer, Montana.

14. Superintendent of the Fort Phil Kearny State Historic Site, Misty Stoll welcomes Indian interpreters at these events and encourages them to tell their stories according to their beliefs, family histories, and traditions. She insists the historic site does not try to delineate what Indian people say or do. She is tired of putting Native Americans in a box. Hannah Wiest, *The Sheridan Press*, December 23, 2013, http://thesheridanpress.com/?p=15838. Non-Indians, looking for exact facts within events, often have trouble understanding the circular "medicine way" of Indian storytelling that, in the non-Indian mind, appears to be more metaphorical than exact but is perfectly logical in the minds of tribal families and individuals.

15. Tiwahe, Tȟašúnke Witcó, *The Authorized Biography of Crazy Horse*, vol. 2, "Defending the Homeland Prior to the 1868 Treaty," DVD produced by Matson, William, and Frethem, Reel Contact, 2007.

16. Joseph Marshall III, *Hundred in the Hand: A Novel* (Golden, CO: Fulcrum Fiction, 2007); Chris Ravenshead to author, correspondence, April 2007; Marshall Sprague, a descendant of Hump, *'Paha Sapa,'—American Use of the Black Hills*, May 16, 2007, a presentation given at Fort Phil Kearny/ Bozeman Trail Historic Site, and courtesy of Starr Zabel from the archives of FPK/Bozeman Trail Museum and Bookstore. Brazil Claymore gave an accurate short biography of Hump to Josephine Waggoner, accessible in Waggoner, *Witness*, 369–70.

17. Alfred Red Cloud tells his family history in Serle L. Chapman, *Promise: Bozeman Trail to Destiny* (Park City, UT: Pavey Western Publishing, 2004), 122–29. Military reports chronicle no officers' bodies being recovered on the north end (bottom) of the fighting on Massacre Ridge.

18. Ibid., 138.

19. Ibid., 144.

20. Ibid., 153.

21. Douglas War Eagle to Lieutenant Colonel Edward Saunders (Ret.), shared with the author, May 30, 2013. The author has heard stories of several soldiers being honored by warriors placing pouches of buffalo hide over their heads after the fight.

22. Fort Phil Kearny/Bozeman Trail Association website, http://amertribes. proboards.com/thread/552/fetterman-fight-1866.

23. Author's conversation with Ted Risingsun at Dull Knife battlefield, Wyoming, 1993.

24. Leo Killsback, "The Legacy of Little Wolf: Rewriting and Righting Our Leaders Back into History," *Wicazo Sa Review* 26, no. 1 (Spring 2011): 85, 106–107;

The Chiefs' Prophecy: Survival of the Northern Cheyenne Nation, a documentary film produced and directed by Leo Killsback (DVD, Dusty Nose Productions, Arizona Public Media, 2009). Today the cultural center at Chief Dull Knife College is named for Little Wolf. The author of this book had the good fortune to be invited, with Dr. Killsback and other esteemed scholars, as a speaker at the symposium and dedication of the Punished Woman Fork Battlefield Historic Site near Scott City, Kansas, in September 2013, where Little Wolf was honored. The ceremonies and symposium hosted hundreds of Northern Cheyennes who had made the journey by bus from Montana to Kansas, including members of a "younger generation." Ted Risingsun would have been pleased.

Chapter 13

1. Stands In Timber and Liberty, *A Cheyenne Voice*, 350.
2. For the Indian eyewitness accounts of the Hayfield and Wagon Box Fights, see White Bull's stories in Vestal, *Warpath: The True Story of the Fighting Sioux*, 70–83, and Fire Thunder's account in Neihardt, *Black Elk Speaks*, 13. For military studies see Jerome A. Greene, "The Hayfield Fight: A Reappraisal of a Neglected Action," *Montana: The Magazine of Western History* 22, no. 4 (Autumn 1972): 30–43; and Jerry Keenan, *The Wagon Box Fight: An Episode of Red Cloud's War* (Conshocken, Penn.: Savas, 2000). See also, Monnett, *Where a Hundred Soldiers Were Killed*, 193–205, and McDermott, *Red Cloud's War*, 407–422.
3. Dee Brown asserts: "For the first time in history the United States Government had negotiated a peace which conceded everything demanded by the enemy and which exacted nothing in return." Brown is mistaken. Brown, *Fort Phil Kearny*, 225.
4. Colin G. Calloway, *First Peoples: A Documentary Survey of American Indian History*, 4th ed. (Boston and New York: Bedford/St. Martin's, 2012), 294–95.
5. Ibid. The army would use some portions of the Bozeman Road once again in 1876–77 for logistical transport during the Great Sioux War.
6. Ibid., 295.
7. Gray, *Centennial Campaign: The Sioux War of 1876*, 11, 15.
8. Teleconference interview with Charlotte A. Black Elk, September 24, 1992, with author consultants for *How the West Was Lost*, Discovery Channel, VHS, vol. 3, segment 1, "A Good Day to Die." Statement by Black Elk in vol. 3, segment 1.
9. Quoted in Edward Lazarus, *Black Hills/White Justice: The Sioux Nation Versus the United States, 1775 to the Present* (New York: HarperCollins, 1991), 61–62.
10. Powell, *People of the Sacred Mountain*, 2:762–63.
11. Quoted in Calloway, *First Peoples*, 304.

12. Ibid.

13. Quoted in Olson, *Red Cloud and the Sioux Problem*, 74–75.

14. In 1906 Red Cloud told Clarence Three Stars, interpreting for Eli S. Ricker, that the boundaries of the Great Sioux Reservation proscribed in the Treaty of 1868 had not been honored. "It has been a puzzle to me and to the Indian people," Red Cloud stated, "how the line came to be where it has been put." Interview with Red Cloud, November 24, 1906, Pine Ridge, South Dakota, Ricker Papers, Nebraska State Historical Society, Tablet 25.

15. Calloway, *First Peoples*, 373–74. The five remaining reservations are Standing Rock, Cheyenne River, Lower Brûlé, Pine Ridge, and Rosebud.

16. Ibid., 374–76. For the Lakota story of the Black Hills fight, see Jeffrey Ostler, *The Lakotas and the Black Hills: The Struggle for Sacred Ground* (New York: Viking, 2010). An excellent up-to-date study of Sioux history to 1890 is Jeffrey Ostler, *The Plains Sioux and U.S. Colonialism from Lewis and Clark to Wounded Knee* (New York: Cambridge University Press, 2004).

17. For the story of the Omisis travails of 1878–79, see Monnett, *Tell Them We are Going Home*; and James N. Leiker and Ramon Powers, *The Northern Cheyenne Exodus: In History and Memory* (Norman: University of Oklahoma Press, 2011). For the struggle to obtain a northern reservation, see Orlan J. Svingen, *The Northern Cheyenne Indian Reservation, 1877–1900* (Niwot, CO: University Press of Colorado, 1993).

18. John Southard, "Beyond 'A Company, B Company' History," *The American Historian* (Organization of American Historians), August 2014, 20–23.

19. Conversations with anthropologist Margot Liberty, Fort Sill, Oklahoma, October 2009, and Conrad Fisher (Northern Cheyenne historian and lobbyist), Scott City, Kansas, September 27, 2013. Battle of Punished Woman's Fork Symposium, talk by Dr. Leo Killsback (Northern Cheyenne, professor, Arizona State University), and Dr. Richard Littlebear (Northern Cheyenne, president, Chief Dull Knife College), Scott City, Kansas, September 28, 2013. For an excellent study of economic colonialism in modern times, see Donald L. Fixico, *The Invasion of Indian Country in the Twentieth Century* (Boulder: University Press of Colorado, 2012). See also Orlan J. Svingen, "Self-Sufficiency: Stock Raising vs. Farming on the Northern Cheyenne Indian Reservation, 1900–1914," *Montana: The Magazine of Western History* 31, no. 4 (Autumn, 1981): 14–23; Hope M. Babcock, "'[This] I Know from My Grandfather:' The Admissibility of Indigenous Oral History as Proof of Tribal Land Claims," *American Indian Law Review* 37, no. 1 (2012–2013): 19–61; Suzanne H. Schrems, "The Northern Cheyennes Fight for Cultural Sovereignty: The Notes of Father Aloysius Van Der Velden, S. J., *Montana: The Magazine of Western History* 45, no. 2 (Spring, 1995): 18–33.

Afterword

1. Raymond DeMallie, review of *Red Cloud's War*, by John D. McDermott, in *North Dakota History: Journal of the Northern Plains* 77, nos. 3–4 (2012): 42–43.

2. Vaughn, *Indian Fights*, 14–90.

3. Monnett, *Where a Hundred Soldiers Were Killed*, 158. In another recent corrective study, Shannon D. Smith considers Vaughn's offense thesis simply as a historiographical "scenario" without drawing decisive conclusions. Indeed, she writes that if Fetterman had directed his troops to cross over the ridge (which he had to have done regardless of motive) "then he is indeed solely responsible for the annihilation of his troops." Shannon D. Smith, *Give Me Eighty Men: Women and the Myth of the Fetterman Fight* (Lincoln: University of Nebraska Press, 2008), 108.

4. See McDermott, *Red Cloud's War*, 2:343–51.

5. Mark W. Johnson, *That Body of Brave Men: The U.S. Regular Infantry and the Civil War in the Far West* (Cambridge, MA: Da Capo Press, 2003), 292–93, 347. Johnson presents an exemplary accounting of the Eighteenth Infantry and all the Regular Army regiments during the Civil War, with follow up of their deployments after the war.

6. M. Carrington, *Absaraka*, 195.

7. Such ironic incidents during the Civil War are examined in James M. McPherson, *This Mighty Scourge: Perspectives of the Civil War* (New York: Oxford University Press, 2007).

8. Records of the Special Commission, NA, RG 75, M470.

9. Ibid.

10. M. Carrington, *Absaraka*, 203–204.

11. These and other quotes are found in: 50th Cong, 1st sess., Senate Exec. Doc. 33, 40–45, and in M. Carrington, *Absaraka*, 203–204.

12. Records of the Special Commission, NA, RG 75, M470.

13. When Fetterman's command reached the summit of Lodge Trail Ridge, the cavalry under the impetuous Lieutenant Grummond rode ahead to Peno Creek or beyond, leaving Fetterman's flanks unprotected for a distance of approximately one mile, possibly to head off the retreating wood train attackers with Fetterman's infantry to close behind. We shall never know if Fetterman ordered this separation or if Grummond bolted ahead on his own volition as he had previously done in combat. The possibilities are documented in Monnett, *Where a Hundred Soldiers Were Killed*, 119–59 and 219–41.

Appendix A

1. Miniconjou, not the Oglala, He Dog.
2. Two Moons gives the name "Swift Hawk" to Little Wolf's younger brother rather than Big Nose, an error that caused confusion in the memory of John Stands In Timber.

For Further Reading

For reader convenience and accessibility I have chosen, for the reasons advanced in the introduction of this book, to present those sources that pertain mainly to Indian views of the Fetterman Fight. For almost a century and a half, historians' theses of the battle were concerned mostly with the military point of view. They have searched for culpability, responsibility, and blame among army officers at Fort Phil Kearny, the Department of the Platte, and among those in Washington, D.C. These views are largely based on the belief that no force of Indians greater in number could defeat an element of the Regular U.S. Army unless some officer blundered. Perhaps the simplest explanation of both the Fetterman Fight and Little Big Horn is that stated by historian Robert M. Utley: that "the soldiers lost because the Indians won." If true, 150 years is long enough to go without giving the Lakotas, Cheyennes, and Arapahos credit for their victory, and to do that without belaboring U.S. Army officers' arguable mistakes. I have attempted to include and favor as many recommended sources as possible that are fairly accessible to readers interested in furthering their knowledge of the Fetterman Fight, its legacy, and those Lakota and Cheyenne ancestors who witnessed the events in this book.

For those interested in comprehensive military histories of the fight, in recent years scholars have focused more on inclusive up-to-date narratives. Shannon D. Smith's *Give Me Eighty Men: Women and the Myth of the Fetterman Fight* (Lincoln: University of Nebraska Press, 2008) focused on the role of Colonel Henry Carrington's consecutive wives, Margaret and Frances, and brings an insightful scholarly interpretation to their original source (but dated) volumes, Margaret I. Carrington, *Absaraka: Home of the Crows* (Philadelphia: Lippincott, 1868), and Frances C. Carrington, *My Army Life: A*

Soldier's Wife at Fort Phil Kearny (Philadelphia: Lippincott, 1910). Both of the Carrington wives' books are available as recent Bison Books from the University of Nebraska Press.

Shortly following this study is my own, *Where a Hundred Soldiers Were Killed: The Struggle for the Powder River Country and the Making of the Fetterman Myth* (Albuquerque: University of New Mexico Press, 2008), which presents a new scholarly interpretive paradigm to a narrative of the Fetterman Fight, integrating both the military and Indian perspectives along with essays that reevaluate both Fetterman and Crazy Horse. In 2010, John D. McDermott published Volume 10 of Arthur C. Clark's "Military Frontier Series," titled *Red Cloud's War* (Norman: University of Oklahoma Press, 2010), in two volumes. It presents a traditional narrative history of the Fetterman Fight as well as all aspects of Red Cloud's War and its results, and incorporates Indian maneuvers during the war. For those interested in the entire military perspective of the war, McDermott offers the most complete bibliography of original source materials.

All three of these recent books exceed in their scope, Dee Brown's *Fort Phil Kearny: An American Saga* (changed to *The Fetterman Massacre*) (Lincoln: University of Nebraska Press, Bison Books edition, 1962), which has been the staple secondary source for years. It basically chronicles the story of the Carrington family at Fort Phil Kearny in 1866. An older study, worth a look for its archaeological insights and available in paperback from the University of Oklahoma Press, is J. W. Vaughn's *Indian Fights: New Facts on Seven Encounters*, 1966. The standard go-to source for original military reports and other records is "Records of the Special Commission to Investigate the Fetterman Massacre and the State of Indian Affairs," M740, RG 75, National Archives. Many of these documents from the Commission are now online on http//freepages.history.ancestry.com.

Two very accessible Indian accounts, also available in paperback editions, are Walter S. Campbell's (a.k.a. Stanley Vestal) *Warpath: The True Story of the Fighting Sioux Told in a Biography of Chief White Bull* (Lincoln: University of Nebraska Press, Bison Books edition, 1962), and George B. Grinnell's *The Fighting Cheyennes* (Norman: University of Oklahoma Press, 1983). The Walter S. Campbell notes on the Fetterman Fight, taken mainly from his interviews with White Bull (Miniconjou), are located in the Walter S. Campbell Papers, Western History Collection, University of Oklahoma Libraries, Norman. These too are accessible online: http//www.digital. libraries.ou.edu. The Eli S. Ricker Interviews are in the Ricker Papers Collection of the Nebraska State Historical Society and available in Eli S. Ricker's *Voices of the American West*, Volume 1: *The Indian Interviews of Eli S. Ricker, 1903–1919, edited and with an Introduction by Richard E. Jensen* (Lincoln: University of Nebraska Press, 2005). Reminiscences of Red Cloud are located in James H. Cook's *Fifty Years on the Old Frontier* (Norman: University of Oklahoma Press paperback reprints, 1980).

Short original biographies are found in Josephine Waggoner's *Witness: A Hunkpapha Historian's Strong-Heart Song of the Lakotas* (Lincoln: University of Nebraska Press, 2013), Charles A. Eastman's (Ohiyesa) *Indian Heroes & Chieftains* (Lincoln: Bison Books edition, 1991), Nicholas Black Elk and John G. Neihardt's *Black Elk Speaks* (Lincoln: University of Nebraska Press, Bison Book edition, 2000), and *The Sixth Grandfather: Black Elk's Teaching Given to John G. Neihardt*, edited by Raymond J. DeMallie (Lincoln: University of Nebraska Press, Bison Books edition, 1985). Of great interest is *Autobiography of Red Cloud: War Leader of the Oglalas*, edited by R. Eli Paul (Helena: Montana Historical Society, 1997). While not specifically dealing with Red Cloud's role in the Fetterman Fight, Paul's book sheds firsthand light on the early years of the great chief's life. For original and second-generation reminiscences of the Cheyennes the best original source is George F. Hyde's *The Life of George Bent Written from His Letters* (Norman: University of Oklahoma paperbacks, 1968). For Wooden Leg, see Thomas B. Marquis' *Wooden Leg, A Warrior Who Fought Custer* (Lincoln: Bison Books, 1986). Although second-generation, for reminiscences of warriors' tales of the Fetterman Fight of much value is John Stands In Timber and Margot Liberty's *Cheyenne Memories* (Lincoln: Bison Books, 1972) and John Stands In Timber and Margot Liberty's *A Cheyenne Voice: The Complete John Stands In Timber Interviews* (Norman: University of Oklahoma Press, 2013).

Other Indian eyewitness testimonial accounts are more difficult to access. All of the George B. Grinnell Notebooks are housed in the Braun Research facility of Autry National Center (formerly the Southwest Museum) in Los Angeles. The Letters of George Bent to George E. Hyde and George B. Grinnell are spread out in the Coe Collection of the Beinecke Manuscript Library at Yale University, History Colorado (formerly, Colorado Historical Society), and the University of Colorado Boulder. Two Moons' statements to William Camp are in the Wm. Camp Papers of the Lily Library, University of Indiana, Bloomington, or the Camp Papers in the Robert S. Ellison Collection of the Western History Department of Denver Public Library. Some of the most interesting unpublished Lakota eyewitness accounts are found in the A. E. Sheldon Papers of the Nebraska State Historical Society. For artistic ledger book representation of Red Cloud's War, see Castle McLaughlin's *A Lakota War Book from the Little Bighorn: The Pictographic Autobiography of Half Moon* (Cambridge: Peabody Museum Press, 2013).

An ethnographical context of the Lakotas, Cheyennes, and Arapahos is important to an understanding of the Fetterman Fight. Always on hand in my research and writing are the works of George B. Grinnell, especially *The Cheyenne Indians: Their History and Way of Life*, 2 vols. (Lincoln: Bison Books, 1972) and *By Cheyenne Campfires* (Lincoln: Bison Books, 1971). Raymond J. DeMallie and Douglas R. Parks' *Sioux Indian Religion: Translations and Innovation* (Norman: University of Oklahoma Press,

1987) is essential. Excellent insight is to be found in Royal B. Hassrick's *The Sioux: The Life and Customs of a Warrior Society* (Norman: University of Oklahoma Press, 1964). See also E. Adamson Hoebel's *The Cheyennes, Indians of the Great Plains* (New York: Holt, Rinehart, and Winston, 1960). Two of the best Cheyenne ethnological surveys are John H. Moore's *The Cheyenne Nation: A Social and Demographic History* (Lincoln: Bison Books, 1987) and also his *The Cheyenne* (Malden, Mass.: Blackwell Publishers, 1999). Of much importance is Peter John Powell's *Sweet Medicine: The Continuing Role of the Sacred Arrows, the Sun Dance, and the Sacred Buffalo Hat in Northern Cheyenne History*, 2 vols. (Norman: University of Oklahoma Press paperbacks, 1969). An essential reference specifically for Oglalas is Catherine Price's *The Oglala People, 1841–1879: A Political History* (Lincoln: Bison Books, 1998). For the Arapahos, see Virginia Cole Trenholm's *The Arapahoes, Our People* (Norman: University of Oklahoma Press paperbacks, 1986).

For secondary sources, the best biography of Red Cloud remains Robert W. Larson's *Red Cloud: Warrior-Statesman of the Lakota Sioux* (Lincoln: Bison Books, 1997). Most interesting is Frank H. Goodyear III's *Photographs of a Lakota Chief* (Lincoln: University of Nebraska Press, 2003). Red Cloud is the most photographed American Indian of the nineteenth Century. The best overall biography of Crazy Horse is Kingsley Bray's *Crazy Horse: A Lakota Life* (Norman: University of Oklahoma Press, 2006). See also Fort Phil Kearny/Bozeman Trail Association's *Portraits of Fort Phil Kearny* (Banner, WY: Fort Phil Kearny/Bozeman Trail Association, 1993).

In addition to the recent studies of the Fetterman Fight listed above, an arguably original but essential source is George E. Hyde's *Red Cloud's Folk: A History of the Oglala Sioux Indians* (Norman: University of Oklahoma Press, 1937, with new printings). An amazing narrative well worth the cost in the used book market is Peter John Powell's *People of the Sacred Mountain: A History of the Northern Chiefs and Warrior Societies, 1830–1974, with an Epilog, 1969–1974*, 2 vols. (San Francisco: Harper & Row, 1981). Suggested recent sources for modern oral testimonies are: Serle L. Chapman's *Promise: Bozeman's Trail to Destiny* (Park City, UT: Pavey Western Publishing, 2004), and Leo Killsback's *The Chief's Prophecy: Survival of the Northern Cheyenne Nation* (DVD: Dusty Noise Productions, 2009). Bill Tall Bull's full account of the Fetterman Fight may be found on www.philkearny.vcn.com/fpk-tallbull.htm.

For further linkage to the "legacy" of the Fetterman Fight three scholarly studies are recommended. See Jeffrey Ostler's *The Plains Sioux and U.S. Colonialism from Lewis and Clark to Wounded Knee* (New York: Cambridge University Press, 2004), and Ostler's *The Lakotas and the Black Hills: The Struggle for Sacred Ground* (New York: Viking, 2010). Finally, for an examination of legal treaty injustice, including the Treaty of 1868, see Paul VanDevelder's *Savages & Scoundrels: The Untold Story of America's Road to Empire Through Indian Territory* (New Haven: Yale University Press, 2009).

Acknowledgments

I have visited the Fetterman battlefield since I was a sixteen-year-old high school student. In those days we had to ask locals where it was located and how to get there. In the company of my father, Howard Norman Monnett, a historian and, in later times, a college president, we had the time in the summer to drive around and locate such places. After all, gasoline was only twenty-two cents a gallon. The only problem was finding the place in the wilds of northern Wyoming prior to superhighways. In any event, we finally located it thanks to local ranchers in July of 1961. I still have vivid memories of standing where Fort Phil Kearny was located and standing up on the hill by the 1905 monument.

The ridges in that broken country area struck my fancy the most. As my dad related the story of Captain Fetterman's demise, I thought at that very first moment of comprehension: "No way. No veteran Civil War Army officer would be so irresponsible as to cross Sullivant Hill and Lodge Trail into a massed force of perhaps 1,500 Indians." I determined then that someday I would get to the bottom of it. Of course, at that time the victors wrote the history of America's Indian Wars and any large force of Indians could not wipe out a command of eighty-one soldiers unless their commanding officer was completely incompetent. Only years later, and through much study, did I realize that Fetterman and his subordinate officers had no idea there might be 1,500 Lakotas and Cheyennes waiting in ambush for them north of the crest of Lodge Trail. I considered: "Maybe he should have, given the size of the villages on the Tongue River." But, "Nope": many came into those villages during the two weeks prior to the fight, swelling the numbers. Then I considered that the troops at Fort Phil Kearny had never faced more than 150 warriors at one time, and that it was unlikely that more than a thousand Indians would commit to an offensive battle at one time. Then I considered other factors, like how hated the Bozeman Trail forts really were, and how intensely the Indians felt they endangered a fragile ecology and threatened their economy and culture—and that there was really no other place as good to go to as the Powder River Country. Somewhere along the line it dawned on me, "These people were not savages." They were a people of complex culture protecting their turf. Logic took over as an essential element of my (or any scholar's) evolving understanding of history. I knew then that to understand this time in our history I needed to understand the Indian perspective, and that that perspective has formed an identification of problems and concerns for America's Native peoples to the present day.

I have my dad to thank for first spurring my interest in history to the extent it would become my life profession. He taught me to think about these things, consider multiple viewpoints, and above all, temper a passion for history with rationality, logic, and objectivity. The result is this book, among several in my career. I have many people and institutions to thank. A portion of the financing for this research was provided by the Charles Redd Center of the American West at Brigham Young University. I would like to thank the wonderful staff archivists at the Nebraska State History Society, the South Dakota State Society, and History Colorado, especially William Convery at the latter. I would be unable to conduct research without the help of Dennis Hagen and Jim Kroll of the Western History Department of the Denver Public Library, one of the finest western history research facilities in the nation. Folks at the Beinecke Research Library at Yale University, and the libraries of the University of Oklahoma, Lilly Library at Indiana University, and the Norlin Library of the University of Colorado, Boulder, and the National Archives have been indispensible. I wish to thank Manola Madrid and Liza Pozas of the Braun Research Library of the Autry Center (formerly, Southwest Museum) for providing me with essential reproductions from the Notebooks of George B. Grinnell without my having to negotiate the streets of Los Angeles in a rental car.

Colleagues at Metropolitan State University of Denver have graciously read parts of my manuscript and made significant necessary suggestions for improvement. They include: Shelby Balik, James Drake, Derek Everett, Margaret Frisbee, Kim Klimik, Stephen Leonard, Laura McCall, Andrea Maejestram, Matthew Maher, and Kevin Rucker. Here in Denver I would like to thank, for their contributions, ideas, and encouragement: Jerome Greene, Geoffrey Hunt, Rebecca Hunt, Layton Hooper, Robert Larson, Gregory Michno, Thomas Noel, and Luther Wilson.

Among academic scholars, a few of whom I have never met in person, but have always looked up to for inspiration derived from their own work, as well as for friendship, I would like to acknowledge: Gary Clayton Anderson, Russell David Edmonds,

Raymond DeMallie, Margot Liberty (our conversations are always lively bordering on raunchy), Sherry L. Smith, Gregory Urwin, Robert M. Utley, and Elliott West (who literally "persevered" with me through festivities at the Western Heritage Center in Oklahoma City). In Wyoming much gratitude goes to Misty Stoll, R. C. Wilson (who straightened out my geography at the battlefield), and Starr Zabel, all of the Fort Phil Kearny State Historic Site, for their hard work at preservation and for their friendship. Fellow author Shannon D. Smith, formerly of my home, Boulder, Colorado, now of Laramie, Wyoming, has given me ideas and inspiration regarding this important event in history.

Among American Indian friends who have supported my ideas and work, I especially would like to recognize and thank all of my Indian students through the past twenty years, and Conrad Fisher, Leo Killsback, who enlightened me on Little Wolf, Richard Littlebear, Chris Ravenshead, the late Ted Risingsun, Chief Rock Red Cherries, Wallace Bearchum, Danny Sioux, Minoma Littlehawk Sills, and Michael Badhand. Others I would like to acknowledge for their contributions, friendship, and their impeccable knowledge are Kingsley Bray, Philip Fetterman, Louis Kraft, John D. McDermott, Billy Markland, Steve Peckel, Col. Ed Saunders, Ken Weidner, Clark Whitehead, and especially Chuck Rankin of the University of Oklahoma Press (a graciously patient editor-in-chief), and all of his terrific editing and production staff, including the two anonymous manuscript referees. All of these wonderful folks have convinced me that the subject of the Indian wars, aside from simply being interesting, is still academically relevant, significant, and worthy of further scholarly research to enhance an understanding of the new directions of American history today.

Index

References to illustrations appear in italic type.

Aarons, Henry E., 164
Absaraka, Home of the Crows
(Carrington), 67
Acherman, Frederick, 163
ACR Consultants, Inc., 127–28
Agate Springs Stock Farm, 54–55
akicitas, 41–42
Allen, Charles, 65
allotment policy, 148
Amberson, Thomas, 165
Ambrose, Stephen, 84
American Horse, 13, 43, *55*, 71, 73,
81, 85, 88; in decoy action, 82; in
Fetterman's death, 56–57, 71, 76,
138–39; on Fort Laramie Treaty,
146; Ricker interview with, 54–57;
role in fight, 56; Sheldon interview
with, 57–60; war club of, *58*; winter
count mnemonic of fight, *40*, 54
Annexation Act (1877), 148
anthropology, 126
Apache Warhorse, 137
Arapaho accounts, 9, 139, 188n6

Arapahos, 24, 48, 146; casualties, 56,
161; role in fight, *6–7*, 56, 104, 105,
110–12, 188n6
archaeological investigation, 126;
of infantry position, 189n6; of
Monument Hill, 206n6; of Sand
Creek Massacre, 127–28
Army Reorganization Act (1866), 153
Arnold, W. F., 155
Augur, C. C., 144, 146, 176
*Authorized Biography of Crazy Horse
and His Family, The* (video series),
138

Bad Face Oglalas, 42, 59, 64, 65, 66,
67, 70, 94–95
Badhand, 137, 206n12
Bad Heart Bull, Amos, 7, 41, 192n1
Baker, James, 165
Baker Massacre, 125
Battle of Beecher Island, 94
Battle of Belly Butte, 148
Battle of Blue Water Creek, 74

Lightning Source UK Ltd.
Milton Keynes UK
UKHW01f0612100818
327043UK00001B/87/P

9 780806 161884